工学结合新思维高职高专财经类“十二五”规划教材

国际商务单证操作

主　编　吴铁群
副主编　汪鼎喜　凌　鸣　刘　珊
参　编　杨楚欣　马　宇　杨　昇　匡一贞
　　　　周　道　龙晓辉　彭　礼

对外经济贸易大学出版社
中国·北京

图书在版编目（CIP）数据

国际商务单证操作：英文、中文／吴铁群主编．—
北京：对外经济贸易大学出版社，2014
工学结合新思维高职高专财经类“十二五”规划教材
ISBN 978-7-5663-1156-6

Ⅰ．①国… Ⅱ．①吴… Ⅲ．①国际贸易-票据-高等
职业教育-教材-英文、中文 Ⅳ．①F740.44

中国版本图书馆 CIP 数据核字（2014）第 200332 号

国际商务单证操作
吴铁群 主编
责任编辑：胡小平 红 梅

对 外 经 济 贸 易 大 学 出 版 社
北京市朝阳区惠新东街 10 号 邮政编码：100029
邮购电话：010-64492338 发行部电话：010-64492342
网址：http://www.uibep.com E-mail：uibep@126.com

北京市山华苑印刷有限责任公司印装 新华书店北京发行所发行
成品尺寸：185mm×260mm 17.25 印张 398 千字
2014 年 9 月北京第 1 版 2014 年 9 月第 1 次印刷

ISBN 978-7-5663-1156-6
印数：0 001-3 000 册 定价：36.00 元

出版说明

工学结合新思维高职高专财经类“十二五”规划教材是对外经济贸易大学出版社贯彻教育部教高［2006］16号《关于全面提高高等职业教育教学质量的若干意见》精神，联合天津商务职业学院（原天津对外经济贸易职业学院）、天津职业大学、河北工业职业技术学院、北京工业职业技术学院、天津国土资源和房屋职业学院、天津海运职业学院等国家、省（直辖市）级示范性高等职业院校推出的一套面向高职高专层次、涵盖不同专业的立体化教材。本系列教材包括国际经贸、财会金融、工商管理、物流管理、电子商务、旅游与酒店管理6个专业。

根据教高［2006］16号文件关于“高等职业院校要积极与行业企业合作开发课程，根据技术领域和职业岗位（群）的任职要求，参照相关的职业资格标准，改革课程体系和教学内容，建立突出职业能力培养的课程标准，规范课程教学的基本要求，提高课程教学质量”的要求，本套教材以提高学生专业实际操作能力和就业能力为宗旨，采取情景模块、案例启发、任务驱动、项目引领、精讲解、重实训的编写方式，让学生在理论够用的基础上，在专业技能培养环节，特别是“教学做一体化”方面有所突破，“确保优质教材进课堂”。

根据国家职业教育的指导思想，目前我国高职高专教育的培养目标是以能力培养和技术应用为本位；根据教育部提出的高等职业教育“与行业企业共同开发紧密结合生产实际的实训教材”的要求，其教材建设突出强调应用性和适用性，既要满足专业教育，又能适应就业导向的“双证书”（毕业证和技术等级证）的人才培养目标需要。本套教材的作者不仅具有丰富的高等职业教育教学经验，而且具有企业第一线实践经历，主持或参加过多项应用技术研究。这是本套教材编写质量与高等职业特色的重要保证。

本套教材配有教师用PPT文稿，方便教师教学参考。

愿本套教材的出版对“十二五”期间我国高等职业教育的创新发展和高职人才培养质量的稳步提升有所助益！

对外经济贸易大学出版社

2011年6月

前　言

中国加入 WTO 以后，进出口贸易额连年递增，特别是近年，我国的贸易总量已跃居世界前列，因此需要大量的国际商务类人才。然而目前的国际商务类人才培养不论是从培养规模还是培养质量上来看，与行业的发展速度都是不匹配的。另外，从职业教育教学改革的角度来看，课程改革则是人才培养的核心环节。根据业务环节的展开情况，模仿真实的贸易背景来编写专业教材是培养高职学生职业岗位能力的关键。

国际商务单证操作技能是进出口业务进程中的一项核心职业技能，实操性强，必须结合基本的国贸实务知识和商务英语知识，在现代的无纸化贸易中还要求一定的计算机操作能力。为此，《国际商务单证操作》一书以项目化教学为编写理念，以进出口单证业务流程为导向，根据国际商务单证员的几大典型岗位能力设置编写项目内容，将业务操作知识仿真化，项目化，将进出口单证操作业务分成十三个工作项目，引入真实的贸易背景和公司单据，并邀请外贸企业和银行国际结算部的业务骨干共同设计，力求将本书打造成体现职教改革理念，体现“岗、证、课”一体，符合岗位需求，同时亦可供行业人士自学的高质量专业用书。

本教材作为国际贸易专业省级示范特色专业的重点建设成果之一，以一名国际商务单证员应完成的一笔完整的单证业务为项目主线，将本书分为信用证审核与修改业务操作、商业单据业务操作、运输单据业务操作、保险单据业务操作、官方单据业务操作、金融单据业务操作及进口单据业务操作等十三个典型工作项目。每个工作项目都从一个典型的工作任务开始，分成项目预期目标、项目实施条件、开篇任务引入及多个子项目等四大板块，不论是典型任务中的业务讲解还是拓展任务中的模拟操作，均采用外贸公司的真实贸易背景、业务单据和图片、数据，充分体现了进出口业务的真实性，同时为了尊重商业机密，部分核心信息如交易双方信息、商品参数等内容已做了技术替换，如不慎发生雷同，实属巧合，谨此声明。

本书可作为中、高职高专院校、本科院校独立学院及成教自考等国际商务类专业的教学用书，亦可作为外贸从业人员的培训用书及参考用书，同时也可以成为外贸从业人员的业务参考。

本书由湖南外贸职业学院吴轶群担任主编并统稿，宁波赛尔集团义乌分公司总经理喻进担任主审，参加编写的人员有湖南外贸职业学院吴轶群（前言、项目二）、湖南外贸职业学院杨楚欣（项目九）、湖南外贸职业学院汪鼎喜（项目七）、湖南外贸职业学院彭礼（项目六）、湖南外贸职业学院刘珊（项目一、项目四）、湖南外贸职业学院凌鸣（项目三、项目十一)、湖南外贸职业学院马宇(项目五)、湖南外贸职业学院周道(项目十二)、湖南外贸职业学院龙晓辉(项目十三)、湖南科技职业学院杨昇(项目十)、重庆能源职业学院匡一贞(项目八)。

本书在编写过程中得到了湖南外贸职业学院副校长魏敏教授、国际商务学院院长吴敏良教授等领导的悉心指导和帮助,还得到了郴州海关关长伍祥刚、光大银行湖南省分行国际结算部周莹经理等外贸业务专家的大力支持,在此一并衷心地感谢。

由于编写时间紧、任务重,书中内容难免出现疏漏和错误,真诚欢迎各位批评指正,以便再版时予以修正。

编　者

2014 年 4 月于长沙

目　录

项目一　国际商务单证业务描述

项目预期目标

通过对国际商务单证员这一岗位的描述以及国际商务单证工作的介绍，使国际商务类相关专业的同学对该岗位的基本职业素养、核心技能以及业务操作准则有基本的了解，为今后单证业务的展开奠定扎实的基础。

表 1-1　　项目预期目标

目标类型	单证员岗位及单证业务介绍
知识目标	熟悉国际商务单证员的岗位要求
	掌握单证工作的基本要求和制单的“三原则”
能力目标	能初步理解国际商务单证员岗位
	能熟悉并整理基本的单据类型
职业素质目标	细心、谨慎的工作态度
	与国外客户和银行沟通衔接能力
	风险控制意识

项目实施条件

1. 组织学生登录国际商务单证员考试中心，了解相关的岗位要求
2. 学生能通过真实案例理解单证工作的重要性
3. 教师必须具备国际商务单证员培训师资格或具备外贸企业单证工作经验

开篇业务引入

2012 年 5 月，国际贸易专业毕业生李望应聘到长沙鹏兴进出口有限公司，成为一名国际商务单证员。李望的主要职责是根据外销合同及信用证及相关资料，并结合具体业务要求完成全套单据的制作，同时负责日常的单证归档及管理工作。

子项目一　单证员岗位描述

一、国际商务单证员岗位职责

（一）具备良好的职业道德

作为单证员应充分认识到单证工作的重要意义，具备良好的职业道德，有严谨的职业操守，责任心强，严格遵守外贸纪律和本企业的规章制度，在工作中能够不断努力学习，更新知识，充实自己。

（二）掌握必要的专业技能

作为单证员应知晓国家对外贸易的有关方针、政策及其最新变化，了解国际贸易发展现状和趋势以及相关国际法规和惯例，掌握进出口业务知识，熟悉进出口合同各项条款内容，特别是与单证相关的内容，能熟练审核信用证并缮制、审核各种单证，了解与国际贸易单证相关的国际标准和国家标准并能熟练使用各种制单专业软件和现代办公设备。

（三）打好扎实的外语基础

目前国际贸易单证工作中使用的语言以英语为主，只有极个别国家要求某些进口单证或个别单证中的某些项目必须使用该本国语言。所以单证员必须能够熟练使用英语缮制单证、阅读合同、信用证和相关单证。

（四）拥有丰富的实践经验

单证员必须在日常工作中不断丰富和积累经验，善于发现问题、处理问题、总结教训，对合同、信用证、相关国际法规和相关国际惯例要吃准吃透，对合同履行的各个环节要烂熟于心，对单证工作涉及的各个部门要了如指掌，经常研究讨论各种业务案例以增强解决问题的实际能力。

（五）坚持认真的工作态度

单证工作内容烦琐，工作量大，时间性强，所以要求单证员必须具有一丝不苟、踏实细致的工作作风和认真负责、严格细致的工作态度。否则，一单之错，甚至一字之差都可能给合同的履行造成障碍和困难，给企业造成经济损失。

二、国际商务单证工作描述

（一）定义

单据证书（export documents）简称单据，是指在出口业务中使用的单据与证书，凭此来处理货物的交付、运输、保险、商检、结汇、报关等工作。

（二）工作流程

审证→制单→审单→制单→交单→归档

（三）用途

1. 国际贸易结算的基本工具

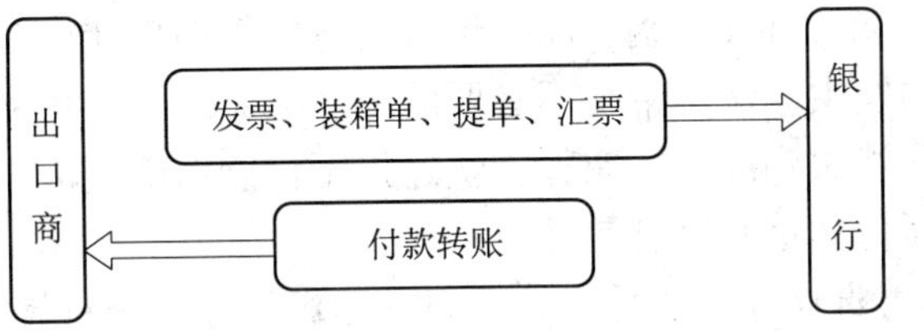

国际间的商品买卖，由于买卖双方处在不同的国家、地区，商品与货币不能简单地直接交换，所以就出现了以单证作为交换的手段。尤其是按 CIF 成交，并以 L/C 为支付方式的合同，是典型的“单据买卖合同”，即所谓的“象征性交货”，当事人处理的是单据而不是实际的货物。因此，在国际贸易中，一套完整、正确的单据是买卖双方及时取得物权凭证的保证，单证的任何差错都会给双方带来不同程度的经济损失。

长沙鹏兴进出口贸易公司出口阿根廷布宜诺斯艾利斯货物一批，合同规定 2013 年 10 月 10 日交货，因 10 月 10 日前无船去该国，立即与进口商联系延续 20 天。对方表示同意以后，我方在 10 月 25 日装船，30 日持全套单据向议付行进行议付。银行审单后，予以拒付。为什么？

2. 交易双方履约的凭证

如在托运环节中：

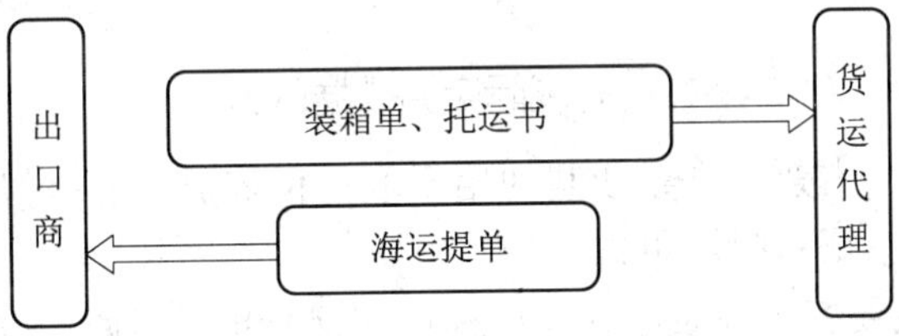

如在商检环节中：

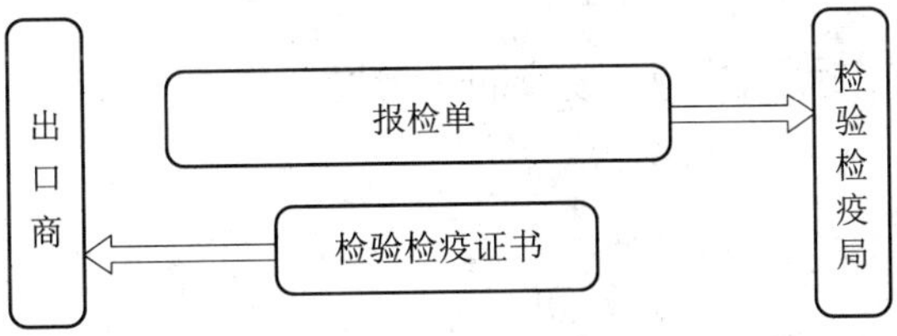

在外贸业务中，无论是使用信用证，还是托收、汇付等支付方式，按《联合国货物销售公约》的规定，出口商不仅有交付货物的义务，同时还必须移交单据。因此，单证是买卖双方履行合同的必然结果，也是完成外贸交易各环节工作的证明文件。

思考：长沙鹏兴进出口有限公司与日商签订一份出口合同。我方按合同规定的品质、数量、交货时间等条款履行后，持全套单据进行了议付。货到达目的地，日商发现货物数量短缺，便直接向我方提出索赔。我方对此予以拒绝。为什么？

3. 经营管理的重要环节

单证工作服务于国际贸易业务的整个过程，它不仅仅是单证的缮制和转递，而且必须妥善地处理各种问题，保证结汇的安全。

例如，单证工作能及时反映货、船、证等业务的管理现状，工作责任性强可及时解决、杜绝差错事故的发生，避免带来不必要的经济损失。

同时，单证工作能做到准确、完整、快速，不仅能保证收汇安全，又能加快收汇，加速资金周转，进而树立企业自身信誉。

思考：长沙鹏兴进出口有限公司与澳大利亚客商签订一份销售合同，目的港为悉尼。由于单证员疏忽，制单时误填为墨尔本，以至进口货物到达该地。你设想一下，会给该公司会带来什么后果？

三、国际商务单据的种类

外贸业务中涉及的单据种类繁多，且有不同的分类，主要有以下几种：

（一）跟单信用证统一规则（UCP600）对国际商务单据的分类

运输单据：海运提单、非转让海运单、租船合约提单、多式联运单据、航空运单、公路、铁路和内陆水运单据、快递收据、邮政收据或邮寄证明。

保险单据：保险单、保险凭证、联合声明、预约保单等。

商业发票及其他单据

它包括装箱单、重量单、产地证明书、普惠制单据、检验检疫证书、受益人声明或受益人证明等。

（二）托收统一规则（URC522）对国际商务单据的分类

金融单据：汇票、本票、支票或其他用于取得付款资金的类似凭证。

商业单据：基本单据、附属单据。

其中，商业单据主要有商业发票、海运提单和保险单；附属单据主要有领事发票、海关发票、原产地证明等官方单证和装箱单、商检证书、受益人证明、装运通知、船公司证明等说明单据。

（三）UN/EDIFACT 标准对国际商务单证的分类

生产单证

订购单证

销售单证

银行单证

保险单证

货运代理服务单证

运输单证

出口单证

进口和转口单证

四、制单的基本原则——“三一致，四要求”

1. 三一致：单证一致，单单一致，单货一致。
2. 四要求：正确、完整、及时、整洁。

子项目二　单证员岗位走岗认知

参观外贸企业的国际商务单证员岗位，了解该岗位的职业要求及基本的单证工作原则，熟悉该单位的单证管理制度。

项目二　信用证审核与修改业务

项目预期目标

通过对该出口销售合同条款的认真解读，结合出口方银行开来的信用证通知书内容，以及 UCP600 等国际惯例，使同学们了解信用证的基本业务操作流程，熟悉跟单信用证的基本结构和重要条款，根据受益人的立场掌握信用证条款的审核与修改。

在项目实施过程中，通过信用证审核与修改任务的分解，在分工与合作中逐渐培养翻译、审核、风险控制等国际商务单证基本职业能力，亦培养独立操作信用证业务和与国外客户或进出口双方银行有效沟通的能力。

表 2-1　项目预期目标

目标类型	信用证的审核与修改
知识目标	熟悉信用证业务操作流程
	理解跟单信用证的基本结构
	掌握信用证条款的审核与翻译
能力目标	能根据合同审核信用证条款
	能根据己方需要对信用证提出适当的修改意见
职业素质目标	独立业务操作能力
	与国外客户和银行沟通衔接能力
	风险控制意识

项目实施条件

1. 组织学生参观中国银行或其他银行的国际结算部，参观外贸公司并收集业务资料
2. 学生能够在网上同虚拟的国外客户或银行交流业务信息
3. 学生可以在教学资源库中查阅信用证业务交易明细
4. 指导教师掌握扎实的国际贸易政策，具备扎实的外贸业务基础

开篇业务引入

2012 年 7 月 5 日，长沙鹏兴进出口有限公司与加拿大的 ELBY 实业有限公司签订了一份马克杯出口的销售合同，根据合同要求，双方以跟单信用证的方式来完成货款的收付。该业务具体由单证员李望负责，并按照合同条款认真审核操作信用证业务。

子项目一 信用证审核与修改

一、定义

信用证：(Letter of Credit，L/C）是银行开立的有条件承诺付款的书面文件。即：(开证行）根据买方（开证申请人）的请求，或自己主动向卖方（受益人）开立的一定金额的，并在一定期限内凭受益人提交符合信用证内所规定的单证，承诺付款的书面文件。

二、特点

1. 信用证是一种银行信用。

信用证一经开出，开证行承担第一性付款责任。只要出口商提交了信用证规定的单据，开证行就必须付款。

2. 信用证是独立于贸易合同之外的自足文件。

信用证一经开出就成为独立性的文件，所有当事人，特别是有关银行，只受信用证条款的约束，不受合同条款的约束。

3. 信用证业务处理的是单据而不是货物。

凭相符单据付款，“认单不认货”。想要安全、迅速结汇，就必须使单据在表面上与信用证条款规定的一致，同时各种单据之间也要一致。即“单证一致、单单一致”。

三、形式

1. 信开本（to open by airmail)：开证银行采用印就的信函格式的信用证，开证后以航空邮寄送通知行。

2. 电开本（to open by cable)：开证银行使用电传、传真、SWIFT 等各种电信方法将信用证条款传达给通知行。

四、基本当事人及主要内容

（一）信用证的主要当事人

1. 开证申请人（applicant)，又称开证人（opener)，指向银行申请开立信用证的人。一般为进出口业务的买方。有时也可能由银行自己主动开证，即为其自身开证。此时则没有开证申请人。

2. 开证银行（opening bank，issuing bank)，也称开证行，指接受开证人委托或为其本身开立信用证的银行，一般为进口地银行。开证银行开出信用证后，即承担保证付款的责任。

3. 受益人（beneficiary)，指信用证上所指定的有权使用该证的人，一般为进出口业务的卖方。受益人通常也是信用证的收件人（addressee)，他有按信用证规定签发汇票向指定的付款银行索取价款的权利，但也在法律上以汇票出票人的地位对其后的持票人负有担保该汇票必获承兑或付款的责任。

4. 通知行（advising bank，notifying bank），指接受开证行的委托，将信用证通知受益人的银行。一般为出口地银行，且通常是开证行的代理行或分行。通知行只证明信用证的真实性，无其他义务。

5. 议付行（negotiating bank），又称押汇银行，是指愿意买入或贴现受益人交来跟单汇票的银行。议付银行可以是由开证银行在信用证条款中指定的银行，也可以是非指定的银行。（议付行的付款有追索权）

6. 付款银行（paying bank，drawee bank），指信用证上指定的付款银行。一般为开证行，但有时也可能是受开证行委托代为付款的另一家银行。付款银行通常是汇票的受票人，故也称受票行（drawee bank）。（付款行如同一般的汇票受票人，一经付款，即使事后发现有误，对受款人也无追索权）

7. 偿付行（reimbursing bank），也称清算银行（clearing bank），是指受开证行的指示或授权，对有关代付行或议付行的索偿予以照付的银行。（此偿付不为终局性付款，因为偿付行并不审查单据、不负单证不符之责。开证行在见单后发现单证不符时，可直接向寄单的议付行、代付行追回已付讫的款项）

8. 保兑行（confirming bank），是指应开证行请求在信用证上加具保兑的银行，它具有与开证行相同的责任和地位。（付款或议付后无追索权）

9. 承兑行（accepting bank），对承兑信用证项下的单据，经审核确认与信用证规定相符时，在汇票正面签字承诺到期付款的银行。

10. 转让行（transferring bank），是应受益人的委托，将可转让信用证转让给信用证的受让人即第二受益人的银行。（转让行一般为通知行，也可是议付行、付款行或保兑行）。

11. 受让人（transferee），也称第二受益人（second beneficiary），在可转让信用证条件下，受益人有权将信用证总金额的全部或一部分转让另一出口人使用，该出口人即为受让人。

（二）信用证的主要内容

1. 自身说明：如信用证的编号（letter of credit No.）、开证日期、到期日（This Credit is valid for payment/negotiation in China until 31st July 2003）（本证至 2003 年 7 月 31 日止在中国付款/议付有效）、到期地点、交单期限等。

2. 兑付方式：即期付款（sight payment）、远期付款（after sight payment）、延期付款（deferred payment）、承兑（acceptance）、议付（negotiation）。

3. 信用证的种类：是否可撤消（可撤销 revocable，不可撤销 irrevocable）、是否经另一家银行保兑（保兑 confirmed，非保兑 unconfirmed）、可否转让（可转让 transferable，不可转让 untransferable）。

4. 信用证的当事人：开证人（applicant）、开证行（opening bank）、受益人（beneficiary）、通知行（advising bank，notifying bank）、付款行（paying bank，drawee bank）、偿付行（reimbursing bank）、承兑行（accepting bank）、议付行（negotiating bank）。

5. 汇票条款：包括汇票的种类、出票人、受票人、付款期限、出票条款及付款日期等。凡不需汇票的信用证无此内容。

6. 货物条款：包括货物的名称、规格、数量、包装、价格。

7. 支付货币和信用证金额：币别、总额。

8. 装运与保险条款。

9. 单据条款。

10. 附属条款。

五、SWIFT 信用证格式简介

目前国际上使用最多的信用证为 SWIFT 格式的信用证，该类信用证的特点是格式简明统一，覆盖全球绝大多数银行，且文件传输速度快，费用较为低廉。其中 MT700 和 MT701 为信用证的开证格式，MT707 为信用证的改证格式，具体格式简介如下：

【MT700 和 MT701 开证格式】

代码 Tag	栏位名称（Field Name）
27	Sequence of Total 电文页次
20	Documentary Credit Number 信用证编号
40E	Applicable Rule 适用条文
45B	Description of Goods and/or Service 货物和/或服务的描述
46B	Documents Required 所需单据
47B	Additional Conditions 附加条款
50	Applicant 申请人
59	Beneficiary 受益人
32B	Currency Code, Amount 币种、金额
39A	Percentage Credit Amount 信用证金额上下浮动允许的最大范围
39B	Maximum Credit Amount 最高信用证金额
39C	Additional Amount Covered 附加金额
41A	Available with... by ... 指定的有关银行及信用证兑付的方式
42C	Drafts at ... 汇票付款日期
42A	Drawee 汇票付款人
42M	Mixed Payment Details 混合付款条款
42P	Deferred Payment Details 延期付款条款
43P	Partial Shipment 分批装运
43T	Transshipment 转运
44A	Loading on Board/Dispatch/Taking in Charge at/from ... 装船、发运和接受监管的地点

续表

代码 Tag	栏位名称（Field Name）
44B	For Transportation to ... 货物发运的最终目的港（地）
44C	Latest Date of Shipment 最迟装船日
44D	Shipment Period 装期
45A	Description of Goods and/or Services 货物与/或服务描述
46A	Documents Required 所需单据
47A	Additional Conditions 附加条款
71B	Charges 费用情况
48	Period for Presentation 交单期限
49	Confirmation Instruction 保兑指示
53A	Reimbursement Bank 偿付银行
78	Instructions to the Paying/Accepting/Negotiating Bank 对付款/承兑/议付银行的指示
57A	Advising through 通知银行
72	Sender to Receiver Information 银行间的备注

（一）跟单信用证开证格式（MT700）简介

必选 20 DOCUMENTARY CREDIT NUMBER（信用证号码）

可选 23 REFERENCE TO PRE-ADVICE（预先 通知 号码）

如果信用证是采取预先通知的方式，该项目内应该填入“PREADV/”，再加上预先通知的编号或日期。

必选 27 SEQUENCE OF TOTAL（电文页次）

可选 31C DATE OF ISSUE（开证日期）

如果这项没有填，则开证日期为电文的发送日期。

必选 31D DATE AND PLACE OF EXPIRY（信用证有效期和有效地点）

该日期为最后交单的日期。

必选 32B CURRENCY CODE, AMOUNT（信用证结算的货币和金额）

可选 39A PERCENTAGE CREDIT AMOUNT TOLERANCE（信用证金额上下浮动允许的最大范围）

该项目的表示方法较为特殊，数值表示百分比的数值，如：5/5，表示上下浮动最大为 5%。

可选 39B MAXIMUM CREDIT AMOUNT（信用证最大限制金额）

39B 与 39A 不能同时出现。

可选 39C ADDITIONAL AMOUNTS COVERED（额外金额）

表示信用证所涉及的保险费、利息、运费等金额。

必选 40A FORM OF DOCUMENTARY CREDIT（跟单信用证形式）

跟单信用证有五种形式：

（1）IRREVOCABLE（不可撤销跟单信用证）

（2）IRREVOCABLE TRANSFERABLE（不可撤销可转让跟单信用证）

（3）REVOCABLE TRANSFERABLE（可撤销可转让跟单信用证）

（4）IRREVOCABLE STANDBY（不可撤销备用信用证）

（5）REVOCABLE STANDBY（可撤销备用信用证）

必选 41a AVAILABLE WITH...BY...（指定的有关银行及信用证兑付的方式）

（1）指定银行作为付款、承兑、议付。

（2）兑付的方式有 5 种：BY PAYMENT（即期付款）；BY ACCEPTANCE（远期承兑）；BY NEGOTIATION（议付）；BY DEF PAYMENT（迟期付款）；BY MIXED PAYMENT（混合付款）。

（3）如果是自由议付信用证，对该信用证的议付地点不做限制，该项目代号为：41D，内容为：ANY BANK IN。

可选 42A DRAWEE（汇票付款人）

必须与 42C 同时出现。

可选 42C DRAFTS AT。（汇票付款日期）

必须与 42A 同时出现。

可选 42M MIXED PAYMENT DETAILS（混合付款条款）

可选 42P DEFERRED PAYMENT DETAILS（迟期付款条款）

可选 43P PARTIAL SHIPMENTS（分装条款）

表示该信用证的货物是否可以分批装运。

可选 43T TRANSSHIPMENT（转运条款）

表示该信用证的货物是直接到达，还是通过转运到达。

可选 44A LOADING ON BOARD/DISPATCH/TAKING IN CHARGE AT/FORM（装船、发运和接收监管的地点）

可选 44B FOR TRANSPORTATION TO...（货物发运的最终目的地）

可选 44C LATEST DATE OF SHIPMENT（最后装船期）

装船的最迟的日期。44C 与 44D 不能同时出现。

可选 44D SHIPMENT PERIOD（船期）

44C 与 44D 不能同时出现。

可选 45A DESCRIPTION OF GOODS AND/OR SERVICES（货物描述）

货物的情况、价格条款。

可选 46A DOCUMENTS REQUIRED（单据要求）

各种单据的要求

可选 47A ADDITIONAL CONDITIONS（特别条款）

可选 48 PERIOD FOR PRESENTATION（交单期限）

表明开立运输单据后多少天内交单。

必选 49 CONFIRMATION INSTRUCTIONS（保兑指示）

其中，CONFIRM：要求保兑行保兑该信用证

MAY ADD：收报行可以对该信用证加具保兑。

WITHOUT：不要求收报行保兑该信用证。

必选 50 APPLICANT（信用证开证申请人）

一般为进口商。

可选 51A APPLICANT BANK（信用证开证的银行）

可选 53A REIMBURSEMENT BANK（偿付行）

可选 57A “ADVISE THROUGH” BANK（通知行）

必选 59 BENEFICIARY（信用证的受益人）

一般为出口商。

可选 71B CHARGES（费用情况）

表明费用是否由受益人（出口商）出，如果没有这一条，表示除了议付费、转让费以外，其他各种费用由开出信用证的申请人（进口商）出。

可选 72 SENDER TO RECEIVER INFORMATION（附言）

可选 78 INSTRUCTION TO THE PAYING/ACCEPTING/NEGOTIATING BANK（给付款行、承兑行、议付行的指示）

【MT707 信用证修改格式】

代码 Tag	栏位名称（Field Name）
20	Sender's Reference 送讯银行的编号
21	Receiver's Reference 受讯银行的编号
23	Issuing Bank's Reference 开证银行的编号
52a	Issuing Bank 开证银行
31c	Date of Issue 开证日期
30	Date of Amendment 修改日期
26E	Number of Amendment 修改序号
59	Beneficiary (before this amendment) 受益人（修改以前的）
31E	New Date of Expiry 新的到期日
32B	Increase of Documentary Credit Amount 信用证金额的增加
33B	Decrease of Documentary Credit Amount 信用证金额的减少
34B	New Documentary Credit Amount After 修改后新的信用证金额
39A	Percentage Credit Amount Tolerance 信用证金额上下浮动允许的最大范围
39B	Maximum Credit Amount 最高信用证金额
39C	Additional Amount Covered 附加金额

续表

代码 Tag	栏位名称（Field Name）
44A	Loading on Board/Dispatch/Taking in Charge at/from ... 装船、发运和接受监管的地点
44B	For Transportation to ... 货物发运的最终目的港（地）
44C	Latest Date of Shipment 最迟装船日
44D	Shipment Period 装期
79	Narrative 说明
72	Sender to Receiver Information 银行间备注

（二）信用证修改（MT707）格式简介

必选 20 SENDER'S REFERENCE（信用证号码）

必选 21 RECEIVER'S REFERENCE（收报行编号）

发电文的银行不知道收报行的编号，填写“NONREF”。

可选 23 ISSUING BANK'S REFERENCE（开证行的号码）

可选 26E NUMBER OF AMENDMENT（修改次数）

该信用证修改的次数，要求按顺序排列。

可选 30 DATE OF AMENDMENT（修改日期）

如果信用证修改没填这项，修改日期就是发报日期。

可选 31C DATE OF ISSUE（开证日期）

如果这项没有填，则开证日期为电文的发送日期。

可选 31E NEW DATE OF EXPIRY（信用证新的有效期）

信用证修改的有效期。

可选 32B INCREASE OF DOCUMENTARY CREDIT AMOUNT（信用证金额的增加）

可选 33B DECREASE OF DOCUMENTARY CREDIT AMOUNT（信用证金额的减少）

可选 34B NEW DOCUMENTARY CREDIT AMOUNT AFTER AMENDMENT（信用证修改后的金额）

可选 39A PERCENTAGE CREDIT AMOUNT TOLERANCE（信用证金额上下浮动允许的最大范围的修改）

该项目的表示方法较为特殊，数值表示百分比的数值，如：5/5，表示上下浮动最大为 5%。39B 与 39A 不能同时出现。

可选 39B MAXIMUM CREDIT AMOUNT（信用证最大限制金额的修改）

39B 与 39A 不能同时出现。

可选 39C ADDITIONAL AMOUNTS COVERED（额外金额的修改）

表示信用证所涉及的保险费、利息、运费等金额的修改。

可选 44A LOADING ON BOARD/DISPATCH/TAKING IN CHARGE AT/FROM（装船、发运和接收监管的地点的修改）

可选 44B FOR TRANSPORTATION TO...（货物发运的最终地的修改）

可选 44C LATEST DATE OF SHIPMENT（最后装船期的修改）

修改装船的最迟的日期。44C 与 44D 不能同时出现。

可选 44D SHIPMENT PERIOD（装船期的修改）

44C 与 44D 不能同时出现。

可选 52a APPLICANT BANK（信用证开证的银行）

必选 59 BENEFICIARY（BEFORE THIS AMENDMENT）（信用证的受益人）

该项目为原信用证的受益人，如果要修改信用证的受益人，则需要在 79 NARRATIVE 修改详述）中写明。

可选 72 SENDER TO RECEIVER INFORMATION（附言）

/BENCON/：要求收报行通知发报行受益人是否接受该信用证的修改。/PHONBEN/：请电话通知受益人（列出受益人的电话号码）。/TELEBEN/：用快捷有效的电讯方式通知受益人。

可选 79 NARRATIVE（修改详述）

详细的修改内容。

六、信用证审核

受益人主要审核信用证的条款，信用证的真实性以及开证行的资信状况则由通知行来审核。审核内容如下：

1. 信用证通知书

在审证之前，要仔细阅读信用证通知书的内容。若认为开证行资信状况差、信用等级低，可要求开证申请人找一家可靠的银行加以保兑，使该信用证成为保兑信用证（Confirmed L/C），获得开证行和保兑行的双重第一性付款保证；若收到的为预先通知信用证时，则需要谨慎处理，因为预先通知信用证在法律上是无效的。

2. 审证依据

（1）外贸合同。信用证是依据外贸合同开立的，其条款应与外贸合同的条款相符。

（2）UCP600。审核信用证时，应遵循 UCP600 的规定来确定是否可以接受信用证的某些条款。

（3）业务实际情况。对于合同中未规定或无法根据 UCP600 来做出判断的信用证条款，应根据业务实际情况来审核。

3. 审证要点

（1）开证申请人和受益人的名称。开证申请人和受益人的名称是出口单证中必不可少的，若信用证开错应及时修改，以免影响安全收汇。

（2）信用证金额。信用证金额必须与外贸合同相符。若外贸合同订有商品数量的“溢短装”条款，信用证金额也应规定相应的机动幅度。若所开的信用证金额已扣除佣金，则不能在信用证上再出现议付行内扣佣金词句。

（3）货物描述。信用证中货物的名称、货号、规格、包装等内容是否与外贸合同完全一致。

（4）信用证有效期。按 UCP600 第 6 条 d 款的规定，信用证必须规定一个交单的有效期。

（5）交单期。信用证还应规定一个运输单据出单日期后必须提交符合信用证条款的单据的特定期限，即“交单期”。

（6）装运期。卖方将货物装上运往目的地（港）的运输工具或交付给承运人的日期。若信用证中未规定装运期，则最迟装运期与信用证有效期为同一天，即通常所称的“双到期”。

（7）运输条款。信用证运输条款中的装运港（地）和目的港（地）应与外贸合同相符，交货地点也必须与价格条款相一致。

若来证指定运输方式、运输工具或运输路线以及要求承运人出具船龄或船籍证明，应及时与承运人联系。

（8）保险条款。若来证要求的投保险别或投保金额超出了外贸合同的规定，除非信用证上表明由此而产生的超保费用由开证申请人承担并允许在信用证项下支取，否则应予修改。若保险加成过高，还需征得保险公司同意，否则应予修改。

（9）单据条款。要仔细审核信用证中的单据条款，特别要注意一些软条款，如商业发票经买方复签生效、1/3 正本提单直接寄给买方等。

（10）银行费用条款。一般情况下，出口方银行费用由受益人承担，进口方银行的费用由开证申请人承担。关于银行费用承担，进出口双方应在谈判时加以明确。

七、信用证的修改

（一）修改原则

在既不影响开证申请人正常利益又维护受益人自己的合法利益的前提下一有如下 5 种常见的处理原则：

（1）对我方有利又不影响对方利益的问题条款，一般不改。

（2）对我方有利但会严重影响对方利益的问题条款，一定要改。

（3）对我方不利但在不增加或基本不增加成本的情况下可以完成的问题条款，可以不改。

（4）对我方不利又要在增加较大成本的情况下可以完成的问题条款，若对方愿意承担成本，则不改；否则，要改。

（5）对我方不利若不改会严重影响安全收汇的问题条款，则坚决要改。

（二）修改流程

（1）受益人给开证申请人发改证函，协商改证事宜；

（2）协商一致后，开证申请人填写改证申请书，向开证行提出改证申请；

（3）开证行同意后，向信用证的原通知行发信用证修改，即 MT707；

（4）原通知行给受益人信用证修改通知和信用证修改，进行信用证修改通知。

（三）UCP600 中对信用证修改的规定

（1）UCP600 第 9 条 d 款规定，经由通知行或第二通知行通知信用证的银行必须经由同一通知行通知信用证的修改。

（2）UCP600 第 10 条 b 款规定，开证行发出修改之时起，即不可撤销地受其约束。保兑行可将其保兑扩展至修改，并自通知该修改之时，即不可撤销地受其约束。但是，保兑行可以选择将修改通知受益人而不对其加具保兑。若然如此，其必须毫不延误地将此告知开证行，并在其给受益人的通知中告知受益人。

（3）UCP600 第 10 条 c 款规定，在受益人告知通知修改的银行其接受该修改之前，原信用证（或含有先前被接受的修改的信用证）的条款对受益人仍然有效。受益人应提供接受或拒绝修改的通知。如果受益人未能给予通知，当交单与信用证以及尚未表示接受的修改的要求一致时，即视为受益人已做出接受修改的通知，并且从此时起，该信用证被修改。

（4）UCP600 第 10 条 e 款规定，对同一修改的内容不允许部分接受，部分接受将被视为拒绝修改的通知。

（5）UCP600 第 10 条 f 款规定，修改中关于“除非受益人在某一时间内拒绝修改否则修改生效”的规定应被不予理会。

子项目二 审证典型业务演示

2012 年 8 月 23 日，根据长沙鹏兴进出口有限公司与加拿大 ELBY 实业有限公司签订的马克杯出口合同，对方向 A 银行申请开立了一份不可撤销跟单信用证，并由中国银行湖南省分行通知鹏兴公司。单证员李望在该项目的任务是认真对照合同审核信用证，并提出修改意见。合同及信用证内容如下：

CONTRACT

Contract No.: CB121039　　　　Date: JUL 5, 2012

THE SELLER: PENGXING IMP&EXP COMPANY
LILING PENGXING CERAMIC FACTORY
WUSHI JIASHU LILING HUNAN, CHINA
TEL: 86-731-23384199　FAX: 86-731-23384298

THE BUYER: ELBY GIFTS INC.
879 INDUSTRIEL BOIS DES FILION
QUEBEC, J6Z 4T3, CANADA
TEL: 514-420-0282　FAX: 514-420-0322

This Contract is made by and between the Buyer and Seller, whereby the Buyer agrees to buy and the Seller agrees to sell the under mentioned goods on the terms and conditions stated below:

Description of Goods, Specifications,	Quantity (set)	Unit Price (U.S.D/set)	Amount (U.S.D)
Ceramic Cups and Bowls		C.I.F Prince Rupert	
V23-234	912	4.05	3,693.60
V23-234F	912	4.05	3,693.60
V23-235	1,520	2.40	3,648.00
V23-236	1,512	2.10	3,175.20
V23-237	1,488	1.95	2,901.6
V23-2348	1,520	2.04	3,100.80
36-062	1,528	2.30	3,514.40
36-063	1,496	2.12	3,171.52
As per the P/I No.: CCB23-36			
Total	10,888		26,898.72

Say total: U.S DOLLARS TWENTY SIX THOUSAND EIGHT HUNDRED AND NINETY EIGHT AND SEVENTY TWO CENTS (USD26,898.72)ONLY.

PACKING: 4 sets packed in a carton(V 23-234/V23-234F), 8 sets packed in a carton for others.

TRANSPORT DETAILS: the goods should be shipped on or before: 5th Sep, 2012, from Shenzhen, China to Prince Rupert Canada, transshipment and partial shipment are all allowed.

INSURANCE: To be effected by the Seller for 110% of invoice value covering all risks and S.R.C.C. as per C.I.C of PICC dated 01/01/1981.

PAYMENT: By irrevocable documentary letter of credit at sight, reaching the seller not later than Aug 5, 2012 and remain valid for negotiation in China for 15 days after shipment.

DOCUMENTS:

+ Signed commercial invoice one original and three copies.
+ Full set of clean on board ocean Bill of Lading made to order of issuing bank.
+ Packing List one original and two copies.
+ Insurance policy endorsed in blank.
+ GSP Form A certified by government authority.

INSPECTION: Quality/Quantity/Weight Discrepancy and Claim: In case the quality and/or quantity/weight are found by the Buyer not to conform with the contract after arrival of the goods at the final destination, the Buyer may lodge a claim against the seller supported by a survey report issued by an inspection organization agreed upon by both parties with the exception of those claims for which the insurance company and/or the shipping company are to be held responsible. Claim for quality discrepancy should be filed by the Buyer within 60 days after arrival of the goods at the final destination while for quantity/weight discrepancy claim should be filed by the Buyer within 30 days after arrival of the goods at the final destination.

FORCE MAJEURE: The Seller shall not be held responsible for failure or delay in delivery of the entire or portion of the goods under this contract in consequence of any Force Majeure incidents.

ARBITRATION: All disputes in connection with this Contract or the execution thereof shall be settled through friendly negotiations. If no settlement can be reached, the case shall then be submitted to the Foreign Trade Arbitration Commission of the China Council for the Promotion of International Trade, Beijing, for settlement by arbitration in accordance with the Commission's Provisional Rules of Procedure. The award rendered by the Commission shall be final and binding on both parties. The arbitration expenses shall be borne by the losing party unless otherwise award by the arbitration organization.

Signed by:

THE SELLER:	**THE BUYER:**
PENGXING IMP&EXP COMPANY	ELBY GIFTS INC.
LILING PENGXING CERAMIC FACTORY	
李 望	Camp Wolf
--	--

以下是该业务信用证：

SEQUENCE OF TOTAL	27:	1/1
FORM OF DC	40A:	IRREVOCABLE
DC NO	20:	DC HMN214479
DATE OF ISSUE	31C:	120705
APPLICABLE RULES	40E:	UCP LATEST VERSION
EXPIRY DATE AND PLACE	31D:	120810 IN CANADA
APPLICANT	50:	ELBY GIFTS INC.876 INDUSTRIEL BOLS DES FITION, QUEBEC, J6Z 4T3, CANADA
BENEFICIARY	59:	PENGXING IMPORT & EXPORT CO. LTD. LILING PENGXING CERAMIC FACTORY WUSHI JIASHU LILING HUNAN, CHINA
AMOUNT	32B:	USD27,010.40
PCT CR AMT TOLERANCE	39A:	10/10
AVAILABLE WITH/BY	41D:	ANY BANK IN CANADA BY NEGOTIATION
DRAFTS AT	42C:	AFTER SIGHT OF 15 DAYS
DRAWEE	42A:	ISSUING BANK

PARTIAL SHIPMENTS	43P:	NOT ALLOWED
TRANSHIPMENT	43T:	ALLOWED
PORT OF LOADING	44E:	SHANGHAI, CHINA
PORT OF DISCHARGE	44F:	PRINCE RUPERT, BC
LATEST DATE OF SHIPMENT	44D:	120901
DESCRIPTION OF GOODS OR SERVICES	45A:	CERAMIC CUP AND BOWL AS PER S/C NO.:CB121089 (CIF PRINCE RUPERT,BC)删 ALL PACKED IN CARTONS AND 4 SETS IN A CARTON.
DOCUMENTS REQUIRED	46A:	+ ORIGINAL SIGNED INVOICE PLUS THREE COPIES. + FULL SET OF CLEAN MULTIMODAL TRANSPORT DOCUMENT PLUS 2 N/N COPIES, MADE TO THE ORDER OF BANK OF CHINA, HUNAN BRANCH SHOWING ON BOARD NOTATION, MARKED FREIGHT COLLECT, AND NOTIFY APPLICANT(STATING FULL NAME AND ADDRESS). + INSURANCE POLICY OR CERTIFICATE BLANK INDORSED, FOR THE INVOICE VALUE PLUS 20% COVERING ALL RISKS AND W.P.A. AND S.R.C.C. FROM WAREHOUSE TO WAREHOUSE. + PACKING LIST IN ONE ORIGINAL AND TWO COPIES. + GSP CERTIFICATE OF ORIGIN FORM A, IN ONE ORIGINAL PLUS 2 COPIES, INDICATING COUNTRY OF ORIGIN, COUNTERCHOPPED BY GOVERNMENT. OR EXPORTER'S STATMENT OF ORIGIN + SHIPPING NOTE INCLUDING SHIPPING MARKS, CTN NO., B/L NO., QUANTITY, VESSEL'S NAME, VOYAGE NO., SHOULD BE SENT TO THE ISSUING BANK ON THE DATE OF SHIPMENT.
ADDITIONAL CONDITIONS	47A:	+ BENEFICIARY'S DETAILS: CTC: MILLER LEE TEL: 86-731-2338-4199

		FAX: 86-731-2338-4298 FOLLOWING CHARGES ARE FOR BENEFICIARY'S ACCOUNT: 1) REIMBURSEMENT/REMITTANCE CHARGES 2) DISCREPANCY FEE OF USD/CAD/EUR100 PLUS ALL RELEVANT CABLE CHARGES WILL BE DEDUCTED FROM EACH PRESENTATION OF DISCREPANT DOCUMENTS UNDER THIS DC.
CHARGES	71B:	ALL BANKING CHARGES ARE FOR ACCOUNT OF BENEFICIARY/EXPORTER
PERIOD OF PRESENTATION	48:	WITHIN 5 DAYS AFTER THE DATE OF SHIPMENT BUT WITHIN THE VALIDITY OF THE CREDIT
CONFIRMATION INSTRUCTIONS	49:	WITHOUT
INFO TO PRESENTING BK	78:	+ UPON RECEIPT OF DOCUMENTS CONFORMING TO THE TERMS OF THIS CREDIT WE UNDERTAKE TO REIMBURSE YOU IN THE CURRENCY OF THIS CREDIT IN ACCORDANCE WITH YOUR INSTRUCTIONS, LESS CABLE CHARGES + FORWARD DOCUMENTS IN ONE LOT BY COURIER AT BENEFICIARY'S EXPENSES TO HSBC BANK CANADA, TRADE AND SUPPLY CHAIN, 5100 SHERBROOKE STREET EAST, SUITE 190, MONTREAL, QUEBEC, H1V 3R9 CANADA. + THE AMOUNT OF EACH DRAWING MUST BE ENDORSED ON THE REVERSE OF THIS DC BY THE NEGOTIATING/PRESENTING BANK.

经审核，该信用证有以下条款需要修改：

1. 31C 开证日期不符，根据合同，开证日期应为 120720 之前
2. 31D 有效期不符，根据合同，有效期应为 120919
3. 31D 到期地点不符，根据合同，到期地点应在中国
4. 59 受益人名称不符，受益人名称应为 LILING PENGXING CERAMIC FACTORY
5. 42C 汇票付款期限不符，汇票付款期限应为 AT SIGHT
6. 41D 信用证议付行应在中国的任意银行
7. 43P 应为允许分批装运

8. 44E 装运港不符，装运港应为 SHENZHEN

9. 44C 最迟装运期不符，最迟装运期应为 120905

10. 45A 品名不符，品名应为 CERAMIC CUPS AND BOWLS

11. 45A 合同号有误，应为 CB121039

12. 45A 包装条款有误，应为 4 SETS PACKED IN A CARTON (V 23-234/V23-234F), 8 SETS PACKED IN A CARTON FOR OTHERS

13. 46A 提单应做成开证行抬头

运费项目错误，应注明 FREIGHT PREPAID

14. 46A 保险单的保险金额错误，应为发票金额的 10%

15. 46A 保险险别应为 ALL RISKS AND S.R.C.C

16. 71B 所有费用由受益人负担不合理

17. 48 交单期应为装运日期后 15 天

18. 50 申请人有误，应为 ELBY GIFTS INC.879 INDUSTRIEL BOIS DES FILION, QUEBEC, J6Z 4T3, CANADA

19. 39A 应删除，该类商品不适用数量机动幅度条款

子项目三 审证拓展业务操作

能力实训项目 1：信用证审核及修改业务操作

根据上海淼睿进出口有限公司第 C-11027 号信用证的要求，2013 年 8 月 31 日，单证员彭婷根据合同开始审核信用证。

1. 合同

SALES CONTRACT

Contract No.:SSW0803

Date: AUG 15,2013

THE SELLER: JIANGSU I-TOUCH BUSINESS SERVICE LTD,
ROOM 117, JIANGSU EDIFICE
ZHANGJIAGANG FREE TRADE ZONE,
JIANGSU, CHINA TEL:86-512-56363783

THE BUYER: M/S. MEMORY STEEL CORPORATION
73/A, LAL MOHAN SHAHA STREET
(DHOLAIKHAL), DHAKA-1100.
BANGLADESH.

This Contract is made by and between the Buyer and Seller, whereby the Buyer agrees to buy and the Seller agrees to sell the under mentioned goods on the terms and conditions stated below:

Description of Goods, Specifications,	Quantity (set)	Unit Price (U.S.D/set)	Amount (U.S.D)
		C.F.R CHITTAGONG	
201/2B SECONDARY GRADE STAINLESS STEEL SHEET OF WIDTH 1,219MM OR MORE THICKNESS 1MM TO 3MM, QTY:25,000KGS AT THE RATE OF USD1.40/KG. AS PER BENIFICIARY'S PROFORMA INVOIVE NO. SK20130802-001 DATED AUG 2,2013	1.2*1,219*2,438 1.5*1,219*2,438 2.0*1,219*2,438 3.0*1,219*2,438	1.40 1.40 1.40 1.40	7,806.40 4,547.20 16,282.00 6,364.40 35,000.00
Total			

Say Total: U.S DOLLARS THIRTY FIVE THOUSAND ONLY.

PACKING: Standard export packing on pallets.

TRANSPORT DETAILS: the goods should be shipped before: 9th Oct, 2013, from any Chinese port To Chittagong Bangladesh,

Transshipment and partial shipment are allowed.

PAYMENT: By sight L/C and remain valid for negotiation in China for 15 days after shipment.

DOCUMENTS:

+ Signed commercial invoice in triplicate, certifying the goods are of Chinese origin and being imported against IRC No.BA-0171646,VAT Registration No.9141093671..

+ Full set (3/3) of clean on board ocean Bill of Lading made out to order of shipper and blank indorsed.

+ Packing List in triplicate.

+ Certificate of origin by CCPIT.

+Beneficiary's Declaration certifying that the country of origin has been printed on goods packing bag.

INSPECTION: Quality/Quantity/Weight Discrepancy and Claim: In case the quality and/or quantity/weight are found by the Buyer not to conform with the contract after arrival of the goods at the final destination, the Buyer may lodge a claim against the seller supported by a survey report issued by an inspection organization agreed upon by both parties with the exception of those claims for which the insurance company and/or the shipping company are To be held responsible. Claim for quality discrepancy should be filed by the Buyer within 60 days after arrival of the goods at the final destination while for quantity/weight discrepancy claim should be filed by the Buyer within 30 days after arrival of the goods at the final destination.

FORCE MAJEURE: The Seller shall not be held responsible for failure or delay in delivery of the entire or portion of the goods under this contract in consequence of any Force Majeure incidents.

ARBITRATION: All disputes in connection with this Contract or the execution thereof shall be settled through friendly negotiations. If no settlement can be reached, the case shall then be submitted to the Foreign Trade Arbitration Commission of the China Council for the Promotion of International Trade, Beijing, for settlement by arbitration in accordance with the Commission's Provisional Rules of Procedure. The award rendered by the Commission shall be final and binding on both parties. The arbitration expenses shall be borne by the losing party unless otherwise award by the arbitration organization.

Signed by:

THE SELLER:	**THE BUYER:**
JIANGSU I-TOUCH BUSINESS CORPORATION.SERVICE LTD	M/S. MEMORY STEEL CORPORATION
彭 婷	John Lee

2. 信用证

SEQUENCE OF TOTAL	27:	1/1
FORM OF DC.	40A:	IRREVOCABLE
DC. NO.	20:	0684130117426
DATE OF ISSUE	31C:	130825
APPLICABLE RULES	40E:	UCP LATEST VERSION
EXPIRY DATE AND PLACE	31D:	130924, IN BANGLADESH
APPLICANT	50:	M/S. MEMORY STEEL CORPORATION 73/A, LAL MOHAN SHAHA STREET, DHAKA-100. BANGLADESH.
BENEFICIARY	59:	JIANGSU I-TOUCH BUSINESS SERVICE LTD, ROOM 117, JIANGSU EDIFICE ZHANGJIAGANG FREE TRADE ZONE, JIANGSU, CHINA TEL:86-512-56363783
AMOUNT	32B:	EUR35,500.00
AVAILABLE WITH/BY	41D:	ANY BANK IN CHINA BY NEGOTIATION
DRAFTS AT	42C:	AT SIGHT FOR FULL INVOICE VALUE
DRAWEE	42A:	M/S. MEMORY STEEL CORPORATION
PARTIAL SHIPMENTS	43P:	PROHIBITTED
TRANSSHIPMENT	43T:	ALLOWED
PORT OF LOADING	44A:	ANY SEA PORT, CHINA

PORT OF DISCHARGE	44B:	CHITTAGONG SEA PORT, BANGLADESH
LATEST DATE OF SHIPMENT	44C:	131109
DESCRIPTION OF GOODS	45A:	201/2B SECONDARY GRADE STAINLESS STEEL SHEET OF WIDTH 1219MM OR MORE THICKNESS 1MM TO 3MM, QTY:25,000KGS AT THE RATE OF USD1.40/KG FOR TOTAL AMOUNT OF USD35,000.00 CIF CHITTAGONG, BANGLADESH. AS PER BENEFICIARY'S PROFORMA INVOICE NO. SK20130807-001 DATED 23.AUG,2013, PACKED IN CARTONS.
DOCUMENTS REQUIRED	46A:	+MANUALLY SIGNED COMMERCIAL INVOICE IN TRIPLICATE CERTIFYING MERCHANDISE TO BE OF CHINA ORIGIN AND INDICATING THAT THE GOODS ARE BEING IMPORTED AGAINST IRC NO.BA-0171646. +CLEAN 'SHIPPED ON BOARD' OCEAN BILL OF LADING IN DUPLICATE, SHOWING 'FREIGHT PREPAID', MADE OUT TO ORDER OF AB BANK LIMITED, NAWABPUR ROAD BRANCH, DHAKA, BANGLADESH AND MARKED NOTIFY OPENERS. + INSURANCE POLICY IN TRIPLICATE FOR THE 110% OF INVOICE VALUE COVERING ALL RISKS AS PER P.I.C.C. +PACKING LIST IN TRIPLICATE SHOWING GROSS WEIGHT, NET WEIGHT. + A CERTIFICATE OF 'COUNTRY OF ORIGIN' MUST BE ISSUED BY THE GOVERNMENT APPROVED AUTHORITY/ORGANIZATION OF THE EXPORTER'S COUNTRY. +BENEFICIARY SHOULD SEND A FAX OR BY COUR-IER TO L/C OPENING BANK WITHIN FIVE DAYS FROM THE OF SHIPMENT, ADVISING THE DATE OF SHIPMENT, VESSEL'S NAME, AMOUNT OF BILL AND L/C NO. A COPY OF THIS FAX SHOULD SIGNED BY THE NOMINATED PERSON OF THE

		APPLICANT AND ACCOMPANY THE SHIPPING DOCUMENTS.
ADDITIONAL CONDITIONS	47A:	+FULL NAME, ADDRESS OF THE APPLICANT, L/C NO. AND DATE TO BE SHOWN IN INVOICE, PACKING LIST AND BILL OF LADING. +SHORT FORM, STALE, CLAUSED BILL OF LADING IS NOT ACCEPTABLE.
CHARGES	71B:	ALL FOREIGN BANK CHARGES ARE FOR THE ACCOUNT OF THE BENEFICIARY.
PERIOD OF PRESENTATION	48:	5 DAYS FROM SHIPMENT DATE BUT WITHIN VALIDITY OF THE CREDIT

请对根据合同对信用证认真进行审核，并结合受益人实际情况对该证提出合理的修改意见。

能力实训项目 2：信用证审核修改业务操作

根据深圳普瑞玛建材有限公司第 DC 13720 号合同的要求，2013 年 8 月 5 日，单证员黄柯根据合同审核信用证。

1. 合同

CONTRACT

Contract No.:BFF0606

Date: JUL 1, 2013

THE SELLER: PRIMA CONSTRUCTION MATERIALS CO., LTD.
1401 ROOM, 38 BUILDING, CHUANGYE GARDEN
BAOAN DISTRICT, SHENZHEN, CHINA

THE BUYER: CONSTRUCTION MOUDULAR SPECIALIST
POSTAL: 13 HARVEY RD.,
SHENTON PK, WA 6008 AUSTRALIA

This Contract is made by and between the Buyer and Seller, whereby the Buyer agrees to buy and the Seller agrees to sell the under mentioned goods on the terms and conditions stated below:

Description of Goods, Specifications,	Quantity (SQM)	Unit Price (U.S.D/SQM)	Amount (U.S.D)
BAMBOO FLOORING ITEM 1 ITEM 2	 100 100	CIF FREMENTLE 20.00 39.50	 2,000.00 3,950.00
AS PER PI NO.: BFF0610			
Total	200		5,950.00

Say total: U.S DOLLARS FIFTY NINE HUNDRED AND FIFTY (USD5,950)ONLY.

PACKING: All packing in seaworthy cartons.

TRANSPORT DETAILS: the goods should be shipped on or before: 20th Sep, 2013, from Shenzhen, China to Frementle Australia, transshipment and partial shipment are all allowed.

INSURANCE: To be effected by the Seller for 110% of invoice value covering ICC(A) risk and ICC(War Risk).

PAYMENT: By irrevocable documentary letter of credit at 30 days after sight, reaching the seller not later than Jul 30,2013 and remain valid for negotiation in China for 15 days after shipment.

DOCUMENTS:

+ Signed commercial invoice three originals and three copies.
+ Full set of clean on board ocean Bill of Lading made to order.
+ Packing List three originals and two copies.
+ Insurance policy endorsed in blank and in triplicate.
+Certificate of Origin in China issued by official authority.

2. 信用证

SEQUENCE OF TOTAL	27:	1/1
FORM OF DC	40A:	IRREVOCABLE
DC NO.	20:	DC 130720
DATE OF ISSUE	31C:	130731
APPLICABLE RULES	40E:	UCP 600
EXPIRY DATE AND PLACE	31D:	130910 IN CHINA
APPLICANT	50:	CONSTRUCTION MOUDULAR SPECIALIST POSTAL: 13 HARVEY RD., SHENTON PK, WA 6008
BENEFICIARY	59:	PRIMA CONSTRUCTION MATERIALS CO., LTD 1041 ROOM, 38 BUILDING, HUANGYE GARDEN BAOAN DISTRICT, SHENZHEN, CHINA
AMOUNT	32B:	USD6,840.00
AVAILABLE WITH/BY	41D:	ANY BANK BY NEGOTIATION
DRAFTS AT	42C:	AT SIGHT
DRAWEE	42A:	DRAWN ON US
PARTIAL SHIPMENTS	43P:	PERMITTED
TRANSHIPMENT	43T:	FORBIDDEN
LOADING PORT	44E:	CHINA MAIN PORT
DISCHARGE PORT	44F:	FREMENTLE, AUSTRALIA
LATEST DATE OF SHIPMENT	44C:	130905

DESCRIPTION OF GOODS	45A:	BAMBOO FLOORING ITEM 1 100 SQM U.S.D39.50/SQM ITEM 2 100 SQM U.S.D20.00/SQM ALL PACKING IN SEA WORTHY CARTONS CFR FREMENTLE AS PER PI NO.: BFF6100
DOCUMENTS REQUIRED	46A:	+ MANUALLY SIGNED COMMECIAL INVOICE 2 ORIGINALS PLUS TWO COPIES. + FULL SET(3/3) OF MARINE BILLS OF LADING, MADE OUT TO ORDER, MARKED FREIGHT COLLECT, AND NOTIFY APPLICANT(STATING FULL NAME AND ADDRESS). + INSURANCE POLICY OR CERTIFICATE IN TRIPLICATE, BLANK INDORSED, FOR THE INVOICE VALUE PLUS 12% COVERING ICC(A) RISK AND ICC(STRIKE). FROM WAREHOUSE TO WAREHOUSE AND I.O.P, PAYABLE AT FREMENTLE IN U.S.D. + PACKING LIST 3 ORIGINALS AND 2 COPIES. +CERTIFICATE OF ORIGIN IN CHINA ISSUED BY OFFICIAL AUTHRORITY. + BENNIFICIALRY'S CERTIFICATE SHOWING THAT A SET OF ORIGINAL SHIPPING DOCUMENTS HAS BEEN MAIL TO THE APPLICANT BY EXPRESS AFTER 2 DAYS OF SHIOMENT.
CHARGES	71B:	ALL BANKING CHARGES ARE FOR BENEFICIARY/'S ACCOUNT.
PERIOD OF PRESENTATION	48:	WITHIN 5 DAYS AFTER THE DATE OF SHIPMENT BUT WITHIN THE VALIDITY OF THE L/C
CONFIRMATION INSTRUCTIONS	49:	WITHOUT

请对根据合同对信用证认真进行审核，并结合受益人实际情况对该证提出合理的修改意见。

项目三　商业单据制作业务

项目预期目标

商业发票是出口交易中最常见、最重要的单据之一，是全套出口单据的核心。装箱单是包装单据的一种，对商业发票进行补充，同时也是货运单据中一种重要单据。通过对信用证下有关商业发票和装箱单条款的解读，理清该笔业务对商业发票和装箱单缮制的具体要求，通过介绍发票和装箱单的定义、种类和作用，引导学生熟悉商业发票和装箱单的格式及内容，重点训练学生掌握商业发票和装箱单的制作要点，并最终能独立完成符合信用证要求的商业发票和装箱单缮制。

在项目实施过程中，有效训练学生对信用证单据条款的阅读理解，培养学生认真细心制单的基本职业能力，并熟悉 UCP600 的相关条款。

表 3-1　　**项目预期目标**

目标类型	商业发票和装箱单的制作
知识目标	了解发票和装箱单的含义、作用和类型
	熟悉商业发票和装箱单的格式及内容
	掌握商业发票和装箱单的缮制要点
能力目标	能根据信用证等相关信息正确制作商业发票
	能根据信用证等相关信息正确制作装箱单
职业素质目标	独立业务操作能力
	认真、细致、严谨的工作态度

项目实施条件

1. 教师演示工作项目和归纳技能要点
2. 学生能够在实训室对该项目进行分组讨论并实施

开篇业务引入

根据第 DC HMN214479 号信用证的要求，长沙鹏兴进出口有限公司需要向进口方 ELBY GIFTS INC.开具商业发票和装箱单，该项目任务具体由单证员李望负责。2012 年 8 月 16 日，单证员李望根据 L/C 规定：“+ ORIGINAL SIGNED INVOICE PLUS THREE

COPIES."、"+ ORIGINAL PACKING LIST PLUS 2 COPIES"，要求完成商业发票和装箱单的缮制。

子项目一 商业发票与装箱单制作

一、商业发票的含义

商业发票（Commercial Invoice）是卖方向买方开具的载有交易货物名称、数量、价格等内容的总清单，是买卖双方交接货物、结算记账的依据，也是进出口申报关税必不可少的单证之一。在国际贸易中，也常常将商业发票简称为发票。我国各外贸公司的商业发票没有统一格式，但主要项目基本相同，主要包括发票的编号、收货人、填制日期、数量、单价、总值和支付方式等项内容。

二、商业发票的作用

（一）商业发票是交易的合法证明文件，是货运单据的中心，也是装运货物的总说明。

（二）商业发票是买卖双方收付货物和记账核算的依据。

（三）商业发票是买卖双方办理报关、纳税的计算依据。

（四）在不使用汇票结算的情况下，发票代替汇票作为付款依据。

（五）商业发票是出口方缮制其他出口单证的依据。

三、发票的类型

发票的种类很多，除了常见的商业发票外，还有形式发票（Pro-forma Invoice）、海关发票（Customs Invoice）、领事发票（Consular Invoice）、厂商发票（Manufacturer's Invoice）等。其中，形式发票不是一种正式发票，一般是不可接受的，仅作参考和预估，待正式成交后需重新制作商业发票。

<table>
<tr><td colspan="2">ISSUER</td><td colspan="3" rowspan="2">COMMERCIAL INVOICE</td></tr>
<tr><td colspan="2">TO</td></tr>
<tr><td colspan="2"></td><td colspan="2">NO.</td><td>DATE</td></tr>
<tr><td colspan="2" rowspan="2">TRANSPORT DETAILS</td><td colspan="2">S/C NO.</td><td>L/C NO.</td></tr>
<tr><td colspan="3">TERMS OF PAYMENT</td></tr>
<tr><td>Marks and Numbers</td><td>Number and Kind of Package
Description of Goods</td><td>Quantity</td><td>Unit Price</td><td>Amount</td></tr>
<tr><td colspan="5"></td></tr>
<tr><td colspan="5">Total:
SAY
TOTAL:</td></tr>
<tr><td colspan="5"></td></tr>
</table>

<table>
<tr><td colspan="3" rowspan="1">ISSUER</td><td colspan="3" rowspan="2">形式发票
PROFORMA INVOICE</td></tr>
<tr><td colspan="3">TO</td></tr>
<tr><td colspan="3" rowspan="1"></td><td colspan="2">NO.</td><td>DATE</td></tr>
<tr><td colspan="3" rowspan="2">TRANSPORT DETAILS</td><td colspan="2">S/C NO.</td><td>L/C NO.</td></tr>
<tr><td colspan="3">TERMS OF PAYMENT</td></tr>
<tr><td>Marks and Numbers</td><td>Number and Kind of Package
Description of Goods</td><td>Quantity</td><td colspan="2">Unit Price</td><td>Amount</td></tr>
<tr><td></td><td></td><td></td><td colspan="2"></td><td></td></tr>
<tr><td colspan="6">Total:
SAY
TOTAL:</td></tr>
<tr><td colspan="6">PORT TO LOADING:
PORT OF DESTINATION:
TIME OF DELIVERY:
INSURANCE:
VALIDITY:
BENEFICIARY
ADVISING BANK:
NEGOTIATING BANK:</td></tr>
</table>

CANADA CUSTOMS INVOICE

Customs and Excise / Douanes et Accise　**FACTURE DES DOUANES CANADIENNES**　of / de

1. Vendor (Name and Address) / Vendeur (Nom et adresse)

AMERIWOOD
INDUSTRIES

2 SPAULDING STREET • DOWAGIAC, USA
Phone: +1-616-　Fax: +1-616-

2. Date of Direct Shipment to Canada / Date d'expédition directe vers le Canada

INVOICE NUMBER

3. Other References (Include Purchaser's Order No.) / Autres références (Inclure le no de commande de l'acheteur)

4. Consignee (Name and Address) / Destinataire (Nom et adresse)

5. Purchaser's Name and Address (If other than Consignee) / Nom et adresse de l'acheteur (s'il diffère de destinataire)

6. Country of Transhipment / Pays de transbordement

7. Country of Origin of Goods / Pays d'orine des marchandises

IF SHIPMENT INCLUDES GOODS OF DIFFERENT ORIGINS ENTER ORIGINS AGAINST ITEMS IN 12. SI L'EXPÉDITION COMPREND DES MARCHANDISES D'ORIGINES DIFFÉRENTES, PRÉCISER LEUR PROVENANCE EN 12.

8. Transportation: Give Mode and Place of Direct Shipment to Canada / Transport: Préciser mode et point d'expédition directe vers le Canada

9. Conditions of Sales and Terms of Purchase (i.e. Sale, Consignment Shipment, Leased Goods, etc.) / Conditions de vente et modalités de paiement (p. ex. vente, expédition en consignation, locate de marchandises, etc.)

10. Currency of Settlement / Devises du paiement

11. No of Pkgs / Nbre de colis	12. Specification of Commodities (Kind of Packages, Marks and Numbers, General Description and Characteristics i.e. Grade, Quality) / Désignation des articles (Nature des colis, marques et numéros, description générale et caractéristiques, p. ex. classe, qualité)	13. Quantity (State unit) / Quantité (Préciser l'unité)	Selling Price / Prix de vente: 14. Unit Price / Prix unitaire	15. Total

18. If any fields 1 to 17 are included on an additional commercial invoice, check this box. / Si tout renseignement relativement aux zone 1 & 17 figure sur une ou des factures commerciales ci-attachées, cocher cette case.　**SEE ATTACHED** ☐

Commercial Invoice No. / No de la facture commerciale ________

16. Total Weight / Poids total: Net / Gross / Brut

17. Invoice Total / Total de la facture

19. Exporter's Name and Address (If other than Vendor) / Nom et adresse de l'exportateur (s'il diffère du vendeur)

20. Originator (Name And Address) / Expéditeur d'origine (Nom et adresse)

21. Departmental Ruling (If applicable) / Décision du Ministère (s'il y a lieu)

22. If fields 23 & 25 are not applicable, check this box. / Si les zones 23 & 25 sont sans objet, cocher cette case. ☐

23. If included in field 17, indicate amount: / Si compris dans le total à la zone 17, préciser:

(i) Transportation charges, expenses and insurance from the place of direct shipment to Canada. / Les frais de transport, dépenses et assurances à partir du point d'expédition directe vers le Canada. ________

(ii) Costs for construction, erection and assembly incurred after importation into Canada. / Les coûts de construction, d'érection et d'assemblage après importation au Canada. ________

(iii) Export Packing / Le coût de l'emballage d'exportation ________

24. If not included in field 17, indicate amount: / Si non compris dans le total à la zone 17, préciser:

(i) Transportation charges, expenses and insurance to the place of direct shipment to Canada. / Les frais de transport, dépenses et assurances à partir du point d'expédition directe vers le Canada. ________

(ii) Amounts for commissions other than buying commissions. / Les commissions autres que celles versées pour l'achat. ________

(iii) Export Packing / Le coût de l'emballage d'exportation ________

25. Check (If applicable) / Cocher (s'il a lieu):

☐ (i) Royalty payment or subsequent proceeds are paid or payable by the purchaser. / Des redevances ou produits ont été or seront versés par l'acheteur.

☐ (ii) The purchaser has supplied goods or services for use in the production of these goods. / L'acheteur a fourni des marchandises ou des services pour la production des marchandises.

四、商业发票的缮制

（一）具体操作

1. 出口方公司名称和地址（Name and Address of the Seller）

（1）填写内容：

根据 UCP600 的规定，若信用证无另外规定，商业发票的出票人为受益人（即出口方）。发票的顶端往往要有醒目的出票人名称和详细地址，且应与信用证或合同一致。许多出口企业在印刷空白发票时已印制这些内容，或将这些内容编入电脑程序一并打印。

（2）实例：

LILING PENGXING CERAMIC FACTORY

WUSHI JIASHU LILING HUNAN, CHINA

TEL: 86-731-23384199　FAX: 86-731-23384298

2. 商业发票名称（Name of Invoice）

（1）填写内容：

根据来证要求填写，若无另外规定，一般标为“商业发票”或“发票”的单据均可接受。

（2）实例：

COMMERCIAL INVOICE 或 INVOICE

3. 收货人或抬头名称和地址（To）

（1）填写内容：

根据 UCP600 的规定，若信用证无另外规定，商业发票的收货人或抬头为开证申请人（即进口方）。名称和地址应与信用证或合同一致。

（2）实例：

To

ELBY GIFTS INC.

879 INDUSTRIEL BOIS DES FILION,QUEBEC,

J6Z 4T3, CANADA

4. 商业发票号码（Invoice No.）

（1）填写内容：

由出口商统一编制，一般采用顺序号，便于查对。因商业发票作为中心票据，其他票据的号码一般此号码保持一致。如：汇票号码、出口报关单号码及附属单据号码等一般都与发票号码一致。

（2）实例：

Invoice No.: PX12IVN1039

5. 商业发票日期（Invoice Date）

（1）填写内容：

通常是指商业发票签发的日期，发票日期应早于提单日期和汇票日期，但不能迟于信用证的议付日期或有效期。根据 UCP600 的规定，如果信用证没有特殊规定，银行可以接受签发日期早于开证日的发票。

（2）实例：

Invoice Date: 2012/8/16

6. 合同号码或信用证号码（S/C No. Or L/C No.）

（1）填写内容：

参照合同和信用证填制。

（2）实例：

S/C No.: CB121039

L/C No.: DC HMN214479

7. 运输路线及工具（From…to…by…）

（1）填写内容：

该栏目为非必须栏目，可以省略。如不省略，起运地和目的地均应明确具体，不能笼统。且按实际情况填制，起讫地应与提单一致。如果货物系转运，转运地点也应明确表示。

（2）实例：

From Shanghai to London, U.K. W/T at Rotterdam by sea

8. 唛头及件号（Marks & Numbers）

（1）填写内容：

凡是来证有指定唛头的，必须完全按照规定制作唛头。若无指定，出口商可自行设计唛头，唛头一般以简明、易于识别为原则。唛头通常包括：收货人名称缩写、参考号码（合同号/发票号码/订单号码等）、目的港、件号四部分组成。如系散装或裸装货物时，无唛头，则可打上 N/M（No Mark）。

（2）实例：

Marks & Numbers

MOMO
HNT (04) 021
KOBE
NO. 1~240

9. 货物描述（Description of Goods）

（1）填写内容：

商业发票的货物描述必须与信用证保持一致，但并不要求如同镜子反射那样一致。货物细节可以在发票中的若干地方表示，当合并在一起与信用证规定一致即可。同时，商业发票中的货物描述必须反映实际装运的货物。

（2）实例：

Description of Goods

12,000 KGS Pu-erh Tea PACKED IN 240 CARTONS AS PER CONTRACT NO. HNT (04) 021

10. 商品的数量（Quantity）

（1）填写内容：

商品的重量或数量应与其他单据相一致，且数量单位应与单价中的数量单位一致。凡出现“约”（About/ABT/more or less）、“大概”、“大约”或类似词语，用于信用证数量时，应理解为有关数量不超过 10%的增减幅度。

（2）实例：

Quantity

100PCS

11. 单价与总值（Unit Price & Amount）

（1）填写内容：

完整的商品单价应由：计价货币、单位价格金额、计量单位、价格术语四部分组成。其中特别注意不要漏填或错填价格术语，且必须与信用证指明的价格术语保持一致，因为它涉及到买卖双方责任的承担、费用的负担和风险的划分等问题，另外，也是海关核定关税的依据。

商业发票中使用的币种应与信用证中使用的币种严格一致。同时，商业发票总金额应该是计算后得出的商品的总价值，且总金额不能超过信用证规定的最大金额。特别注意，当来证要求商业发票必须显示折扣或佣金时，应如实照办。当出现既含折扣又含佣金时，应先减扣折扣，再减扣佣金。例如，来证要求“5% DISCOUNT AND 5% COMMISSION TO BE DEDUCTED FROM INVOICE VALUE”，那么商业发票应显示如下：

Quantity	Unit Price	Amount
4000PCS	USD3.10/PC CIFC5 NEWYORK	USD12,400.00
	LESS 5% DISCOUNT	USD620.00
		USD11,780.00
	LESS 5% COMMISSION	USD589.00
	NET:	USD11,191.00

如果来证要求显示 FOB 价格，或要求分别注明运费、保险费和 CIF 价格，应严格按信用证要求来制作商业发票。如：

Quantity	Unit Price	Amount
500 sets	USD50.00/set FOB Shanghai	USD25,000.00
	Freight	USD1,000.00
	Insurance	USD1,500.00
	TOTAL CIF VALUE	USD27,500.00

单价和总值是商业发票的重要项目，必须准确计算、正确缮打，并认真复核。特别要注意小数点的位置是否正确，金额和数量的横乘、竖加是否有矛盾。凡出现“约”

（About/ABT/more or less）、“大概”、“大约”或类似词语，用于信用证金额、单价时，应理解为有关金额或单价有不超过 10%的增减幅度。

（2）实例：

Quantity	Unit Price	Amount
200 PCS	EUR80.00/PC CFR BANGKOK	EUR16,000.00

12. 来证要求加注特殊内容（Other Special Requirements）

（1）填写内容：

有时信用证要求在商业发票上加注各种费用金额、特定号码、某些权威机构认证等证明文句，在可以接受和做到的情况下，一般将这些内容打在商业发票商品栏以下的空白处。常见的有如：加注运费或保费等，注明许可证号码等，注明货物原产自中国，加注“发展中国家声明”等等。因此，在审证时，则应将这些特殊条款标出，以免遗漏。如若难以办到，则应及时要求对方修改条款。

（2）实例：

WE HEREBY CERTIFY THAT THE ABOVE GOODS ARE TRUE AND CORRECT.

或 WE HEREBY CERTIFY THAT THE ABOVE GOODS ARE OF CHINESE ORIGIN.

13. 出票人签章（Signature）

（1）填写内容：

除非信用证另有规定，商业发票只能由信用证中规定的受益人出具，且由出票人一般在发票正面右下角签章。如果以影印、自动或电脑处理或复写方法制作的商业发票作为正本者，应在商业发票上注明“正本”（ORIGINAL）字样，并由出单人签字。

UCP600 规定商业发票可不必签字，但有时来证规定商业发票需要签字的，则必须照办，如来证要求“SIGNED COMMERCIAL INVOICE…”。在没有手签要求的情况下，可以使用印鉴；但若来证明确要求手签（MANULLY SIGNED 或 HAND SIGNED），则必须手签。

（2）实例：

HUNAN TEA IMPORT & EXPORT COPORATION
WUYI ROAD, CHANGSHA, HUNAN, CHINA
李 萍

（二）《UCP600》对商业发票的规定和注意事项

1.《UCP600》第 18 条规定：商业发票

a. i. 必须看似由受益人出具；

ii. 必须出具成以申请人为抬头；

iii. 必须与信用证的货币相同；

iv. 无须签名。

b. 按指定行事的指定银行、保兑行（如有的话）或开证行可以接受金额大于信用证允许金额的商业发票，其决定对有关各方均有约束力，只要该银行对超过信用证允许金额的部分未作承付或者议付。

c. 商业发票上的货物、服务或履约行为的描述应该与信用证中的描述一致。

2. 制作商业发票的注意事项

（1）应根据来证要求，提交数量准确的正本与副本商业发票。

（2）注意商业发票的格式整齐。若出现多种货号的商品，每一货号商品内容和总数排列要有序，做到：横排是每一货号的商品内容，竖排是个货号商品内容的总和。

五、装箱单的含义及作用

装箱单（Packing List）又称为花色码单或包装单，是列明出口商品的包装形式、规格、数量、毛净重、体积等的一种包装单据。它是商业发票的补充，同时也是货运单据中的一项重要单据。通常可以将其有关内容加列在商业发票上，但是在信用证有明确要求时，就必须严格按信用证约定制作。

装箱单主要用于补充商业发票内容的不足，通过列明包装件数、规格、体积、重量、运输标志等，详尽描述了商品的包装情况，便于进口方掌握和核查交易商品的包装及数量等细节情况，同时也便于进口国海关查验核对货物。

装箱单的内容应与商品实际包装情况相符，并与其他单据所列内容保持一致。一般包括：合同号码、发票号码、唛头、货物描述、体积、重量、收货人名称及地址、运输路线等等。有的来证规定“SEAWORTHY PACKING”（适用于海运包装）、“PACKING SUITABLE FOR LONG VOYAGE”（适合于长途海运包装）或“STRONG WOODEN CASE PACKING”（坚固木箱装运）等，信用证中的这些表达都应在商业发票和装箱单中照抄。

<table>
<tr><td colspan="3">**ISSUER**</td><td colspan="4">**PACKING LIST**</td></tr>
<tr><td colspan="3" rowspan="2">**TO**</td><td colspan="2">**INVOICE NO.**</td><td colspan="2">**DATE**</td></tr>
<tr><td colspan="2"></td><td colspan="2"></td></tr>
<tr><td>**Marks and Numbers**</td><td>**Number and Kind of Package**</td><td>**Quantity**</td><td>**PACKAGE**</td><td>**A.W**</td><td>**N.W**</td><td>**Meas.**</td></tr>
<tr><td></td><td>**Description of Goods**</td><td></td><td></td><td></td><td></td><td></td></tr>
<tr><td></td><td></td><td></td><td></td><td></td><td></td><td></td></tr>
<tr><td colspan="7"></td></tr>
<tr><td>**SAY TOTAL:**</td><td></td><td>Total:</td><td colspan="4"></td></tr>
<tr><td colspan="7"></td></tr>
</table>

装箱单样本

六、装箱单的缮制

（一）具体操作

1. 单据名称（Name of Document）

（1）填写内容：

按信用证要求的类型和名称提供，如要求“Detailed Packing List”，可通过在单据中详细显示单件货物的毛、净重和体积加以实现；如要求“Neutral Packing List”（中性装箱单），所提供的单据只要不打印受益人名称，不签章就可满足要求；如要求提供重量单，则名称应写为“Weight List”；如要求提供尺码单，则名称应写为“Measurement List”。ISBP规定，只要单据中包括了装箱细节，即使没有单据名称也视为符合信用证规定。

（2）实例：

PACKING LIST

2. 抬头（To）

（1）填写内容：

内容与商业发票相同，一般填写开证申请人即买方的公司名称及地址。也有不列抬头而注明“As per Inv.”或“To whom it may concern”。除非信用证特别要求，否则银行可以接受装箱单表面无抬头的表示。

（2）实例：

TO: ELBY GIFTS INC.

879 INDUSTRIEL BOIS DES FILION QUEBEC, J6Z 4T3, CANADA

3. 出单日期（Date）

（1）填写内容：

实务中，因为装箱单通常是商业发票内容的补充，所以装箱单的出单日期可以按商业发票的日期填写，也可晚于发票日，但不能晚于提单的签发日。如信用证未做规定，也可不注明出单日。

（2）实例：

Date: APR.15,2013

4. 合同号码或销售确认书号码或商业发票号码（Contract No./Sales Confirmation No./Invoice No.）

（1）填写内容：

根据合同、销售确认书、商业发票如实填写即可。

（2）实例：

S/C NO.: DD145

L/C NO.: DE4578FF

INVOICE NO.: RT084

5. 唛头（Marks & No.s）

（1）填写内容：

唛头须与商业发票、信用证及实物印刷完全一致，也可以只注明“As Per Invoice

No.×××”。

（2）实例：

Marks & No.s

TOTO

BHI7821

DUBAI

NO. 1-565

6. 货物描述及数量（Description of Goods & Quantity）

（1）填写内容：

装箱单中所列明的货物应与商业发票中所描述的货物一致，但可用与其他单据无矛盾的统称表示。

（2）实例：

Description of Goods	Quantity
LADIES JACKET NO.112 NO.113	 1,520PCS 1,230PCS

7. 包装件数（Number & Kind of Package/Package/PKGS）

（1）填写内容：

特别注意该栏目要求填写货物的运输包装单位的数量，而不是计价单位的数量。

（2）实例：

Package

560CTNS

8. 毛重（Gross Weight/G.W.）、净重（Net Weight/N.W.）和体积（Measurement/Meas.）

（1）填写内容：

毛重应注明每个包装件的毛重和此包装件内不同规格、品种、花色货物各自的总毛重，最后在合计栏处标注所有货物的总毛重。净重应注明每个包装件的净重和此包装件内不同规格、品种、花色货物各自的总净重，最后在合计栏处标注所有货物的总净重。注意重量都是以千克（KG）为单位，保留整数。

体积则要求注明每个包装件的尺寸和总体积。注意体积单位是立方米（m^3或 CBM），且保留三位小数。

（2）实例：

Package	G.W.	N.W.	Measurement
560CTNS	3,500KGS	3,250KGS	35.876CBM

9. 签署（Signature）

（1）填写内容：

通常由受益人完成，如信用证没有要求，可以不签字盖章。

（2）实例：

SHANGHAI GARMENT CORPORATION

王晓丽

（二）注意事项

1. 装箱单的内容必须完全符合信用证的要求，既包括包装的货物内容，也包括包装的种类和件数、每件毛净重和总毛净重、总体积。

2. 装箱单可以不显示货物的价格、运输路线和收货人，除非特别规定。

3. 若信用证对装箱单有特殊规定，必须在单据中充分体现出来。如：要求加注信用证号或者详细描述货物的包装细节。

子项目二　商业发票及装箱单典型业务演示

上接项目二，根据信用证审核并修改后的条款并结合合同的要求，鹏兴公司完成了该笔业务货物的准备，接下来单证员李望应完成的工作任务包括：

任务 1：根据资料和信用证相关条款要求，完成商业发票的缮制。

任务 2：根据资料和信用证相关条款要求，完成装箱单的缮制。

1. 信用证：

SEQUENCE OF TOTAL	27:	1/1
FORM OF DC	40A:	IRREVOCABLE
DC NO	20:	DC HMN214479
DATE OF ISSUE	31C:	120720
APPLICABLE RULES	40E:	UCP LATEST VERSION
EXPIRY DATE AND PLACE	31D:	120919 IN COUNTRY OF BENEFICIARY
APPLICANT	50:	ELBY GIFTS INC.879 INDUSTRIEL BOIS DES FILION,QUEBEC, J6Z 4T3, CANADA
BENEFICIARY	59:	LILING PENGXING CERAMIC FACTORY WUSHI JIASHU LILING HUNAN, CHINA
AMOUNT	32B:	USD27,010.40
PCT CR AMT TOLERANCE	39A:	10/10
AVAILABLE WITH/BY	41D:	ANY BANK BY NEGOTIATION
DRAFTS AT	42C:	AT SIGHT FOR FULL INVOICE VALUE
DRAWEE	42A:	ISSUING BANK
PARTIAL SHIPMENTS	43P:	ALLOWED
TRANSHIPMENT	43T:	ALLOWED
PORT OF LOADING	44E:	SHENZHEN, CHINA
PORT OF DISCHARGE	44F:	PRINCE RUPERT, BC
LATEST DATE OF SHIPMENT	44D:	120905

DESCRIPTION OF GOODS OR SERVICES	45A:	CERAMIC CUPS AND BOWLS AS PER S/C NO.:CB121039 CIF PRINCE RUPERT,BC ALL PACKED IN CARTONS.
DOCUMENTS REQUIRED	46A:	+ ORIGINAL SIGNED INVOICE PLUS THREE COPIES. + FULL SET OF CLEAN MULTIMODAL TRANSPORT DOCUMENT PLUS 2 N/N COPIES, MADE TO THE ORDER OF HSBC BANK CANADA, SHOWING ON BOARD NOTATION, MARKED FREIGHT PREPAID, AND NOTIFY APPLICANT(STATING FULL NAME AND ADDRESS). + INSURANCE POLICY OR CERTIFICATE BLANK INDORSED, FOR THE INVOICE VALUE PLUS 10% COVERING ALL RISKS AND S.R.CC. FROM WAREHOUSE TO WAREHOUSE. + ORIGINAL PACKING LIST PLUS 2 COPIES + GSP CERTIFICATE OF ORIGIN FORM A, IN ONE ORIGINAL PLUS 2 COPIES, INDICATING COUNTRY OF ORIGIN, COUNTERCHOPPED BY GOVERNMENT AUTHORITIES OR EXPORTER'S STATMENT OF ORIGIN + SHIPPING NOTE INCLUDING SHIPPING MARKS, CTN NO., B/L NO., QUANTITY, VESSEL'S NAME, VOYAGE NO., SHOULD BE SENT TO THE ISSUING BANK ON THE DATE OF SHIPMENT.
ADDITIONAL CONDITIONS	47A:	+ BENEFICIARY'S DETAILS: CTC: MILLER LEE TEL: 86-731-2338-4199 FAX: 86-731-2338-4298 FOLLOWING CHARGES ARE FOR BENEFICIARY'S ACCOUNT: 1) REIMBURSEMENT/REMITTANCE CHARGES 2) DISCREPANCY FEE OF USD/CAD/EUR100 PLUS ALL RELEVANT CABLE CHARGES WILL BE DEDUCTED FROM EACH PRESENTATION OF

		DISCREPANT DOCUMENTS UNDER THIS DC.
CHARGES	71B:	ALL BANKING CHARGES OUTSIDE COUNTRY OF ISSUE FOR ACCOUNT OF BENEFICIARY/EXPORTER
PERIOD OF PRESENTATION	48:	WITHIN 15 DAYS AFTER THE DATE OF SHIPMENT BUT WITHIN THE VALIDITY OF THE CREDIT
CONFIRMATION INSTRUCTIONS	49:	WITHOUT
INFO TO PRESENTING BK	78:	+ UPON RECEIPT OF DOCUMENTS CONFORMING TO THE TERMS OF THIS CREDIT WE UNDERTAKE TO REIMBURSE YOU IN THE CURRENCY OF THIS CREDIT IN ACCORDANCE WITH YOUR INSTRUCTIONS, LESS CABLE CHARGES, + FORWARD DOCUMENTS IN ONE LOT BY COURIER AT BENEFICIARY'S EXPENSES TO HSBC BANK CANADA, TRADE AND SUPPLY CHAIN, 5100 SHERBROOKE STREET EAST, SUITE 190, MONTREAL, QUEBEC, H1V 3R9 CANADA. + THE AMOUNT OF EACH DRAWING MUST BE ENDORSED ON THE REVERSE OF THIS DC BY THE NEGOTIATING/PRESENTING BANK.

2. 合同

CONTRACT

Contract No.: CB121039
Date: JUL 5, 2012

THE SELLER: PENGXING IMP&EXP COMPANY
LILING PENGXING CERAMIC FACTORY
WUSHI JIASHU LILING HUNAN, CHINA
TEL: 86-731-23384199　FAX: 86-731-23384298

THE BUYER: ELBY GIFTS INC.
879 INDUSTRIEL BOIS DES FILION
QUEBEC, J6Z 4T3, CANADA

TEL: 514-420-0282 FAX: 514-420-0322

This Contract is made by and between the Buyer and Seller, whereby the Buyer agrees to buy and the Seller agrees to sell the under mentioned goods on the terms and conditions stated below:

Description of Goods, Specifications,	Quantity (set)	Unit Price (U.S.D/set)	Amount (U.S.D)
Ceramic Cups and Bowls		C.I.F Prince	
V23-234	912	Rupert	3,693.60
V23-234F	912	4.05	3,693.60
V23-235	1,520	4.05	3,648.00
V23-236	1,512	2.40	3,175.20
V23-237	1,488	2.10	2,901.6
V23-2348	1,520	1.95	3,100.80
36-062	1,528	2.04	3,514.40
36-063	1,496	2.30	3,171.52
As per the P/I No.: CCB23-36		2.12	
Total	10,888		26,898.72

Say total: U.S DOLLARS TWENTY SIX THOUSAND EIGHT HUNDRED AND NINETY EIGHT AND CENTS SEVENTY TWO (USD26,898.72) ONLY.

PACKING: 4 sets packed in a carton(V 23-234/V23-234F), 8 sets packed in a carton for others.

TRANSPORT DETAILS: the goods should be shipped on or before: 5th Sep, 2012, from Shenzhen, China to Prince Rupert

Canada, transshipment and partial shipment are all allowed.

INSURANCE: To be effected by the Seller for 110% of invoice value covering all risks and S.R.C.C as per C.I.C of PICC dated 01/01/1981.

PAYMENT: By irrevocable documentary letter of credit at sight, reaching the seller not later than Aug 5,2012 and remain valid for negotiation in China for 15 days after shipment.

DOCUMENTS:

+ Signed commercial invoice one original and three copies.
+ Full set of clean on board ocean Bill of Lading made to order of issuing bank.
+ Packing List one original and two copies.
+ Insurance policy endorsed in blank.
+ GSP Form A certified by government authority.

INSPECTION: Quality/Quantity/Weight Discrepancy and Claim: In case the quality and/or quantity/weight are found by the Buyer not to conform with the contract after arrival of the goods at the final destination, the Buyer may lodge a claim against the seller supported by a survey report issued by an inspection organization agreed upon by both parties with the exception of those claims for which the insurance company and/or the shipping company are to be held responsible. Claim for quality discrepancy should be filed by the Buyer within 60 days after arrival of the goods at the final destination while for quantity/weight discrepancy claim should be filed by the Buyer within 30 days after arrival of the goods at the final destination.

FORCE MAJEURE: The Seller shall not be held responsible for failure or delay in delivery of the entire or portion of the goods under this contract in consequence of any Force Majeure incidents.

ARBITRATION: All disputes in connection with this Contract or the exccution thereof shall be settled through friendly negotiations. If no settlement can be reached, the case shall then be submitted to the Foreign Trade Arbitration Commission of the China Council for the Promotion of International Trade, Beijing, for settlement by arbitration in accordance with the Commission's Provisional Rules of Procedure. The award rendered by the Commission shall be final and binding on both parties. The arbitration expenses shall be borne by the losing party unless otherwise award by the arbitration organization.

Signed by:

THE SELLER:	THE BUYER:
PENGXING IMP&EXP COMPANY LILING PENGXING CERAMIC FACTORY	ELBY GIFTS INC.
李 望	Camp Wolf

据此，单证员李望完成了该笔业务下商业发票和装箱单的制作。

PENGXING IMP&EXP COMPANY

LILING PENGXING CERAMIC FACTORY

WUSHI JIASHU LILING HUNAN CHINA

TEL: 86-731-23384199 FAX: 86-731-23384298

COMMERCIAL INVOICE

To:	ELBY GIFTS INC. 879 INDUSTRIEL BOIS DES FILION QUEBEC, J6Z 4T3, CANADA	**Invoice No.:**	PX12IVN1039
		Invoice Date:	AUG. 16, 2012
		S/C No.:	S/C NO.:CB121039
		S/C Date:	JUL. 5, 2012
From:	SHENZHEN, CHINA	**To:**	PRINCE RUPERT, BC, CANADA
Letter of Credit No.:	DC HMN214479	**Issued By:**	HSBC BANK, MONTREAL CANADA

Marks and Numbers	Number and kind of package Description of goods	Quantity	Unit Price U.S.D/set	Amount
	CERAMIC CUPS AND BOWLS		CIF PRINCE RUPERT, BC	
ELBY		CTN	U.S.D	U.S.D
S/C NO.:CB121039	V23-234	228	4.05	3,693.60
NO: 1-1589	V23-234F	228	4.05	3,693.60
	V23-235	190	2.40	3,648.00
	V23-236	189	2.10	3,175.20
	V23-237	186	1.95	2,901.60
	V23-238	190	2.04	3,100.80
	36-062	191	2.30	3,514.40
	36-063	187	2.12	3,171.52
	Total:	1,589 CTNS		U.S.D 26,898.72

Say Total: U.S DOLLARS TWENTY SIX THOUSAND EIGHT HUNDRED AND NINETY EIGHT AND CENTS SEVENTY TWO (USD26,898.72) ONLY

PENGXING IMP&EXP COMPANY

李 望

PENGXING IMP&EXP COMPANY

LILING PENGXING CERAMIC FACTORY
WUSHI JIASHU LILING HUNAN CHINA
TEL: 86-731-23384199 FAX: 86-731-23384298

PACKING LIST

To: ELBY GIFTS INC. **Date** AUG. 16, 2012
879 INDUSTRIEL BOIS DES FILION **Invoice No.:** PX12IVN1039
QUEBEC, J6Z 4T3, CANADA

From: SHENZHEN, CHINA **To:** PRINCE RPERT, BC, CANADA

Item No.	Description of goods	Quantity				Sets/CTN	G.W/N.W		Dimension			Meas.
V23-234	CERAMIC CUPS AND BOWLS	912	SETS	228	CTNS	4	11.8	9.6	38.9*	29.0*	26.6	6.84
V23-234F	CERAMIC CUPS AND BOWLS	912	SETS	228	CTNS	4	11.8	9.6	38.9*	29.0*	26.6	6.84
V23-235	CERAMIC CUPS AND BOWLS	1,520	SETS	190	CTNS	8	15.0	12.8	48.6*	31.6*	43.6	12.72
V23-236	CERAMIC CUPS AND BOWLS	1,512	SETS	189	CTNS	8	10.6	8.4	50.4*	27.0*	.34.8	8.95
V23-237	CERAMIC CUPS AND BOWLS	1,488	SETS	186	CTNS	8	8.4	6.4	31.0*	28.2*	39.2	6.37
V23-238	CERAMIC CUPS AND BOWLS	1,520	SETS	190	CTNS	8	10.5	8.0	48.6	28.2*	39.2	10.21
36-062	CERAMIC CUPS AND BOWLS	1,528	SETS	191	CTNS	8	12.0	9.6	49.0*	28.9*	38.2	10.33
36-063	CERAMIC CUPS AND BOWLS	1,496	SETS	187	CTNS	8	8.4	6.4	34.4*	33.0*	27.6	5.86
	Total:	10,888	SETS	1,589	CTNS		17,654.4	14,138.0				68.13

ALL PACKED IN CARTONS

SAY TOTAL: ONE THOUSAND FIVE HUNDRED AND EIGHTY NINE (1,589CTNS) CARTONS ONLY

子项目三　商业发票及装箱单拓展业务操作

能力实训项目 1：商业发票和装箱单业务操作

根据出口商 Jiangsu 1-Touch Business Service Ltd.第 0684130117426 号信用证及合同的要求，2013 年 9 月 13 日，单证员彭婷制作了商业发票和装箱单。

1. 信用证：

SEQUENCE OF TOTAL	27:	1/1
FORM OF DC.	40A:	IRREVOCABLE
DC. NO.	20:	0684130117426
DATE OF ISSUE	31C:	130825
APPLICABLE RULES	40E:	UCP LATEST VERSION
EXPIRY DATE AND PLACE	31D:	131024,CHINA
APPLICANT	50:	M/S. MEMORY STEEL CORPORATION 73/A, LAL MOHAN SHAHA STREET (DHOLAIKHAL), DHAKA-1100. BANGLADESH.
BENEFICIARY	59:	JIANGSU I-TOUCH BUSINESS SERVICE LTD, ROOM 117, JIANGSU EDIFICE ZHANGJIAGANG FREE TRADE ZONE, JIANGSU, CHINA TEL:86-512-56363783
AMOUNT	32B:	USD35,000.00
AVAILABLE WITH/BY	41D:	ANY BANK IN CHINA BY NEGOTIATION
DRAFTS AT	42C:	AT SIGHT FOR FULL INVOICE VALUE
DRAWEE	42A:	DRAWN ON US
PARTIAL SHIPMENTS	43P:	ALLOWED
TRANSSHIPMENT	43T:	ALLOWED
PORT OF LOADING	44A:	ANY SEA PORT, CHINA
PORT OF DISCHARGE	44B:	CHITTAGONG SEA PORT, BANGLADESH
LATEST DATE OF SHIPMENT	44C:	131009
DESCRIPTION OF GOODS	45A:	201/2B SECONDARY GRADE STAINLESS STEEL SHEET OF WIDTH 1219MM THICKNESS 1MM TO 3MM, QTY:25,000KGS AT THE RATE OF USD1.40/KG FOR TOTAL AMOUNT OF USD35,000.00 CFR CHITTAGONG, BANGLADESH. AS PER BENEFICIARY'S PROFORMA INVOICE NO.

		SK20130802-001 DATED AUG 2,2013
DOCUMENTS REQUIRED	46A:	+MANUALLY SIGNED COMMERCIAL INVOICE IN TRIPLICATE CERTIFYING MERCHANDISE TO BE OF CHINA ORIGIN AND INDICATING THAT THE GOODS ARE BEING IMPORTED AGAINST IRC NO.BA-0171646, TI NO.157-107-0121, VAT REGISTRATION NO.9141093671. +FULL SET OF CLEAN 'SHIPPED ON BOARD' OCEAN BILL OF LADING SHOWING' FREIGHT PREPAID' MADE OUT TO ORDER OF SHIPPER AND BLANK INDORSED, NOTIFY APPLICANT. +PACKING LIST IN TRIPLICATE SHOWING GROSS WEIGHT, NET WEIGHT. +CERTIFICATE OF ORIGIN ISSUED AND LEGALED BY CCPIT + BENEFICIARY'S DECLARATION SHOULD CERTIFY THAT THE COUNTRY OF ORIGIN HAS BEEN PRINTED ON GOODS PACKING BAG. +BENEFICIARY SHOULD SEND A FAX OR BY COUR-IER TO L/C OPENING BANK WITHIN FIVE DAYS FROM THE OF SHIPMENT, ADVISING THE DATE OF SHIPMENT, VESSEL'S NAME, AMOUNT OF BILL AND L/C NO. AND A COPY OF THIS FAX SHOULD ACCOMPANY THE SHIPPING DOCUMENTS. +SHIPMENT BY ISRAELI LINER IS PROHIBITED AND A CERTIFICATE TO THIS EFFECT ISSUED BY THE SHIPPING COMPANY MUST ACCOMPANY THE ORIGINAL DOCUMENTS.
CHARGES	71B:	ALL FOREIGN BANK CHARGES ARE FOR THE ACCOUNT OF THE BENEFICIARY.
PERIOD OF PRESENTATION	48:	15 DAYS FROM SHIPMENT DATE BUT WITHIN VALIDITY OF THE CREDIT

2. 合同：

SALES CONTRACT

Contract No.:SSW0803
Date: AUG 15,2013

THE SELLER: JIANGSU I-TOUCH BUSINESS SERVICE LTD,
ROOM 117, JIANGSU EDIFICE
ZHANGJIAGANG FREE TRADE ZONE,
JIANGSU, CHINA TEL:86-512-56363783

THE BUYER: M/S. MEMORY STEEL CORPORATION
73/A, LAL MOHAN SHAHA STREET
(DHOLAIKHAL), DHAKA-1100.
BANGLADESH.

This Contract is made by and between the Buyer and Seller, whereby the Buyer agrees to buy and the Seller agrees to sell the under mentioned goods on the terms and conditions stated below:

Description of Goods, Specifications,	Size (mm)	Unit Price (U.S.D/set)	Amount (U.S.D)
		C.F.R	CHITTAGONG
201/2B SECONDARY GRADE STAINLESS STEEL SHEET OF WIDTH 1,219MM OR MORE THICKNESS 1MM TO 3MM, QTY:25,000KGS AT THE RATE OF USD1.40/KG. AS PER BENIFICIARY'S PROFORMA INVOIVE NO. SK20130802-001 DATED AUG 2,2013	1.2×1,219×2,438	1.40	7,806.40
	1.5×1,219×2,438	1.40	4,547.20
	2.0×1,219×2,438	1.40	16,282.00
	3.0×1,219×2,438	1.40	6,364.40
			35,000.00
Total			

Say total: U.S DOLLARS THIRTY FIVE THOUSAND ONLY.

PACKING: Standard export packing on pallets.

TRANSPORT DETAILS: the goods should be shipped before: 9th Oct, 2013, from any Chinese port to Chittagong Bangladesh, transshipment and partial shipment are allowed.

PAYMENT: By sight L/C and remain valid for negotiation in China for 15 days after shipment.

DOCUMENTS:

+ Signed commercial invoice in triplicate, certifying the goods are of Chinese origin and being imported against IRC No.BA-0171646,VAT Registration No.9141093671.

+ Full set (3/3) of clean on board ocean Bill of Lading made out to order of shipper and blank

indorsed.
+ Packing List in triplicate.
+ Certificate of origin by CCPIT.
+Beneficiary's Declaration certifying that the country of origin has been printed on goods packing bag.

INSPECTION: Quality/Quantity/Weight Discrepancy and Claim: In case the quality and/or quantity/weight are found by the Buyer not to conform with the contract after arrival of the goods at the final destination, the Buyer may lodge a claim against the seller supported by a survey report issued by an inspection organization agreed upon by both parties with the exception of those claims for which the insurance company and/or the shipping company are to be held responsible. Claim for quality discrepancy should be filed by the Buyer within 60 days after arrival of the goods at the final destination while for quantity/weight discrepancy claim should be filed by the Buyer within 30 days after arrival of the goods at the final destination.

FORCE MAJEURE: The Seller shall not be held responsible for failure or delay in delivery of the entire or portion of the goods under this contract in consequence of any Force Majeure incidents.

ARBITRATION: All disputes in connection with this Contract or the execution thereof shall be settled through friendly negotiations. If no settlement can be reached, the case shall then be submitted to the Foreign Trade Arbitration Commission of the China Council for the Promotion of International Trade, Beijing, for settlement by arbitration in accordance with the Commission's Provisional Rules of Procedure. The award rendered by the Commission shall be final and binding on both parties. The arbitration expenses shall be borne by the losing party unless otherwise award by the arbitration organization.

Signed by:

THE SELLER:	**THE BUYER:**
JIANGSU I-TOUCH BUSINESS SERVICE LTD	M/S. MEMORY STEEL CORPORATION.
彭 婷	John Lee

据此，请完成商业发票与装箱单制作：

ISSUER		**COMMERCIAL INVOICE**		
TO		**NO.**		**DATE**
TRANSPORT DETAILS		**S/C NO.**		**L/C NO.**
		TERMS OF PAYMENT		
Marks and Numbers	**Number and Kind of Package** **Description of Goods**	**Quantity**	**Unit Price**	**Amount**
	Total:			
SAY				
TOTAL:				

×××× Import & Export Co., Ltd

Add: No. 1, ××× Road, ××× District, xxx City, ××× Prov., P R China

Tel: Fax:

PACKING LIST

Contract No.	**Date:.**
L/C No.	**Date:**
From:	**To:**

Marks	**Description**	**Quantity**	**G.W.**	**N.W.**	**Meas.**

Total:

能力实训项目 2：商业发票和装箱单业务操作

根据出口商 PRIMA CONSTRUCTION MATERIALS CO., LTD 第 DC 13724 号信用证的要求，2013 年 8 月 22 日，单证员黄柯制作了商业发票和装箱单。

1. 信用证

SEQUENCE OF TOTAL	27:	1/1
FORM OF DC	40A:	IRREVOCABLE
DC NO.	20:	DC 130720
DATE OF ISSUE	31C:	130720
APPLICABLE RULES	40E:	UCP 600
EXPIRY DATE AND PLACE	31D:	130920 IN CHINA
APPLICANT	50:	CONSTRUCTION MOUDULAR SPECIALIST POSTAL: 13 HARVEY RD., SHENTON PK, WA 6008 AUSTRALIA
BENEFICIARY	59:	PRIMA CONSTRUCTION MATERIALS CO., LTD 1401 ROOM, 38 BUILDING, CHUANGYE GARDEN BAOAN DISTRICT, SHENZHEN, CHINA
AMOUNT	32B:	USD6,840.00
AVAILABLE WITH/BY	41D:	ANY BANK BY NEGOTIATION
DRAFTS AT	42C:	AT 30DAYS AFTER SIGHT
DRAWEE	42A:	DRAWN ON US
PARTIAL SHIPMENTS	43P:	ALLOWED
TRANSHIPMENT	43T:	ALLOWED
LOADING PORT	44E:	CHINA MAIN PORT
DISCHARGE PORT	44F:	FREMENTLE, AUSTRALIA
LATEST DATE OF SHIPMENT	44C:	130905
DESCRIPTION OF GOODS	45A:	BAMBOO FLOORING ITEM 1 100 SQM U.S.D20.00/SQM ITEM 2 100 SQM U.S.D39.50/SQM ALL PACKING IN SEA WORTHY CARTONS CIF FREMENTLE AS PER PI NO.: BFF0610
DOCUMENTS REQUIRED	46A:	+ MANUALLY SIGNED COMMECIAL INVOICE 3 ORIGINALS PLUS THREE COPIES. + FULL SET(3/3) OF MARINE BILLS OF LADING, MADE OUT TO ORDER, MARKED FREIGHT PREPAID, AND NOTIFY

		APPLICANT (STATING FULL NAME AND ADDRESS). + INSURANCE POLICY OR CERTIFICATE IN TRIPLICATE, BLANK INDORSED, FOR THE INVOICE VALUE PLUS 10% COVERING ICC(A) RISK AND ICC(STRIKE). FROM WAREHOUSE TO WAREHOUSE AND I.O.P, PAYABLE AT FREMENTLE IN U.S.D. + PACKING LIST 3 ORIGINALS AND 2 COPIES. +CERTIFICATE OF ORIGIN IN CHINA ISSUED BY OFFICIAL AUTRORITY. + BENNIFICIALRY'S CERTIFICATE SHOWING THAT A SET OF ORIGINAL SHIPPING DOCUMENTS HAS BEEN MAIL TO THE APPLICANT BY EXPRESS AFTER 2 DAYS OF SHIOMENT.
CHARGES	71B:	ALL BANKING CHARGES OUTSIDE COUNTRY OF ISSUE ARE FOR BENEFICIARY/'S ACCOUNT.
PERIOD OF PRESENTATION	48:	WITHIN 15 DAYS AFTER THE DATE OF SHIPMENT BUT WITHIN THE VALIDITY OF THE L/C
CONFIRMATION INSTRUCTIONS	49:	WITHOUT

2. 合同

CONTRACT

Contract No.: BFF0606

Date: JUL 1, 2013

THE SELLER: PRIMA CONSTRUCTION MATERIOLS CO., LTD
1401 ROOM, 38 BUILDING, CHUANGYE GARDEN
BAOAN DISTRICT, SHENZHEN, CHINA

THE BUYER: CONSTRUCTION MOUDULAR SPECIALIST
POSTAL: 13 HARVEY RD.,
SHENTON PK, WA 6008 AUSTRALIA

This Contract is made by and between the Buyer and Seller, whereby the Buyer agrees to buy and the Seller agrees to sell the under mentioned goods on the terms and conditions stated below:

Description of Goods, Specifications,	Quantity (SQM)	Unit Price (U.S.D/SQM)	Amount (U.S.D)
BAMBOO FLOORING ITEM 1 ITEM 2 AS PER PI NO.: BFF0610	 100 100	CIF FREMENTLE 20.00 39.50	 2,000.00 3,950.00
Total	200		5,950.00

Say total: U.S DOLLARS FIFTY NINE HUNDRED AND FIFTY (USD5,950) ONLY.

PACKING: ALL PACKING IN SEA WORTHY CARTONS.

TRANSPORT DETAILS: the goods should be shipped on or before: 20th Sep, 2013, from Shenzhen, China to Frementle Australia, transshipment and partial shipment are all allowed.

INSURANCE: To be effected by the Seller for 110% of invoice value covering ICC(A) risk and ICC(War Risk).

PAYMENT: By irrevocable documentary letter of credit at 30 days after sight, reaching the seller not later than Jul 30, 2013 and remain valid for negotiation in China for 15 days after shipment.

DOCUMENTS:

+ Signed commercial invoice three originals and three copies.
+ Full set of clean on board ocean Bill of Lading made to order.
+ Packing List three originals and two copies.
+ Insurance policy endorsed in blank and in triplicate.
+Certificate of Origin in China issued by official authority.

据此，请完成商业发票及装箱单制作：

<table>
<tr><td colspan="2">ISSUER</td><td colspan="3" rowspan="2">COMMERCIAL INVOICE</td></tr>
<tr><td colspan="2" rowspan="2">TO</td></tr>
<tr><td>NO.</td><td colspan="2">DATE</td></tr>
<tr><td colspan="2" rowspan="2">TRANSPORT DETAILS</td><td>S/C NO.</td><td colspan="2">L/C NO.</td></tr>
<tr><td colspan="3">TERMS OF PAYMENT</td></tr>
<tr><td>Marks and Numbers</td><td>Number and Kind of Package
Description of Goods</td><td>Quantity</td><td>Unit Price</td><td>Amount</td></tr>
<tr><td colspan="5">Total:

SAY

TOTAL:</td></tr>
</table>

×××× Import & Export Co., Ltd

Add: No. 1, ××× Road, ××× District, xxx City, ××× Prov., P R China

Tel: Fax:

PACKING LIST

Contract No.	**Date:.**
L/C No.	**Date:**
From:	**To:**

Marks	**Description**	**Quantity**	**G.W.**	**N.W.**	**Meas.**

Total:

项目四　保险单据制作业务

项目预期目标

通过对信用证项下保险条款的认真解读，结合该项目提供的商业发票等相关单据，介绍保险的相关知识，使同学们了解保险单据的种类，熟悉保险险别和保险条款，掌握保险单的缮制。

在项目实施过程中，通过对填制保险单和办理投保手续的任务训练，培养学生的审核、制单、业务核算等国际商务单证基本职业能力，亦培养学生独立操作业务和沟通能力。

表 4-1　项目预期目标

目标类型	制作投保单和办理保险操作
知识目标	了解国际货物运输保险的有关知识、投保程序以及保单的种类
	掌握国际货物运输保险单的基本格式及内容
	掌握其签订和履行的基本过程
能力目标	能够缮制国际货物运输保险单
	掌握填写保险单据的技巧
职业素质目标	独立业务操作能力
	与国外客户沟通衔接能力

项目实施条件

1. 组织学生参观中国人民保险公司
2. 学生能够在实训室对该项目进行分组讨论并实施
3. 指导教师掌握扎实的国际贸易政策，具备扎实的外贸业务基础

开篇业务引入

完成托运手续确认船期后，长沙鹏兴进出口有限公司向中国人民保险公司办理投保手续。该项目任务具体由单证员李望负责。2012 年 8 月 22 日，单证员李望根据 L/C 规定："+ INSURANCE POLICY OR CERTIFICATE BLANK INDORSED, FOR THE INVOICE VALUE PLUS 10% COVERING ALL RISKS AND S.R.CC. FROM WAREHOUSE TO WAREHOUSE"，以及缮制好的商业发票、装箱单正本，制作投保单，准备投保单据向保险公司办理投保手续。

子项目一　保险单据制作

一、保险单的含义

保险单据一般被理解为保险单，简称保单，是保险人对被保险人的承保证明，又是双方之间权利义务的契约，在被保险货物遭受损失时，它是被保险人索赔和保险人理赔的主要依据。

由于国际贸易大多数是通过海上运输来实现的，在海上运输途中，船只和货物都有可能由于自然灾害和意外事故而造成各种损失，因而进行保险是十分必要的。因此，海上运输保险单也就成为国际贸易中不可或缺的货运单据之一。

二、保险单据的内容

国际贸易中保单的格式不尽相同，但内容基本一致，一份完整的保险单据其基本内容应该包括如下几点：

（1）发票号码和保单号码。

（2）投保人即被保险人名称。

（3）货物描述、唛头、件数、包装情况。

（4）船名、起讫地、预计起运日期。

（5）保险金额和货币单位。

（6）承保险别、投保加成。

（7）保费给付地点及理赔地点。

（8）出单日期。

（9）保险公司签章。

三、保险单据的种类

（1）保险单（Insurance Policy）：俗称大保单，这是一种正规的保险合同，是完整独立的保险文件。除载明被保险人（投保人）的名称、被保险货物（标的物）的名称、数量或重量、唛头、运输工具、保险的起讫地点、承保险别、保险金额、出单日期等项目外，还在保险单的背面列有保险人的责任范围，以及保险人与被保险人各自的权利、义务等方面的详细条款。可由被保险人背书，随物权的转移而转让。

（2）保险凭证（Insurance Certificate）：俗称小保单，中国人民保险公司发出的保险凭证是表示保险公司已经接受保险的一种证明文件，这是一种比较简化的保险单据。它包括了保险单的基本内容，但不附有保险条款全文。这种保险凭证与保险单有同等的法律效力。

（3）联合凭证（Combined Certificate），又称承保证明（Risk Note）。是我国保险公司特别使用的，比保险凭证更简化的保险单据。保险公司仅将承保险别、保险金额及保险编号加注在我国进出口公司开具的出口货物发票上，并正式签章即作为已经保险的证据。

这种单据不能转让，是最简单的保险单据。

（4）预约保险单（Open Policy）：预约保险单又称开口保险单，它一般适用于经常有相同类型货物需要陆续装运的保险条款。预约保险单上载明保险货物的范围、险别、保险费率、每批运输货物的最高保险金额以及保险费的结付、赔款处理等项目，凡属于此保险单范围内的进出口货物，一经起运，即自动按保险单所列条件承保。但被保险人在获悉每批保险货物起运时，应立即将货物装船详细情况包括货物名称、数量、保险金额、运输工具种类和名称、航程起讫地点、开船日期等情况通知保险公司和进口商。

（5）保险批单。保险单出立后，如需变更其内容，可由保险公司另出的凭证注明更改或补充的内容，称为批单。其须粘在保险单上并加盖骑缝章，作为保险单不可分割的一部分。

四、保险条款和险别

我国为适应对外经济贸易业务发展的需要，由中国人民保险公司（PICC）根据我国的实际情况，分别制定了海洋、陆地、航空等多种运输方式的货物保险条款，总称为《中国保险条款》（China Insurance Clause, CIC）。

在国际保险市场上，最有影响力的保险条款当属英国伦敦保险协会制定的《协会货物条款》（Institute Cargo Clauses, ICC）。

（一）我国海运货物保险条款及险别

我国现行的货物保险条款是 1981 年 1 月 1 日的修订本，根据不同的运输方式分别订有用不同运输方式的保险条款，以《海洋运输货物保险条款》使用最普遍，其主要内容有：保险人承保责任范围、除外责任、责任起讫、被保险人的义务和索赔期限。

保险人的承保责任范围：海运货物保险险别分为基本险和附加险两类。

基本险又称主险，是可以独立投保的险别，包括平安险、水渍险和一切险；

附加险是对基本险的补充和扩展，它不能单独投保，只能在投保了基本险的基础上加保，包括一般附加险和特殊附加险。

1. 基本险

（1）平安险（F.P.A）

平安险是我国保险业的习惯叫法，英文原意是“单独海损不赔”。平安险承诺以下八项责任：

① 被保险货物在运输途中由于恶劣气候、雷电、海啸、地震、洪水自然灾害造成整批货物的全部损失或推定全损。当被保险人要求赔付推定全损时，须将受损货物及其权利委付给保险公司。

② 由于运输工具遭搁浅、触礁、沉没、互撞，与流域一其他物体碰撞以及失火、爆炸等外事故造成被保险货物的全部或部分损失。

③ 只要运输工具曾经发生搁浅、触礁、沉没、焚毁等意外事故，不论这个意外事故发生之前或者以后曾在海上遭恶劣气候、雷电、海啸等自然灾害所造成的被保险货物的部分损失。

④ 在装卸转船过程中，被保险货物一件或数件落海所造成的全部损失或部分损失。

⑤ 被保险人对遭受承保责任内危险的货物采取抢救，防止或减少货损的措施而支付的合理费用，但以不超过这批被救货物的保险金额为限。

⑥ 运输工具遭自然或灾害或意外事故，需要在中途的港口或者在避难港口停靠，因而引起的卸货、装货、存仓以及运送货物所产生的特别费用。

⑦ 发生共同海损所引起的牺牲、公摊费和救助费用。

⑧ 运输契约订有“船舶互撞责任”条款，根据该条款规定应由货方偿还船方的损失。

（2）水渍险（W.P.A）

水渍险亦是我国保险业的习惯叫法，英文原意是“负责单独海损”。水渍险承保的责任范围是：

① 平安保险承担的全部责任。

② 被保险货物由于恶劣气候、雷电、海啸、地震、洪水自然灾害所造成的部分损失。

（3）一切险（All Risks）

一切险的承保范围是：

① 水渍险承保的全部责任一切险均给予承保。

② 一切险负责被保险货物在运输途中，由于一般外来风险所致的全部或部分损失。

2. 附加险

（1）一般附加险（General Additional Risks）。

一般附加险承保一般外来风险所造成的损失，共有 11 种。

① 偷窃、提货不着险（Theft, Pilferage and Non-delivery risks, T.P.N.D） ② 淡水雨淋险（Fresh Water and Damage Risks, F.W.R.D） ③ 渗漏险（Leakage Risks） ④ 短量险（Shortage Risks） ⑤ 混杂、玷污险（Intermixture and Contamination Risks） ⑥ 碰撞、破碎险（Clash and Breakage Risks） ⑦ 钩损险（Hook Damage Risks） ⑧ 锈损险（Rust Risks） ⑨ 串味险（risk of Odour） ⑩ 包装破裂险（Breakage of Packing Risks） ⑪ 受潮受热险（sweating and Heating Risks）。

（2）特殊附加险（Special Additional Risks）

① 交货不到险（Failure to Deliver Risks） ② 进口关税险（Import Duty Risks） ③ 舱面险（On Deck Risks） ④ 黄曲霉素险（Aflatoxin Risks） ⑤ 拒收险（Rejection Risks） ⑥ 出口货物到香港（包括九龙在内）或澳门存仓火险责任扩展条款（Fine Risk Extension Clause for Storage of Cargo at Destination HongKong, Including Kowloon,or Macao,简称 F.R.E.C） ⑦ 战争险（War Risks） ⑧ 罢工险（Strikes Risks）。

（二）英国伦敦保险协会海运货物保险条款

现行英国伦敦《协会货物条款》是 1982 年 1 月 1 日的修订本，与我国现行保险条款相比，其形式和内容都有所不同。该条款共有六种险别。它们是：

1. 协会货物条款（A）[ICC（A）]；2. 协会货物条款（B）[ICC（B）]；3. 协会货物条款（C）[ICC（C）]4. 协会战争险条款；5. 协会罢工险条款；6. 恶意损害险条款。

前三种是主险，后三种是附加险，其中战争险条款和罢工险条款在征得保险人同意时，可以作为独立的险别进行投保。

（三）保险责任起讫

保险的责任起讫，是指保险人对被保险货物承担保险责任的有效时间。被保险货物如果在保险有效期内发生保险责任范围内的风险损失，被保险人有权进行索赔，否则就无权进行索赔。

根据国际保险市场的习惯做法，我们应注意以下两个保险条款：

1. 仓至仓条款（Warehouse to Warehouse Clause，简称 W/W）

它是指保险人的承保责任从被保险货物运离保险单所载明的起运地发货人仓库开始，直至该项货物被运抵保险单所载明的收货人仓库或被保险人用作分配、分派或非正常运输的其他储存处所为止。

如未抵达上述仓库或储存处所，则以被保险货物在最后卸货港全部卸离海轮后满 60 天为止。

如在上述 60 天内被保险货物需转运至非保险单所载明的目的地时，则该项货物开始转运时终止。

2. 水上条款

战争险的责任起讫与基本险所采用的“仓之仓条款”不同，而是以“水上危险”为限，是指保险人的承保责任自货物装上保险单所载明的启运港的海轮或驳船开始，到卸离保险单所载明的目的港的海轮或驳船为止。

如果货物不卸离海轮或驳船，则从海轮到达目的港当日午夜起算满 15 日为止，等再装上续运海轮时，保险责任才继续有效。

五、保险金额和保险费

（一）保险金额

保险金额的定义：保险公司承担赔偿或者给付保险金责任的最高限额，也是保险公司计算保险费的基础。

保险金额一般是根据保险价值确定的。

保险金额的计算公式：

保险金额=CIF（CIP）价×（1+投保加成率）

保险费的计算：

保险费=保险金额×保险费率

PICC	中国人民保险公司 **The People's Insurance Company of China** 总公司设于北京　　一九四九年创立 Head Office Beijing　　Established in 1949

货物运输保险单
CARGO TRANSPORTATION INSURANCE POLICY

发票号(INVOICE NO.)		保单号次 POLICY NO.	
合同号(CONTRACT NO.)			

信用证号 (L/C NO.)	
被保险人: INSURED:	

中国人民保险公司(以下简称本公司)根据被保险人的要求，由被保险人向本公司缴付约定的保险费，按照本保险单承保险别和背面所载条款与下列特款承保下述货物运输保险，特立本保险单。
THIS POLICY OF INSURANCE WITNESSES THAT THE PEOPLE'S INSURANCE COMPANY OF CHINA (HEREINAFTER CALLED "THE COMPANY") AT THE REQUEST OF THE INSURED AND IN CONSIDERATION OF THE AGREED PREMIUM PAID TO THE COMPANY BY THE INSURED, UNDERTAKES TO INSURE THE UNDERMENTIONED GOODS IN TRANSPORTATION SUBJECT TO THE CONDITIONS OF THIS POLICY AS PER THE CLAUSES PRINTED OVERLEAF AND OTHER SPECIAL CLAUSES ATTACHED HEREON.

标　记 MARKS&NOS	包装及数量 QUANTITY	保险货物项目 DESCRIPTION OF GOODS	保险金额 AMOUNT INSURED

总保险金额 TOTAL AMOUNT INSURED:	

保费: PERMIUM:	AS ARRANGED	启运日期 DATE OF COMMENCEMENT:		装载运输工具: PER CONVEYANCE:	
自 FROM:		经 VIA		至 TO	

承保险别:
CONDITIONS:

<table>
<tr><td colspan="3">所保货物，如发生保险单项下可能引起索赔的损失或损坏，应立即通知本公司下述代理人查勘。如有索赔，应向本公司提交保单正本(本保险单共有_____份正本)及有关文件。如一份正本已用于索赔，其余正本自动失效。</td></tr>
<tr><td colspan="3">IN THE EVENT OF LOSS OR DAMAGE WHICH MAY RESULT IN A CLAIM UNDER THIS POLICY, IMMEDIATE NOTICE MUST BE GIVEN TO THE COMPANY'S AGENT AS MENTIONED HEREUNDER. CLAIMS, IF ANY, ONE OF THE ORIGINAL POLICY WHICH HAS BEEN ISSUED IN _____ ORIGINAL(S) TOGETHER WITH THE RELEVANT DOCUMENTS SHALL BE SURRENDERED TO THE COMPANY. IF ONE OF THE ORIGINAL POLICY HAS BEEN ACCOMPLISHED. THE OTHERS TO BE VOID.</td></tr>
<tr><td colspan="2"></td><td rowspan="2">中国人民保险公司
The People's Insurance Company of China</td></tr>
<tr><td>赔款偿付地点
CLAIM
PAYABLE AT</td><td></td></tr>
<tr><td>出单日期</td><td rowspan="2"></td><td rowspan="2">Authorized Signature</td></tr>
<tr><td>ISSUING
DATE</td></tr>
</table>

图 中国人民保险公司保险单样本

一、保险单填制

1 栏 被保险人（Insured）

（1）填写内容：

填在“at the request of”后面，被保险人有以下几种填法：

① 如 L/C 和合同无特别规定，或要求“Endorsed in blank”此栏一般填信用证的受益人，即出口公司名称。可不填详细地址，但出口公司应在保险单背面背书。

② 若来证指定以××公司为被保险人，则应在此栏填×× CO.。出口公司不要背书。

③ 若来证规定以某银行为抬头，如：“TO ORDER OF ××× BANK”，则在此栏先填上受益人名称，再填上“HELD TO THE ORDER OF ××× BANK”。受益人均须在背面作空白背书。

如：TO ORDER，则应填 THE APPLICANT +出口企业名称，FOR THE ACCOUNT OF WHOM IT MAY CONCERN。

（2）实例：

① at the request of: JIANGXI JINYUAN IMPORT & EXPORT CO., LTD.

② at the request of: JIANGXI JINYUAN IMPORT & EXPORT CO., LTD. HELD TO THE ORDER OF ××× BANK

2 栏 发票号码、合同号和信用证号（Invoice No., Contract no. and L/C no.）

（1）填写内容：

该栏目要根据商业发票以及合同、信用证信息进行填写。

（2）实例：

发票号（INVOICE NO.） LJ08071

合同号（CONTRACT NO.）ZJJY0739

信用证号（L/C NO.）YZF07699

3 栏 标记&唛头（Marks & Nos.）

（1）填写内容：

按信用证规定，保险单上标记应与发票，提单上一致。可单独填写，若来证无特殊规定，一般可简单填成“AS PER INV. NO. ×××”

（2）实例：

Marks & Nos:

SIK

ZJJY0739

L357/L358

DUBAI, U.A.E.

C/NO:1-166

4 栏 包装及数量（Quantity）

（1）填写内容：

此栏填制大包装件数，并应与提单上同一栏目内容相同。有包装但以重量计价的，应把包装重量与计价重量都注上；裸装货物要注明本身件数；煤炭、石油等散装货注明“IN BULK”再填净重；如以单位包装件数计价者，可只填总件数。

（2）实例：

Quantity：166 BALES

5 栏 保险物资项目（Description of Goods）

（1）填写内容：

根据投保单填写，要与提单此栏目的填写一致。一般允许使用统称，但不同类别的多种货物应注明不同类别的各自总称。

（2）实例：

Description of Goods：LADIES JACKET

6 栏 保险金额（Amount Insured ）和 总保险金额（Total Amount Insured）

（1）填写内容：

保险金额可小写，例如：USD70,638.00

总保险金额大写。

注意：

① 保险货币与信用证一致，大小写要一致。

② 保险金额应严格按照信用证和合同上的要求填制，保险金额应为发票金额加上投保加成后的金额，如信用证和合同无明确规定，一般都以发票金额加一成（即 110%的发票金额）填写。

③ 保险金额不要小数，出现小数时无论多少一律向上进位。

（2）实例：

Amount Insured：USD70,638.00

Total Amount Insured：SAY U.S. DOLLARS SEVENTY THOUSAND SIX HUNDRED THIRTY EIGHT ONLY

7 栏 保险费及保险费率（Premium and Rate）

（1）填写内容：

此栏一般由保险公司填制或已印好 AS ARRANGED，除非信用证另有规定，如 “INOURANCE POLICY ENDORSED IN BLANK FULL INVOICE VALUE PLUS10% MARKED PREMIUM PAID” 时，此栏就填入“PAID”或把已印好的“AS ARRANGED”删去加盖校对章后打上“PAID”字样。

8 栏 装载运输工具（Per Conveyance）

（1）填写内容：

要与运输单据一致，并应按照实际情况填写。

海运方式下填写船名和航次；如整个运输由两段或两段以上运程完成时，应分别填写一程船名及二程船名，中间用“/”隔开；例如：提单中一程船名为“DOGXING”，二程船为“HUAIHAI”，则填“DONGXING/HUAIHAI”。

铁路运输加填运输方式为 BY RAILWAY 或 BY TRAI，最好再加车号，如：BY TRAIN：WAGON NO.××；航空运输为“BY AIR”，邮包运输为“BY PARCEL POST”。

（2）实例：

Per conveyance: MSC SARAH VOY. NO.60A

9 栏 启运日期（Date of Commencement）

（1）填写内容：

此栏填制应按 B/L 中的签发日期或签发日期前 5 天内的任何一天填，或可简单填上 AS PER B/L。

（2）实例：

Date of Commencement: MAR. 20, 2010

10 栏 起讫地点（FROM…TO…）

（1）填写内容：

与提单一致。填装运港，目的港及转运港。当信用证中未明确列明具体的起运港口和目的的港口时，如：ANY CHINESE PORT 或 ANY JAPANESE PORT，填制时应根据货物实际装运选定一个具体的港口，如 SHANGHAI 或 OSAKA 等。

（2）实例：

FROM SHANGHAI TO NEW YORK

11 栏 承保险别（Conditions）

（1）填写内容：

本栏系保险单的核心内容，填写时应注意保险险别及文句与信用证严格一致，应根据信用证或合同中的保险条款要求填制,即使信用证中有重复语句，为了避免混乱和误解，最好按信用证规定的顺序填写。

注意：① 应严格按照信用证的险别投保。最好注明险别的依据及生效时间。

② 如信用证没有规定具体险别，或只规定“MARINE RISK”、“USUAL RISK”或

"TRANSPORT RISK"等，则可投保一切险（ALL RISKS）、水渍险（WA 或 WPA）、平安险（FPA）三种基本险中的任何一种。另外还可以加保一种或几种附加险。

③ 如来证要求的险别超出了合同规定，或成交价格为 FOB 或 CFR，但来证却由卖方保险，这种情况下，如果买方同意支付额外保险费，可按信用证办理。

④ 保险单据可以援引任何除外责任条款（An insurance document may contain reference to any exclusion clause）

⑤ 保险单据可以注明受免赔率或免赔额（减除额）约束。如果信用证要求的保险不计免索赔（Irrespective of percentage, I.O.P.）,那么该保单不能含有免赔率和超过部分减扣（an excess deductible）的约束条款。

（2）实例：

CONDITIONS: COVERING ALL RISKS AND WAR RISK OF PICC (1/1/1981) INCL. WAREHOUSE TO WAREHOUSE AND I.O.P

12 栏 赔款偿付地点（Claim payable at）

（1）填写内容

① 此栏应严格按照信用证或合同规定填制地点和币种两项内容，地点按信用证或投保单，币种应与保险金额一致。

② 如来证未具体规定，一般将目的地作为赔付地点。

③ 如信用证规定不只一个目的港或赔付地，则应全部照填。

（2）实例：

CLAIM PAYABLE AT：DUBAI，U.A.E.

13 栏 投保日期（Date）

（1）填写内容

此栏填制保险单的日期。以保险手续要求货物离开出口仓库前办理，保险单的签发日期应为货物离开仓库的日期或至少填写早于提单签发的日期、发运日或接受监管日。

（2）实例：

Apr.10，2010

14 栏 保险公司签章（Authorized signature）

（1）填写内容：

此栏盖与第一栏相同的保险公司印章及其负责人的签字。实际操作中其签章一般已经印刷在保险单上。保险单需经保险公司签章后方才生效。

（2）实例：

PICC Property and Casualty Limited Qingdao Branch

李 阳

15 栏 保险单的正本份数（Originals of the policy）

正本保险单上必须有"ORIGINAL"字样。UCP600 规定：如保险单据表明所出具正本单据系一份以上，则必须提交全部正本保险单据。如保险单据表明有要求或信用证条款要求，所有正本必须表面看来已被会签。

子项目二 保险单典型业务演示

上接项目二、项目三，根据信用证审核的结果及商业发票的制作情况，在已完成报关、报检的环节后，该项目中单证员李望应完成的工作任务包括：

任务 1：认真审核信用证中的保险条款并准备好商业发票和装箱单。

任务 2：根据上述资料及具体业务要求缮制保险单。

任务 3：办理投保手续。

1. 信用证：

SEQUENCE OF TOTAL	27:	1/1
FORM OF DC	40A:	IRREVOCABLE
DC NO	20:	DC HMN214479
DATE OF ISSUE	31C:	120720
APPLICABLE RULES	40E:	UCP LATEST VERSION
EXPIRY DATE AND PLACE	31D:	120919 IN COUNTRY OF BENEFICIARY
APPLICANT	50:	ELBY GIFTS INC.879 INDUSTRIEL BOIS DES FILION,QUEBEC, J6Z 4T3, CANADA
BENEFICIARY	59:	LILING PENGXING CERAMIC FACTORY WUSHI JIASHU LILING HUNAN, CHINA
AMOUNT	32B:	USD27,010.40
PCT CR AMT TOLERANCE	39A:	10/10
AVAILABLE WITH/BY	41D:	ANY BANK BY NEGOTIATION
DRAFTS AT	42C:	AT SIGHT FOR FULL INVOICE VALUE
DRAWEE	42A:	ISSUING BANK
PARTIAL SHIPMENTS	43P:	ALLOWED
TRANSHIPMENT	43T:	ALLOWED
PORT OF LOADING	44E:	SHENZHEN, CHINA
PORT OF DISCHARGE	44F:	PRINCE RUPERT,BC
LATEST DATE OF SHIPMENT	44D:	120905
DESCRIPTION OF GOODS OR SERVICES	45A:	CERAMIC CUPS AND BOWLS AS PER S/C NO.:CB121039 CIF PRINCE RUPERT,BC ALL PACKED IN CARTONS.
DOCUMENTS REQUIRED	46A:	+ ORIGINAL SIGNED INVOICE PLUS THREE COPIES. + FULL SET OF CLEAN MULTIMODAL TRANSPORT DOCUMENT PLUS 2 N/N COPIES, MADE TO THE ORDER OF HSBC BANK

CANADA, SHOWING ON BOARD NOTATION, MARKED FREIGHT PREPAID, AND NOTIFY APPLICANT(STATING FULL NAME AND ADDRESS).

+ INSURANCE POLICY OR CERTIFICATE BLANK INDORSED, FOR THE INVOICE VALUE PLUS 10% COVERING ALL RISKS AND S.R.CC. FROM WAREHOUSE TO WAREHOUSE.

+ ORIGINAL PACKING LIST PLUS 2 COPIES

+ GSP CERTIFICATE OF ORIGIN FORM A, IN ONE ORIGINAL PLUS 2 COPIES, INDICATING COUNTRY OF ORIGIN, COUNTERCHOPPED BY GOVERNMENT AUTHORITIES OR EXPORTER'S STATMENT OF ORIGIN

+ SHIPPING NOTE INCLUDING SHIPPING MARKS, CTN NO., B/L NO., QUANTITY, VESSEL'S NAME, VOYAGE NO., SHOULD BE SENT TO THE ISSUING BANK ON THE DATE OF SHIPMENT.

ADDITIONAL CONDITIONS 47A: + BENEFICIARY'S DETAILS:

CTC: MILLER LEE

TEL: 86-731-2338-4199

FAX: 86-731-2338-4298

FOLLOWING CHARGES ARE FOR BENEFICIARY'S ACCOUNT:

1) REIMBURSEMENT/REMITTANCE CHARGES

2) DISCREPANCY FEE OF USD/CAD/EUR100 PLUS ALL RELEVANT CABLE CHARGES WILL BE DEDUCTED FROM EACH PRESENTATION OF DISCREPANT DOCUMENTS UNDER THIS DC.

CHARGES 71B: ALL BANKING CHARGES OUTSIDE COUNTRY OF ISSUE FOR ACCOUNT OF BENEFICIARY/EXPORTER

PERIOD OF PRESENTATION 48: WITHIN 15 DAYS AFTER THE DATE OF SHIPMENT BUT WITHIN THE VALIDITY OF THE CREDIT

CONFIRMATION INSTRUCTIONS 49: WITHOUT

INFO TO PRESENTING BK 78: + UPON RECEIPT OF DOCUMENTS

CONFORMING TO THE TERMS OF THIS CREDIT WE UNDERTAKE TO REIMBURSE YOU IN THE CURRENCY OF THIS CREDIT IN ACCORDANCE WITH YOUR INSTRUCTIONS, LESS CABLE CHARGES,

+ FORWARD DOCUMENTS IN ONE LOT BY COURIER AT BENEFICIARY'S EXPENSES TO HSBC BANK CANADA, TRADE AND SUPPLY CHAIN, 5100 SHERBROOKE STREET EAST, SUITE 190, MONTREAL,QUEBEC,H1V 3R9 CANADA.

+ THE AMOUNT OF EACH DRAWING MUST BE ENDORSED ON THE REVERSE OF THIS DC BY THE NEGOTIATING/PRESENTING BANK.

2. 商业发票：

PENGXING IMP&EXP COMPANY

LILING PENGXING CERAMIC FACTORY

WUSHI JIASHU LILING HUNAN CHINA

TEL: 86-731-23384199 FAX: 86-731-23384298

COMMERCIAL INVOICE

To:	ELBY GIFTS INC. 879 INDUSTRIEL BOIS DES FILION QUEBEC, J6Z 4T3, CANADA	**Invoice No.:**	PX12IVN1039
		Invoice Date:	AUG. 16, 2012
		S/C No.:	S/C NO.:CB121039
		S/C Date:	JUL. 5, 2012
From:	SHENZHEN, CHINA	**To:**	PRINCE RUPERT, BC, CANADA
Letter of Credit No.:	DC HMN214479	**Issued By:**	HSBC BANK, MONTREAL CANADA

Marks and Numbers	Number and kind of package Description of goods	Quantity	Unit Price U.S.D/set	Amount
	CERAMIC CUPS AND BOWLS		CIF PRINCE RUPERT, BC	
ELBY		CTN	U.S.D	U.S.D
S/C NO.:CB121039	V23-234	228	4.05	3,693.60
NO: 1-1589	V23-234F	228	4.05	3,693.60
	V23-235	190	2.40	3,648.00
	V23-236	189	2.10	3,175.20
	V23-237	186	1.95	2,901.60
	V23-238	190	2.04	3,100.80
	36-062	191	2.30	3,514.40
	36-063	187	2.12	3,171.52
	Total:	1,589 CTNS		U.S.D 26,898.72

Say Total: U.S DOLLARS TWENTY SIX THOUSAND EIGHT HUNDRED AND NINETY EIGHT AND CENTS SEVENTY TWO (USD26,898.72) ONLY

PENGXING IMP&EXP COMPANY

李 望

3. 其他信息：

保险单号：SH01/173071

预计开航日期：AS PER B/L

据此，单证员李望缮制了一份保险单。

Policy of insurance

PICC	中国人民保险公司 **The People's Insurance Company of China** 总公司设于北京 一九四九年创立 Head Office Beijing Established in 1949

货物运输保险单

CARGO TRANSPORTATION INSURANCE POLICY

发票号(INVOICE NO.)	PX12IVN1039	保单号次 POLICY NO.	SH01/173071
合同号(CONTRACT NO.)	CB121039		

信用证号(L/C NO.)	DC HMN214479
被保险人： INSURED:	LILING PENGXING CERAMIC FACTORY WUSHI JIASHU LILING HUNAN, CHINA

中国人民保险公司(以下简称本公司)根据被保险人的要求，由被保险人向本公司缴付约定的保险费，按照本保险单承保险别和背面所载条款与下列特款承保下述货物运输保险，特立本保险单。

THIS POLICY OF INSURANCE WITNESSES THAT THE PEOPLE'S INSURANCE COMPANY OF CHINA (HEREINAFTER CALLED "THE COMPANY") AT THE REQUEST OF THE INSURED AND IN CONSIDERATION OF THE AGREED PREMIUM PAID TO THE COMPANY BY THE INSURED, UNDERTAKES TO INSURE THE UNDERMENTIONED GOODS IN TRANSPORTATION SUBJECT TO THE CONDITIONS OF THIS POLICY AS PER THE CLAUSES PRINTED OVERLEAF AND OTHER SPECIAL CLAUSES ATTACHED HEREON.

标 记 MARKS&NOS	包装及数量 QUANTITY	保险货物项目 DESCRIPTION OF GOODS	保险金额 AMOUNT INSURED
AS PRE INVOICE NO. PX12IVN1039	1,589 CTNS	CERAMIC CUPS AND BOWLS	US$29,588.59

总保险金额 TOTAL AMOUNT INSURED:	SAY U.S.DOLLARS TWENTY NINE THOUSAND FIVE HUNDRED AND EIGHTY EIGHT AND CENTS FIFTY NINE ONLY

保费： PERMIUM:	AS ARRANGED	启运日期 DATE OF COMMENCEMENT:	AS PER B/L	装载运输工具： PER CONVEYANCE:	COSCO SEATTLE VOY. NO.0078E

自 FROM:	SHENZHEN	经 VIA		至 TO	PRINCE RUPERT

<table>
<tr><td colspan="3">承保险别：
CONDITIONS:</td></tr>
<tr><td colspan="3">COVERING ALL RISKS AND S.R.CC. OF CIC OF PICC(1/1/1981) INCL.WAREHOUSE TO WAREHOUSE</td></tr>
<tr><td colspan="3">所保货物，如发生保险单项下可能引起索赔的损失或损坏，应立即通知本公司下述代理人查勘。如有索赔，应向本公司提交保单正本(本保险单共有 1 份正本)及有关文件。如一份正本已用于索赔，其余正本自动失效。</td></tr>
<tr><td colspan="3">IN THE EVENT OF LOSS OR DAMAGE WHICH MAY RESULT IN A CLAIM UNDER THIS POLICY, IMMEDIATE NOTICE MUST BE GIVEN TO THE COMPANY'S AGENT AS MENTIONED HEREUNDER. CLAIMS, IF ANY, ONE OF THE ORIGINAL POLICY WHICH HAS BEEN ISSUED IN ONE ORIGINAL(S) TOGETHER WITH THE RELEVANT DOCUMENTS SHALL BE SURRENDERED TO THE COMPANY. IF ONE OF THE ORIGINAL POLICY HAS BEEN ACCOMPLISHED. THE OTHERS TO BE VOID.</td></tr>
<tr><td colspan="2"></td><td rowspan="2">中国人民保险公司
The People's Insurance Company of China

SHENZHEN</td></tr>
<tr><td>赔款偿付地点
CLAIM
PAYABLE AT</td><td>PRINCE RUPERT
IN USD</td></tr>
<tr><td>出单日期</td><td rowspan="2">Aug.23,2012</td><td rowspan="2">* * * * * *</td></tr>
<tr><td>ISSUING DATE</td></tr>
</table>

子项目三 保险单拓展业务操作

能力实训项目 1：保险单业务操作

根据以下资料填制保险单

1. 信用证：

+INSURANCE POLICY/CERTIFICATE IN DUPLICATE ENDORSED IN BLANK FOR 110% INVOICE VALUE, COVERING ALL RISKS OF CIC OF PICC(1/1/1981) INCL.WAREHOUSE TO WAREHOUSE AND I.O.P AND SHOWING THE CLAIMING CURRENCY IS THE SAME AS THE CURRENCY OF CREDIT

2. 商业发票：

ZHEJIANG INTERNATIONAL IMP. & EXP. CORP.

8TH FLOOR FOREIGN TRADER BUILDING
200 ZHANQIAN ROAD, JIANGWANG BUILDING

COMMERCIAL INVOICE

TO:	MCHIME CORPORATION 2-2 NAKANOSHINA 3-CHOME, KITA-KU KOBE, 632-8620, JAPAN	**INVOICE NO.:**	05AO-P001
		INVOICE DATE:	MAR. 10, 2013
		S/C NO.:	J515
		L/C NO.:	DCMTN55123

FROM: SHANGHAI **TO:** KOBE

Marks and Numbers	Number and kind of package Description of goods	Quantity	Unit Price	Amount
			CIF KOBE	
J-515 KOBE PKG. NO. 1-166	100PCT COTTON GREIGE PRINT CLOTH ART. NO. 3,042 FIRST QUALITY SIZE:30×30 68×68 50” EXPORT PACKING IN 166 SEAWORTHY BALES OF 1,200 EACH THIS IS TO CERTIFY THAT THE GOODS IS CHINESE ORIGIN	199,200YDS	CIF KOBE USD 0.32/YD	USD63,744.00
	Total:	199,200YDS		USD63,744.00

SAY TOTAL: U.S. DOLLARS SIXTY THREE THOUSAND SEVEN HUNDRED AND FORTY FOUR ONLY

ZHEJIANG INTERNATIONAL IMP. & EXP. CORP.

XXX

3. 其他信息：
保险单号：CGC0318
船名航次：HAIXIN V.213
预计开航日期：MAR. 20, 2013

<table>
<tr><td colspan="2">PICC</td><td colspan="4">中国人民保险公司
The People's Insurance Company of China
总公司设于北京 一九四九年创立
Head Office Beijing Established in 1949</td></tr>
<tr><td colspan="6">货物运输保险单
CARGO TRANSPORTATION INSURANCE POLICY</td></tr>
<tr><td colspan="2">发票号(INVOICE NO.)</td><td></td><td rowspan="2">保单号次
POLICY NO.</td><td colspan="2" rowspan="2"></td></tr>
<tr><td colspan="2">合同号(CONTRACT NO.)</td><td></td></tr>
<tr><td>信用证号
(L/C NO.)</td><td colspan="5"></td></tr>
<tr><td>被保险人：
INSURED:</td><td colspan="5"></td></tr>
<tr><td colspan="6">中国人民保险公司(以下简称本公司)根据被保险人的要求，由被保险人向本公司缴付约定的保险费，按照本保险单承保险别和背面所载条款与下列特款承保下述货物运输保险，特立本保险单。
THIS POLICY OF INSURANCE WITNESSES THAT THE PEOPLE'S INSURANCE COMPANY OF CHINA (HEREINAFTER CALLED "THE COMPANY") AT THE REQUEST OF THE INSURED AND IN CONSIDERATION OF THE AGREED PREMIUM PAID TO THE COMPANY BY THE INSURED, UNDERTAKES TO INSURE THE UNDERMENTIONED GOODS IN TRANSPORTATION SUBJECT TO THE CONDITIONS OF THIS POLICY AS PER THE CLAUSES PRINTED OVERLEAF AND OTHER SPECIAL CLAUSES ATTACHED HEREON.</td></tr>
<tr><td colspan="2">标　记
MARKS&NOS</td><td>包装及数量
QUANTITY</td><td>保险货物项目
DESCRIPTION OF GOODS</td><td colspan="2">保险金额
AMOUNT INSURED</td></tr>
<tr><td colspan="2"></td><td></td><td></td><td colspan="2"></td></tr>
<tr><td colspan="2">总保险金额
TOTAL AMOUNT INSURED:</td><td colspan="4"></td></tr>
<tr><td>保费：
PERMIUM:</td><td>AS ARRANGED</td><td>启运日期
DATE OF COMMENCEMENT:</td><td></td><td>装载运输工具：
PER CONVEYANCE:</td><td></td></tr>
<tr><td>自
FROM:</td><td></td><td>经
VIA</td><td></td><td>至
TO</td><td></td></tr>
</table>

<table>
<tr><td colspan="3">承保险别：
CONDITIONS:</td></tr>
<tr><td colspan="3"></td></tr>
<tr><td colspan="3">所保货物，如发生保险单项下可能引起索赔的损失或损坏，应立即通知本公司下述代理人查勘。如有索赔，应向本公司提交保单正本(本保险单共有份正本)及有关文件。如一份正本已用于索赔，其余正本自动失效。</td></tr>
<tr><td colspan="3">IN THE EVENT OF LOSS OR DAMAGE WHICH MAY RESULT IN A CLAIM UNDER THIS POLICY, IMMEDIATE NOTICE MUST BE GIVEN TO THE COMPANY'S AGENT AS MENTIONED HEREUNDER. CLAIMS, IF ANY, ONE OF THE ORIGINAL POLICY WHICH HAS BEEN ISSUED IN ORIGINAL(S) TOGETHER WITH THE RELEVANT DOCUMENTS SHALL BE SURRENDERED TO THE COMPANY. IF ONE OF THE ORIGINAL POLICY HAS BEEN ACCOMPLISHED. THE OTHERS TO BE VOID.</td></tr>
<tr><td colspan="2"></td><td rowspan="2">中国人民保险公司
The People's Insurance Company of China</td></tr>
<tr><td>赔款偿付地点
CLAIM PAYABLE AT</td><td></td></tr>
<tr><td>出单日期</td><td></td><td>Authorized Signature</td></tr>
</table>

能力实训项目 2：保险单业务操作

根据深圳比高进出口有限公司第 NK2-136 号信用证的要求，2013 年 10 月 18 日，单证员黄柯备齐信用证、商业发票和装箱单等资料向中国人民保险公司办理保险手续。

1. 信用证

SEQUENCE OF TOTAL	27:	1/1
FORM OF DC	40A:	IRREVOCABLE
DC NO	20:	DC 13810
DATE OF ISSUE	31C:	130810
APPLICABLE RULES	40E:	UCP 600
EXPIRY DATE AND PLACE	31D:	130920 IN CHINA
APPLICANT	50:	CONSTRUCTION MOUDULAR SPECIALIST POSTAL: 13 HARVEY RD., SHENTON PK, WA 6008
BENEFICIARY	59:	PRIMA CONSTRUCTION MATERIALS CO., LTD 1401 ROOM, 38 BUILDING, CHUANGYE GARDEN BAOAN DISTRICT, SHENZHEN,

		CHINA
AMOUNT	32B:	USD6,840.00
AVAILABLE WITH/BY	41D:	ANY BANK BY NEGOTIATION
DRAFTS AT	42C:	AT 30DAYS AFTER SIGHT
DRAWEE	42A:	DRAWN ON US
PARTIAL SHIPMENTS	43P:	ALLOWED
TRANSHIPMENT	43T:	ALLOWED
LOADING PORT	44E:	CHINA MAIN PORT
DISCHARGE PORT	44F:	FREMENTLE, AUSTRALIA
LATEST DATE OF SHIPMENT	44C:	130905
DESCRIPTION OF GOODS	45A:	BAMBOO FLOORING ITEM 1 100 SQM U.S.D20.00/SQM ITEM 1 100 SQM U.S.D39.50/SQM ALL PACKING IN SEA WORTHY CARTONS CIF FREMENTLE AS PER PI NO.: BFF0610
DOCUMENTS REQUIRED	46A:	+ MANUALLY SIGNED COMMECIAL INVOICE 3 ORIGINALS PLUS THREE COPIES. + FULL SET(3/3) OF MARINE BILLS OF LADING, MADE OUT TO ORDER, MARKED FREIGHT PREPAID, AND NOTIFY APPLICANT(STATING FULL NAME AND ADDRESS). + INSURANCE POLICY OR CERTIFICATE IN TRIPLICATE, BLANK INDORSED, FOR THE INVOICE VALUE PLUS 10% COVERING ICC(A) RISK AND ICC(STRIKE). FROM WAREHOUSE TO WAREHOUSE AND I.O.P, PAYABLE AT FREMENTLE IN U.S.D. + PACKING LIST 3 ORIGINALS AND 2 COPIES. +CERTIFICATE OF ORIGIN IN CHINA ISSUED BY OFFICIAL AUTRORITY. + BENNIFICIALRY'S CERTIFICATE SHOWING THAT A SET OF ORIGINAL SHIPPING DOCUMENTS HAS BEEN MAIL TO THE APPLICANT BY EXPRESS AFTER 2 DAYS OF SHIOMENT.
CHARGES	71B:	ALL BANKING CHARGES OUTSIDE

		COUNTRY OF ISSUE ARE FOR BENEFICIARY/'S ACCOUNT.
PERIOD OF PRESENTATION	48:	WITHIN 15 DAYS AFTER THE DATE OF SHIPMENT BUT WITHIN THE VALIDITY OF THE L/C
CONFIRMATION INSTRUCTIONS	49:	WITHOUT

2. 商业发票

Prima Construction Materials Co., Ltd

Add: 1401Room, 38building, Chuangye Gardern, Baoan District, Shenzhen China

Tel: 0086-755-32076630 Fax: 0086-755-32076630

COMMERCIAL INVOICE

Contract No.: CBF130724		**No.:PR-20130820**		
L/C No.: DC 13720		**Date: AUG. 22, 2013**		
From: SHENZHEN		**To: FREMENTLE**		
Marks & No.	**Description of Goods**	**Quantity**	**Unit Price($)**	**Amount**
	BAMBOO FLOORING		CIF FREMENTLE	
CMS FREMENTLE CBF130724 NO.:1-109	CARBONISED BAMBOO FLOORING	100SQM	$ 20.00	$2,000.00
	STRAND WOVEN BAMBOO FLOORING DECKING	100SQM	$39.50	$3,950.00
			TOTAL EXW PRICE	$5,950.00
			LCL CHARGE	$ 450.00
			INSURANCE COST	$ 60.00
			FREIGHT	$ 380.00
			CIF VALUE	$6,480.00

3. 其他信息

保险单号：CBFP302

船名航次：VESSEL/VOYAGE：MOL　INTEGRITY/102W

预计开航日期：130830

PICC	中国人民保险公司 **The People's Insurance Company of China** 总公司设于北京　　一九四九年创立 Head Office Beijing　　Established in 1949

货物运输保险单

CARGO TRANSPORTATION INSURANCE POLICY

发票号(INVOICE NO.)		保单号次 POLICY NO.	
合同号(CONTRACT NO.)			
信用证号 (L/C NO.)			
被保险人： INSURED:			

中国人民保险公司(以下简称本公司)根据被保险人的要求，由被保险人向本公司缴付约定的保险费，按照本保险单承保险别和背面所载条款与下列特款承保下述货物运输保险，特立本保险单。

THIS POLICY OF INSURANCE WITNESSES THAT THE PEOPLE'S INSURANCE COMPANY OF CHINA (HEREINAFTER CALLED "THE COMPANY") AT THE REQUEST OF THE INSURED AND IN CONSIDERATION OF THE AGREED PREMIUM PAID TO THE COMPANY BY THE INSURED, UNDERTAKES TO INSURE THE UNDERMENTIONED GOODS IN TRANSPORTATION SUBJECT TO THE CONDITIONS OF THIS POLICY AS PER THE CLAUSES PRINTED OVERLEAF AND OTHER SPECIAL CLAUSES ATTACHED HEREON.

标　记 MARKS&NOS	包装及数量 QUANTITY	保险货物项目 DESCRIPTION OF GOODS	保险金额 AMOUNT INSURED

总保险金额 TOTAL AMOUNT INSURED:	

保费： PERMIUM:	AS ARRANGED	启运日期 DATE OF COMMENCEMENT:		装载运输工具： PER CONVEYANCE:	
自 FROM:		经 VIA		至 TO	

承保险别： CONDITIONS:
所保货物，如发生保险单项下可能引起索赔的损失或损坏，应立即通知本公司下述代理人查勘。如有索赔，应向本公司提交保单正本(本保险单共有份正本)及有关文件。如一份正本已用于索赔，其余正本自动失效。
IN THE EVENT OF LOSS OR DAMAGE WHICH MAY RESULT IN A CLAIM UNDER THIS POLICY, IMMEDIATE NOTICE MUST BE GIVEN TO THE COMPANY'S AGENT AS MENTIONED HEREUNDER. CLAIMS, IF ANY, ONE OF THE ORIGINAL POLICY WHICH HAS BEEN ISSUED IN ORIGINAL(S) TOGETHER WITH THE RELEVANT DOCUMENTS SHALL BE SURRENDERED TO THE COMPANY. IF ONE OF THE ORIGINAL POLICY HAS BEEN ACCOMPLISHED. THE OTHERS TO BE VOID.

		中国人民保险公司 The People's Insurance Company of China
赔款偿付地点 CLAIM PAYABLE AT		
出单日期		Authorized Signature

项目五　原产地证的申领和制作业务

项目预期目标

通过对信用证项下原产地证条款的认真解读，结合该项目提供的商业发票等相关单据，并介绍几种原产地证的背景知识，使同学们了解原产地证的申领流程，熟悉普惠制原产地证的产生背景，掌握原产地证的缮制。

在项目实施过程中，通过产地证申领和制作任务的分解，在分工与合作中逐渐培养审核、制单、归类等国际商务单证基本职业能力，亦培养独立操作业务和与其他业务或政府部门有效沟通的能力。

表 5-1　　项目预期目标

目标类型	原产地证的申领与制作
知识目标	熟悉原产地制度及贸易政策
	理解原产地证的申领程序
	掌握几种重要的产地证制作
能力目标	能办理原产地证的申领业务
	能根据实际业务需要缮制不同的原产地证
职业素质目标	独立业务操作能力
	与政府部门沟通衔接能力

项目实施条件

1. 组织学生参观贸促会或出入境检验检疫局
2. 学生能够在实训室对该项目进行分组讨论并实施
3. 学生能够登陆产地证网上申报系统界面
4. 指导教师掌握扎实的国际贸易政策，具备扎实的外贸业务基础

开篇业务引入

根据第 DC HMN214479 号信用证的要求，长沙鹏兴进出口有限公司可以向湖南省出入境检验检疫局申领普惠制原产地证。该项目任务具体由单证员李望负责。2012 年 8 月 19 日，单证员李望根据 L/C 规定："+ CETIFICATE OF GSP FORM A CETIFIED BY

OFFICIAL AUTHORIZED”，以及缮制好的商业发票、装箱单正本，申领和制作普惠制原产地证。

子项目一　原产地证制作

一、原产地证的含义及使用场合

原产地证明书，简称产地证。它是由出口国政府相关机构签发的一种证明货物的原产地或制造地的法律文件。它主要用于进口国海关实行差别关税、进口限制、不同进口配额和税率的依据，同时也是进出口通关和贸易统计的重要依据。原产地证明书是出口商按进口商的要求提供的，有着多种形式，其中应用最多的是原产地证书和普惠制产地证，通常多用于不需要提供海关发票或领事发票的国家或地区。

二、原产地证的主要种类

1. 普惠制原产地证（Generalized System of Preference Certificate of Origin，简称 GSP 产地证）

普遍优惠制是发达国家对发展中国家向其出口的制成品或半成品货物，普遍给予的一种关税优惠待遇的制度。它使发展中国家与发达国家在贸易上能开展有效的竞争。至今，世界上目前给予我国普惠制待遇的国家共 39 个：欧盟 27 国（比利时、丹麦、英国、德国、法国、爱尔兰、意大利、卢森堡、荷兰、希腊、葡萄牙、西班牙、奥地利、芬兰、瑞典、波兰、捷克、斯洛伐克、拉脱维亚、爱沙尼亚、立陶宛、匈牙利、马耳他、塞浦路斯、斯洛文尼亚、保加利亚、罗马尼亚）、挪威、瑞士、土耳其、列支敦士登、俄罗斯、白俄罗斯、乌克兰、哈萨克斯坦、日本、加拿大、澳大利亚和新西兰。

受惠国凡是要求享受普惠制待遇的出口商品，都必须持有能证明其原产资格和符合直运规则的证明文件。证明原产资格的文件就是《普遍优惠制原产地证明书（申报与证明联合）格式 A》，简称 GSP FORM A 格式（见图 1）。它是受惠国的产品出口到给惠国时，产品享受普惠制关税减免待遇时必备的凭证。

出口企业在货物出运前 5 天自行缮制好证书，连同申请及商业发票一份送交当地商检机构审核，商检机构接受申请后，审核无误即予签发（一正两副，副本由出口商自己签章，正本进行议付）。签发机构通常不接受货物出运后才递交的原产地证申请。

申请时一般需要提交下列文件：

（1）《普惠制产地证书申请书》一份（见图 1）；

（2）出口商业发票（副本）一份；

（3）装箱单一份；

（4）普惠制产地证书一套；

（5）对含有进口成份的出口商品申请签证，申请人应填写《含进口成份商品成本明细单》；

（6）商检机构认为有必要提供的其他有关单证（如信用证、合同、报关单等），并如实解答商检机构提出的有关问题。

普惠制原产地证明书申请书

注册号：__________

申请单位（盖章）： 证书号：__________

申请人郑重声明： 组织机构代码：__________

本人是被正式授权代表出口单位办理和签署本申请书的。

本申请书及普惠制产地证格式 A 所列内容正确无误，如发现弄虚作假，冒充格式 A 所列货物，擅改证书，自愿接受签证机关的处罚及负法律责任。现将有关情况申报如下：

<table>
<tr><td colspan="2">生产单位</td><td colspan="2"></td><td colspan="2">生产单位联系人电话</td><td colspan="2"></td></tr>
<tr><td colspan="2">商品名称
（中英文）</td><td colspan="2"></td><td colspan="2">H.S 税目号
（以六位数码计）</td><td colspan="2"></td></tr>
<tr><td colspan="3">商品（FOB）总值（以美元计）</td><td colspan="2"></td><td>发票号</td><td colspan="2"></td></tr>
<tr><td colspan="2">最终销售国</td><td></td><td colspan="2">证书种类划“√”</td><td>加急证书</td><td colspan="2">普通证书</td></tr>
<tr><td colspan="3">货物拟出运日期</td><td colspan="5"></td></tr>
<tr><td colspan="8">贸易方式和企业性质（请在试用处划“√”）</td></tr>
<tr><td>正常贸易
C</td><td>来料加工进
L</td><td>补偿贸易
B</td><td>中外合资
H</td><td>中外合作
Z</td><td>外商独资
D</td><td>零 售
Y</td><td>展 卖
M</td></tr>
<tr><td></td><td></td><td></td><td></td><td></td><td></td><td></td><td></td></tr>
<tr><td colspan="3">包装数量或毛重或其他数量</td><td colspan="5"></td></tr>
<tr><td colspan="8">原产地标准：
本项商品系在中国生产，完全符合该给惠国方案规定，其原产地情况符合以下第 条；
（1）“P”（完全国产，未使用任何进口原材料）：
（2）“W”其 H.S 税目号为__________（含进口成分）；
（3）“F”（对加拿大出口产品，其进口成分不超过产品出厂价的 40%）。
本批产品系： 1. 直接运输从__________到__________；
2. 转口运输从__________中转国（地区）__________到__________；</td></tr>
<tr><td colspan="6">申请人说明</td><td colspan="2">领证人（签名）
电 话：
日期 年 月 日</td></tr>
</table>

现提交出口商业发票副本一份，普惠制产地证明书格式 **A（FORM A）** 一正二副，以及其他附件 份，请予审核签证。

注：凡含有进口成分的商品，必须按要求提交《含进口成分受惠商品成分明细单》。

检验检疫局联系记录

上海出入境检验检疫局制

图 1 普惠制原产地证明书申请书样本

ORIGINAL

<table>
<tr><td colspan="3">1. Goods consigned form (Exporter's business name, address, country)</td><td colspan="3" rowspan="2">Reference No.
GENERALIZED SYSTEM OF PREFERENCES
CERTIFICAT OF ORIGIN
(Combined declaration and certificate)
FORM A
issued in the People's Republic of China
…………………………………………………………
(country)
See Notes Overleaf</td></tr>
<tr><td colspan="3">2. Goods consigned to (Consignee's name, address, country)</td></tr>
<tr><td colspan="3">3. Means of transport and route (as far as known)</td><td colspan="3">4. For official use</td></tr>
<tr><td>5. item number</td><td>6. Marks & No.</td><td>7. Number and kind of packages; description of goods</td><td>8. Origin criterion (see Notes overleaf)</td><td>9. Gross weight or other quantity</td><td>10. Number and date of invoices</td></tr>
<tr><td colspan="3">11. Certifcation
It is hereby certified, on the basis of control carried out, that the declaration by the exporter is correct.

…………………………………………………….
Place and date, signature and stamp of certifying authority</td><td colspan="3">12. Declaration by the exporter
The undersigned hereby declares that above details and statements are correct; that all goods were produced in
……………….. ……………………... ...
(country)
and that they comply with the original requirements specified for those goods in the generalized system of preferences for goods exported to
………………… …………... ...

…………………………………………………....
Place and date, signature and stamp of certifying authority</td></tr>
</table>

图 2　普惠制原产地证样本

2. 一般原产地证（Certificate of Origin）

简称 C/O，它是证明中国出口货物符合《中华人民共和国出口货物原产地规则》，货物确系中华人民共和国原产的证明文件，也是进口国海关采取不同国别政策和关税待遇的依据。我国使用的一般原产地证书有以下四种：

检验检疫机构出具的《中华人民共和国一般原产地证书》；

贸促会出具的《中华人民共和国一般原产地证书》；

出口商出具的《原产地证书》；

生产厂家出具的《原产地证书》。

ORIGINAL

<table>
<tr><td colspan="2">1. Exporter</td><td colspan="3" rowspan="2">Certificate No.

CERTIFICATE OF ORIGIN
OF
THE PEOPLE'S REPUBLIC OF
CHINA</td></tr>
<tr><td colspan="2">2. Consignee</td></tr>
<tr><td colspan="2">3. Means of transport and route</td><td colspan="3" rowspan="2">5. For certifying authority use only</td></tr>
<tr><td colspan="2">4. Country/region of destination</td></tr>
<tr><td>6. Marks and numbers</td><td>7. Number and kind of packages; description of goods</td><td>8. H.S. Code</td><td>9. Quantity</td><td>10. Number and date of invoices</td></tr>
<tr><td></td><td></td><td></td><td></td><td></td></tr>
</table>

11. Declaration by the exporter The undersigned hereby declares that the above details and statements are correct, that all the goods were produced in China and that they comply with the Rules of Origin of the People's Republic of China. -- Place and date, signature and stamp of authorized signatory	12. Certification It is hereby certified that the declaration by the exporter is correct. -- Place and date, signature and stamp of certifying authority

图 3　一般原产地证样本

3. 区域性经济集团互惠原产地证

区域性经济集团互惠原产地证主要有《〈中国-东盟自由贸易区〉优惠原产地证明书》（FORM E）、《亚太贸易协定》原产地证明书（FORM B）、《〈中国与巴基斯坦优惠贸易安排〉优惠原产地证明书》（FORM P）、《〈中国—智利自贸区〉原产地证书》（FORM F）等。区域优惠原产地证书是具有法律效力的在协定成员国之间就特定产品享受互惠减免关税待遇的官方凭证。

4. 专用原产地证

专用原产地证书是国际组织和国家根据政策和贸易措施的特殊需要，针对某一特殊行业的特定产品规定的原产地证书。主要有对美国出口的原产地声明书（Declaration of Country Origin），简称 DCO 产地证，输往欧盟纺织品产地证（Certificate of Origin of Textile Products），该证书的效用等同于配额，因此在我国由商务部签发，此外还有输往欧盟蘑菇罐头原产地证明书、烟草真实性证书等。

三、具体单据业务操作

（一）一般原产地证的缮制

1 栏　产地证编号（Certificate No.）

（1）填写内容：

该栏填写由签证机关编订的证书号。

（2）实例：

Certificate No.：CCPIT040377950

2 栏 出口方（Exporter）

（1）填写内容：

该栏填写出口公司的名称、详细地址以及国家（地区）名。如有中间商，则先在出口商信息后填写 VIA，再写中间商名称地址及国家（地区）名。

（2）实例：

Exporter

HUNAN TEXTILE IMP & EXP CORP.

4E WUYI RD., CHANGSHA, CHINA

3 栏 收货方（Consignee）

（1）填写内容：

该栏填写最终收货人的名称、详细地址以及国家（地区）名，一般为合同中的买方或信用证提单条款中的被通知人。如有中间商，则先在收货人信息后填写 VIA，再写中间商名称地址及国家（地区）名。

有时在转口贸易中信用证要求所有单据的收货人一栏留空，而原产地证该栏不得留空，此时，我们应在该栏注明“TO WHOM IT MAY CONCERN”或“TO ORDER”。

（2）实例：

Consignee

K.ASLAM AND CO: 16-A DUBAI MAKET,

SHORAB KATRAK MARKET,

SADDAR KARACHI

4 栏 运输方式及路线（Means of Transport and Route）

（1）填写内容：

该栏填写货物的装运港、目的港以及运输方式，如有转运港也必须注明。

（2）实例：

Means of Transport and Route

FORM CHANGSHA TO KARACHI BY TRAIN AND BY VESSEL VIA SHANGHAI

5 栏 最终目的国（地区）（Country/Region of Destination）

（1）填写内容：

不论货物是否发生转运，该栏应填实际的最终收货人所在国家或地区名称。

（2）实例：

Country/Region of Destination

PAKISTAN

6 栏 签证机关用栏（For Certifying Authority Use Only）

该栏一般留空，仅供签证机关在签发后发、补发证书或加注其他声明时使用。

7 栏 运输标志（Marks and Numbers）

（1）填写内容：

该栏参照信用证的要求或者按商业发票填写商品的详细唛头，不能填写诸如（As per

invoice No.）之类统称，无唛头时填写（N/M）。

（2）实例：

Marks and Numbers

KAAC

KARACHI

JWBS01311

NO.1-500 CTNS

8 栏 商品描述、包装数量及种类（Number and Kind of Packages, Description of Goods）

（1）填写内容：

该栏填写商品描述及包装数量。品名应避免使用食品（Food）之类的泛称，包装数量应用中英文描述，通常格式为在阿拉伯数字后加英文描述。最后可在该栏加注表示结束的分隔符。

（2）实例：

Number and Kind of Packages, Description of Goods

TRANSISTOR

500 CTNS (FIVE HUNDRED CARTONS)

9 栏 商品编码（H.S. Code）

（1）填写内容

该栏填写统一的海关商品编码，多种商品应分别填写商品编码。

（2）实例：

H.S. Code

2106.1000

10 栏 数量（Quantity）

（1）填写内容

该栏填写货物的毛重或净重或其他计量单位。

（2）实例：

Quantity

25,200.00KGS (G.W)

11 栏 发票号码及日期（Number and Date of Invoice）

（1）填写内容

该栏应按照国际标准格式填写商业发票的号码及日期。

（2）实例：

Number and Date of Invoice

SEP 1ST, 2013

12 栏 出口方声明（Declaration by the Exporter）

（1）填写内容

该栏填写申报单位地点、申报日期及经手人签名。

（2）实例：

Declaration by the Exporter

CHANGSHA, SEP 7TH,2013

雷淼

13 栏 签证机关证明（Certification）

（1）填写内容

该栏填写签证地点及日期，并由签证机关如贸促会官员在审查合格后在此栏签名盖章。

（2）实例：

CHANGSHA, SEP 7TH, 2013

章小东

（二）普惠制原产地证（格式 A）的缮制

1 栏 证书编号（Reference No.）

（1）填写内容：

该栏填写由检验检疫机构编订的证书号。

（2）实例：

Reference No.：XSW893489027

2 栏 货物产自（Goods Consigned From）

（1）填写内容：

该栏必须填写出口公司的名称、详细地址包括街道名、门牌号以及国家（地区）名。

（2）实例：

Goods Consigned From

HUNAN TEXTILE IMP & EXP CORP.

4E WUYI RD., CHANGSHA, CHINA

3 栏 货物运至（Goods Consigned to）

（1）填写内容：

该栏应参照信用证的要求填写给惠国最终收货人的名称、详细地址以及国家（地区）名，但不得填写中间商。欧盟成员国一般对该栏不作要求。

（2）实例：

Goods Consigned to

ABC HAND TOOL INC.

P.O. BOX 235，QUEEN AVENUE,

LIVERPOOL, U.K

4 栏 运输方式及路线（Means of Transport and Route）

（1）填写内容：

该栏填写货物的装运港、目的港以及运输方式，如有转运港也必须注明。

（2）实例：

Means of Transport and Route

FORM CHANGSHA TO KARACHI BY TRAIN AND BY VESSEL VIA SHANGHAI

5 栏 供官方使用（For Official Use）

申报单位一般将该栏留空，由签证机关在特殊情况下使用。签发后发、补发证书或加注其他声明时使用。

7 栏 运输标志（Marks and Numbers）

（1）填写内容：

该栏参照信用证的要求或者按商业发票填写商品的详细唛头，不能填写诸如（As per invoice No.）之类统称，无唛头时填写（N/M）。

（2）实例：

Marks and Numbers

KAAC

KARACHI

JWBS01311

NO.1-500 CTNS

8 栏 商品描述、包装数量及种类（Number and Kind of Packages, Description of Goods）

（1）填写内容：

该栏填写商品描述及包装数量。品名应避免使用食品（Food）之类的泛称，包装数量应用中英文描述，通常格式为在阿拉伯数字后加英文描述。最后可在该栏加注表示结束的分隔符。

（2）实例：

Number and Kind of Packages, Description of Goods

TRANSISTOR

500 CTNS (FIVE HUNDRED CARTONS)

9 栏 商品编码（H.S. Code）

（1）填写内容

该栏填写统一的海关商品编码，多种商品应分别填写商品编码。

（2）实例：

H.S. Code

2,106.1000

10 栏 数量（Quantity）

（1）填写内容

该栏填写货物的毛重或净重或其他计量单位。

（2）实例：

Quantity

25,200.00KGS (G.W)

11 栏 发票号码及日期（Number and Date of Invoice）

（1）填写内容

该栏应按照国际标准格式填写商业发票的号码及日期。

（2）实例：

Number and Date of Invoice

SEP 1ST, 2013

12 栏 出口方声明（Declaration by the Exporter）

（1）填写内容

该栏填写申报单位地点、申报日期及经手人签名。

（2）实例：

Declaration by the Exporter

CHANGSHA, SEP 7TH,2013

雷淼

13 栏 签证机关证明（Certification）

（1）填写内容

该栏填写签证地点及日期，并由签证机关如贸促会官员在审查合格后在此栏签名盖章。

（2）实例：

CHANGSHA, SEP 7TH,2013

章小东

子项目二　普惠制及一般原产地证典型业务演示

上接项目二、项目三，根据信用证审核的结果及商业发票的制作情况，在该项目中单证员李望应完成的工作任务包括：

任务 1：认真审核信用证中的原产地证书条款并准备好商业发票和装箱单。

任务 2：根据上述资料及具体业务要求缮制原产地证。

任务 3：办理一般原产地证或普惠制原产地证。

1. 信用证

SEQUENCE OF TOTAL	27:	1/1
FORM OF DC	40A:	IRREVOCABLE
DC NO	20:	DC HMN214479
DATE OF ISSUE	31C:	120720
APPLICABLE RULES	40E:	UCP LATEST VERSION
EXPIRY DATE AND PLACE	31D:	120919 IN COUNTRY OF BENEFICIARY
APPLICANT	50:	ELBY GIFTS INC.879 INDUSTRIEL BOIS DES FILION,QUEBEC, J6Z 4T3, CANADA
BENEFICIARY	59:	LILING PENGXING CERAMIC FACTORY

		WUSHI JIASHU LILING HUNAN, CHINA
AMOUNT	32B:	USD27,010.40
PCT CR AMT TOLERANCE	39A：	10/10
AVAILABLE WITH/BY	41D:	ANY BANK BY NEGOTIATION
DRAFTS AT	42C:	AT SIGHT FOR FULL INVOICE VALUE
DRAWEE	42A:	ISSUING BANK
PARTIAL SHIPMENTS	43P:	ALLOWED
TRANSHIPMENT	43T:	ALLOWED
PORT OF LOADING	44E:	SHENZHEN, CHINA
PORT OF DISCHARGE	44F:	PRINCE RUPERT,BC
LATEST DATE OF SHIPMENT	44D:	120905
DESCRIPTION OF GOODS OR SERVICES	45A:	CERAMIC CUPS AND BOWLS AS PER S/C NO.:CB121039 CIF PRINCE RUPERT,BC ALL PACKED IN CARTONS.
DOCUMENTS REQUIRED	46A:	+ ORIGINAL SIGNED INVOICE PLUS THREE COPIES. + FULL SET OF CLEAN MULTIMODAL TRANSPORT DOCUMENT PLUS 2 N/N COPIES, MADE TO THE ORDER OF HSBC BANK CANADA, SHOWING ON BOARD NOTATION, MARKED FREIGHT PREPAID, AND NOTIFY APPLICANT(STATING FULL NAME AND ADDRESS). + INSURANCE POLICY OR CERTIFICATE BLANK INDORSED, FOR THE INVOICE VALUE PLUS 10% COVERING ALL RISKS AND S.R.CC. FROM WAREHOUSE TO WAREHOUSE. + ORIGINAL PACKING LIST PLUS 2 COPIES + GSP CERTIFICATE OF ORIGIN FORM A, IN ONE ORIGINAL PLUS 2 COPIES, INDICATING COUNTRY OF ORIGIN, COUNTERCHOPPED BY GOVERNMENT AUTHORITIES OR EXPORTER'S STATMENT OF ORIGIN + SHIPPING NOTE INCLUDING SHIPPING MARKS, CTN NO., B/L NO., QUANTITY, VESSEL'S NAME, VOYAGE NO., SHOULD BE

SENT TO THE ISSUING BANK ON THE DATE OF SHIPMENT.

ADDITIONAL CONDITIONS 47A: + BENEFICIARY'S DETAILS:
CTC: MILLER LEE
TEL: 86-731-2338-4199
FAX: 86-731-2338-4298

FOLLOWING CHARGES ARE FOR BENEFICIARY'S ACCOUNT:
1) REIMBURSEMENT/REMITTANCE CHARGES
2) DISCREPANCY FEE OF USD/CAD/EUR100 PLUS ALL RELEVANT CABLE CHARGES WILL BE DEDUCTED FROM EACH PRESENTATION OF DISCREPANT DOCUMENTS UNDER THIS DC.

CHARGES 71B: ALL BANKING CHARGES OUTSIDE COUNTRY OF ISSUE FOR ACCOUNT OF BENEFICIARY/EXPORTER

PERIOD OF PRESENTATION 48: WITHIN 15 DAYS AFTER THE DATE OF SHIPMENT BUT WITHIN THE VALIDITY OF THE CREDIT

CONFIRMATION INSTRUCTIONS 49: WITHOUT

INFO TO PRESENTING BK 78: + UPON RECEIPT OF DOCUMENTS CONFORMING TO THE TERMS OF THIS CREDIT WE UNDERTAKE TO REIMBURSE YOU IN THE CURRENCY OF THIS CREDIT IN ACCORDANCE WITH YOUR INSTRUCTIONS, LESS CABLE CHARGES,

+ FORWARD DOCUMENTS IN ONE LOT BY COURIER AT BENEFICIARY'S EXPENSES TO HSBC BANK CANADA, TRADE AND SUPPLY CHAIN, 5100 SHERBROOKE STREET EAST,SUITE 190, MONTREAL,QUEBEC,H1V 3R9 CANADA.

+ THE AMOUNT OF EACH DRAWING MUST BE ENDORSED ON THE REVERSE OF THIS DC BY THE NEGOTIATING/PRESENTING BANK.

2. 商业发票

PENGXING IMP&EXP COMPANY

LILING PENGXING CERAMIC FACTORY

WUSHI JIASHU LILING HUNAN CHINA

TEL: 86-731-23384199 FAX: 86-731-23384298

COMMERCIAL INVOICE

To:	ELBY GIFTS INC. 879 INDUSTRIEL BOIS DES FILION QUEBEC, J6Z 4T3, CANADA	**Invoice No.:**	PX12IVN1039
		Invoice Date:	AUG. 16, 2012
		S/C No.:	S/C NO.: CB121039
		S/C Date:	JUL. 5, 2012
From:	SHENZHEN, CHINA	**To:**	PRINCE RUPERT, BC, CANADA
Letter of Credit No.:	DC HMN214479	**Issued By:**	HSBC BANK, MONTREAL CANADA

Marks and Numbers	Number and kind of package Description of goods	Quantity	Unit Price U.S.D/set	Amount
	CERAMIC CUPS AND BOWLS		CIF PRINCE RUPERT, BC	
ELBY		CTN	U.S.D	U.S.D
S/C NO.:CB121039	V23-234	228	4.05	3,693.60
NO: 1-1589	V23-234F	228	4.05	3,693.60
	V23-235	190	2.40	3,648.00
	V23-236	189	2.10	3,175.20
	V23-237	186	1.95	2,901.60
	V23-238	190	2.04	3,100.80
	36-062	191	2.30	3,514.40
	36-063	187	2.12	3,171.52
	Total:	1,589 CTNS		U.S.D 26,898.72

Say Total: U.S DOLLARS TWENTY SIX THOUSAND EIGHT HUNDRED AND NINETY EIGHT AND CENTS SEVENTY TWO(USD26,898.72)ONLY

PENGXING IMP&EXP COMPANY

李 望

据此，单证员李望缮制了一份普惠制原产地证。

ORIGINAL

1. Goods consigned from (Exporter's business name, address, country) PENGXIANG IMP&EXP CORP. WUSHI JIASHU LILING HUNAN, CHINA	Reference No. Z12470ZC40401388 GENERALIZED SYSTEM OF PREFERENCES CERTIFICATE OF ORIGIN (Combined declaration and certificate) FORM A Issued in THE PEOPLE'S REPUBLIC OF CHINA (country) See Notes overleaf
2. Goods consigned to (Consignee's name, address, country) ELBY GIFTS INC.879 INDUSTRIEL BOIS DES FILION,QUEBEC, J6Z 4T3, CANADA	
3. Means of transport and route (as far as known) FROM SHENZHEN CHINA TO BOIS DES FILION, CANADA BY VESSEL	4. For official use

5. Item number	6. Marks and numbers of packages	7. Number and kind of packages; description of goods	8. Origin criterion (see Notes overleaf)	9. Gross weight or other quantity	10. Number and date of invoices
1	N/M	CERAMIC CUPS AND BOWLS TOTAL: ONE THOUSAND FIVE HUNDRED EIGHTY NINE (1589) CARTONS COUNTRY OF ORIGIN: CHINA **	"P"	10888SETS	PX12IVN1039 AUG. 16, 2012

<table>
<tr>
<td>11. Certification
It is hereby certified, on the basis of control carried out, that the declaration by the exporter is correct.

C.I.Q

SHENZHEN,AUG 16，2012

Place and date, signature and stamp of certifying authority</td>
<td>12. Declaration by the exporter
The undersigned hereby declares that the above details and statements are correct, that all the goods were
CHINA
produced in ....
(country)
and that they comply with the origin requirements specified for those goods in the Generalized System of Preferences for goods exported to
CANADA
....
SHENZHEN, AUG 16，2012

Place and date, signature and stamp of authorized signatory</td>
</tr>
</table>

子项目三　普惠制及一般原产地证拓展业务操作

能力实训项目 1：一般原产地证业务操作

根据上海淼睿进出口有限公司第 0684130117426 号信用证的要求，2013 年 9 月 16 日，单证员彭婷备齐信用证、商业发票等资料向上海市贸促会申领一般原产地证

1. 信用证

SEQUENCE OF TOTAL	27:	1/1
FORM OF DC.	40A:	IRREVOCABLE
DC. NO.	20:	0684130117426
DATE OF ISSUE	31C:	130825
APPLICABLE RULES	40E:	UCP LATEST VERSION
EXPIRY DATE AND PLACE	31D:	131024,CHINA
APPLICANT	50:	M/S. MEMORY STEEL CORPORATION 73/A, LAL MOHAN SHAHA STREET (DHOLAIKHAL),　DHAKA-1100. BANGLADESH.
BENEFICIARY	59:	JIANGSU I-TOUCH BUSINESS SERVICE LTD, ROOM 117, JIANGSU EDIFICE ZHANGJIAGANG FREE TRADE ZONE,

		JIANGSU, CHINA TEL:86-512-56363783
AMOUNT	32B:	USD35,000.00
AVAILABLE WITH/BY	41D:	ANY BANK IN CHINA BY NEGOTIATION
DRAFTS AT	42C:	AT SIGHT FOR FULL INVOICE VALUE
DRAWEE	42A:	DRAWN ON US
PARTIAL SHIPMENTS	43P:	ALLOWED
TRANSSHIPMENT	43T:	ALLOWED
PORT OF LOADING	44A:	ANY SEA PORT, CHINA
PORT OF DISCHARGE	44B:	CHITTAGONG SEA PORT, BANGLADESH
LATEST DATE OF SHIPMENT	44C:	131009
DESCRIPTION OF GOODS	45A:	201/2B SECONDARY GRADE STAINLESS STEEL SHEET OF WIDTH 1219MM THICKNESS 1MM TO 3MM, QTY:25,000KGS AT THE RATE OF USD1.40/KG FOR TOTAL AMOUNT OF USD35,000.00 CFR CHITTAGONG, BANGLADESH. AS PER BENEFICIARY'S PROFORMA INVOICE NO. SK20130802-001 DATED AUG 2,2013
DOCUMENTS REQUIRED	46A:	+MANUALLY SIGNED COMMERCIAL INVOICE IN TRIPLICATE CERTIFYING MERCHANDISE TO BE OF CHINA ORIGIN AND INDICATING THAT THE GOODS ARE BEING IMPORTED AGAINST IRC NO.BA-0171646, TI NO.157-107-0121, VAT REGISTRATION NO.9141093671. +FULL SET OF CLEAN 'SHIPPED ON BOARD' OCEAN BILL OF LADING SHOWING' FREIGHT PREPAID' MADE OUT TO ORDER AND BLANK INDORSED, NOTIFY APPLICANT. +PACKING LIST IN TRIPLICATE SHOWING GROSS WEIGHT, NET WEIGHT. +CERTIFICATE OF ORIGIN ISSUED AND LEGALED BY CCPIT + BENEFICIARY'S DECLARATION SHOULD CERTIFY THAT THE COUNTRY OF ORIGIN HAS BEEN PRINTED ON GOODS PACKING BAG.

		+BENEFICIARY SHOULD SEND A FAX OR BY COUR-IER TO L/C OPENING BANK WITHIN FIVE DAYS FROM THE OF SHIPMENT, ADVISING THE DATE OF SHIPMENT, VESSEL'S NAME, AMOUNT OF BILL AND L/C NO. AND A COPY OF THIS FAX SHOULD ACCOMPANY THE SHIPPING DOCUMENTS. +SHIPMENT BY ISRAELI LINER IS PROHIBITED AND ACERTIFICATE TO THIS EFFECT ISSUED BY THE SHIPPING COMPANY MUST ACCOMPANY THE ORIGINAL DOCUMENTS.
CHARGES	71B:	ALL FOREIGN BANK CHARGES ARE FOR THE ACCOUNT OF THE BENEFICIARY.
PERIOD OF PRESENTATION	48:	15 DAYS FROM SHIPMENT DATE BUT WITHIN VALIDITY OF THE CREDIT

2. 商业发票

<table>
<tr><td colspan="2" align="center">Jiangsu I-Touch Business Service Ltd.,
Add: Room117, Jinggang Edifice Zhangjiagang Free Trade Zone,
Jiangsu Province, China
Tel: 0086-512-56363783 Fax:: 0086-512-56366780</td></tr>
<tr><td colspan="2">COMMERCIAL INVOICE
To: M/S. MEMORY STEEL CORPORATION73/A, LAL MOHAN SHAHA STREET (DHOLAIKHAL), DHAKA-1100. BANGLANDESH.</td></tr>
<tr><td>Contract No.: C20130807</td><td>No.: 67080-9</td></tr>
<tr><td>L/C No.: 0684130117426</td><td>Date: SEP. 13, 2013</td></tr>
<tr><td>From: SHANGHAI, CHINA</td><td>To: CHITTAGONG, BANGLANDESH</td></tr>
</table>

Marks	Description of Goods Size(mm)	Quantity (G.W/KG)	Unit Price (USD/KG)	Amount
	STAINLESS STEEL SHEET		CFR CHITTAGONG	
N/M	201/2B SECONDARY GRADE			
	1.2*1,219*2,438	5,728.00	1.4000	7,806.40
	1.5*1,219*2,438	3,315.20	1.4000	4,547.20
	2.0*1,219*24,38	11,894.0	1.4000	16,282.00
	1,219MM OR MORE THICKNESS 1MM TO 3MM			
	3.0*1,219*2,438	4,663.70	1.4000	6,364.40
	TOTAL:	25,600.90		35,000.00

SAY U.S.DOLLARS THIRTY FIVE THOUSAND ONLY

WE HEREBY CERTIFY THAT ABOVE MERCHANDISE TO BE OF CHINA ORIGIN AND ARE BEING IMPORTED AGAINST IRC NO. BA-0171646,TI NO. 157-107-0121,VAT REGISTRATION NO.9141093671 AND L.C.A. NO. 101804 UNDER H.S. CODE NO. 721933.00, 721934.00

Jiangsu I-Touch Business Service Ltd.

彭 婷

3. 其他信息

商品编码：6200.2100

产地证编号：CCPIT11051039

据此，请完成一般原产地证的填制：

ORIGINAL

1. Exporter	Certificate No. **CERTIFICATE OF ORIGIN** **OF** **THE PEOPLE'S REPUBLIC OF CHINA**
2. Consignee	
3. Means of transport and route	5. For certifying authority use only
4. Country/region of destination	

6. Marks and numbers	7. Number and kind of packages; description of goods	8. H.S. Code	9. Quantity	10. Number and date of invoices

11. Declaration by the exporter The undersigned hereby declares that the above details and statements are correct, that all the goods were produced in China and that they comply with the Rules of Origin of the People's Republic of China.	12. Certification It is hereby certified that the declaration by the exporter is correct.
   -- Place and date, signature and stamp of authorized signatory	 -- Place and date, signature and stamp of certifying authority

能力实训项目 2：普惠制原产地证业务操作

根据深圳普瑞玛建材有限公司第 DC 13810 号信用证的要求，2013 年 8 月 29 日，单证员黄柯备齐信用证、商业发票等资料向广东省出入境检验检疫局申领普惠制原产地证

1. 信用证

SEQUENCE OF TOTAL	27:	1/1
FORM OF DC	40A:	IRREVOCABLE
DC NO	20:	DC 13810
DATE OF ISSUE	31C:	130810
APPLICABLE RULES	40E:	UCP 600
EXPIRY DATE AND PLACE	31D:	130920 IN CHINA
APPLICANT	50:	CONSTRUCTION MOUDULAR SPECIALIST POSTAL: 13 HARVEY RD., SHENTON PK, WA 6008
BENEFICIARY	59:	PRIMA CONSTRUCTION MATERIALS CO., LTD 1401 ROOM, 38 BUILDING, CHUANGYE GARDEN BAOAN DISTRICT, SHENZHEN, CHINA
AMOUNT	32B:	USD6,840.00
AVAILABLE WITH/BY	41D:	ANY BANK BY NEGOTIATION
DRAFTS AT	42C:	AT 30DAYS AFTER SIGHT
DRAWEE	42A:	DRAWN ON US
PARTIAL SHIPMENTS	43P:	ALLOWED

TRANSHIPMENT	43T:	ALLOWED
LOADING PORT	44E:	CHINA MAIN PORT
DISCHARGE PORT	44F:	FREMENTLE, AUSTRALIA
LATEST DATE OF SHIPMENT	44C:	130905
DESCRIPTION OF GOODS	45A:	BAMBOO FLOORING ITEM 1 100 SQM U.S.D20.00/SQM ITEM 1 100 SQM U.S.D39.50/SQM ALL PACKING IN SEA WORTHY CARTONS CIF FREMENTLE AS PER PI NO.: BFF0610
DOCUMENTS REQUIRED	46A:	+ MANUALLY SIGNED COMMECIAL INVOICE 3 ORIGINALS PLUS THREE COPIES. + FULL SET(3/3) OF MARINE BILLS OF LADING, MADE OUT TO ORDER, MARKED FREIGHT PREPAID, AND NOTIFY APPLICANT(STATING FULL NAME AND ADDRESS). + INSURANCE POLICY OR CERTIFICATE IN TRIPLICATE, BLANK INDORSED, FOR THE INVOICE VALUE PLUS 10% COVERING ICC(A) RISK AND ICC(STRIKE). FROM WAREHOUSE TO WAREHOUSE AND I.O.P, PAYABLE AT FREMENTLE IN U.S.D. + PACKING LIST 3 ORIGINALS AND 2 COPIES. +CERTIFICATE OF ORIGIN IN CHINA ISSUED BY OFFICIAL AUTRORITY. + BENNIFICIALRY'S CERTIFICATE SHOWING THAT A SET OF ORIGINAL SHIPPING DOCUMENTS HAS BEEN MAIL TO THE APPLICANT BY EXPRESS AFTER 2 DAYS OF SHIOMENT.
CHARGES	71B:	ALL BANKING CHARGES OUTSIDE COUNTRY OF ISSUE ARE FOR BENEFICIARY/'S ACCOUNT.
PERIOD OF PRESENTATION	48:	WITHIN 15 DAYS AFTER THE DATE OF SHIPMENT BUT WITHIN THE VALIDITY OF THE L/C
CONFIRMATION INSTRUCTIONS	49:	WITHOUT

2. 商业发票

Prima Construction Materials Co., Ltd.

Add: 1401Room, 38building, Chuangye Gardern, Baoan District, Shenzhen China

Tel: 0086-755-32076630 Fax: 0086-755-32076630

COMMERCIAL INVOICE

Contract No.: CBF130724		No.:PR-20130820		
L/C No.: DC 13720		Date: AUG. 22, 2013		
From: SHENZHEN		To: FREMENTLE		
Marks&Nos. No	**Description of Goods**	**Quantity**	**Unit Price**	**Amount**
	BAMBOO FLOORING		CIF FREMENTLE	
CMS FREMENTLE CBF130724 NO.:1-109	CARBONISED BAMBOO FLOORING	100SQM	$ 20.00	$2,000.00
	STRAND WOVEN BAMBOO FLOORING DECKING	100SQM	$39.50	$3,950.00
			TOTAL EXW PRICE	$5,950.00
			LCL CHARGE	$ 450.00
			INSURANCE COST	$ 60.00
			FREIGHT	$ 380.00
			CIF VALUE	$6,480.00

Prima Construction Materials Co., Ltd.

黄 柯

3. 其他信息

该商品全部生产环节均在中国完成。

普惠制产地证编号：BF2013810

Prima Construction Materials Co., Ltd.

Add: 1401Room, 38building, Chuangye Gardern, Baoan District, Shenzhen China

Tel: 0086-755-32076630　　Fax: 0086-755-32076630

COMMERCIAL INVOICE

To: CONSTRUCTION MOUDULAR SPECIALIST
POSTAL: 13 HARVEY RD.,SHENTON PK, WA 6008 AUSTRALIA

Contract No.: CBF130724	**No.:PR-20130820**
L/C No.: DC 13724	**Date: AUG. 22, 2013**
From: SHENZHEN	**To: FREMENTLE**

Marks&Nos. No	**Description of Goods**	**Quantity**	**Unit Price**	**Amount**
CMS FREMENTLE CBF130724 NO.:1-109	BAMBOO FLOORING		CIF FREMENTLE	
	CARBONISED BAMBOO FLOORING	100SQM	$ 20.00	$2,000.00
	STRAND WOVEN BAMBOO FLOORING DECKING	100SQM	$39.50	$3,950.00
TOTAL			EXW PRICE	$5,950.00
			LCL CHARGE	$ 450.00
			INSURANCE COST	$ 60.00
			FREIGHT	$ 380.00
			CIF VALUE	$6,480.00

Prima Construction Materials Co., Ltd.

黄　柯

据此，请完成普惠制原产地证的填制：

ORIGINAL

<table>
<tr>
<td colspan="3">1. Goods consigned form (Exporter's business name, address, country)</td>
<td colspan="3" rowspan="2">Reference No.
GENERALIZED SYSTEM OF PREFERENCES
CERTIFICAT OF ORIGIN
(Combined declaration and certificate)
FORM A
issued in the People's Republic of China
……………………………………………………
(country)

See Notes Overleaf</td>
</tr>
<tr>
<td colspan="3">2. Goods consigned to (consignee's name, address, country)</td>
</tr>
<tr>
<td colspan="3">3. Means of transport and route (as far as known)</td>
<td colspan="3">4. For official use</td>
</tr>
<tr>
<td>5. item number</td>
<td>6. Marks & No.</td>
<td>7. Number and kind of packages; description of goods</td>
<td>8. Origin criterion (see Notes overleaf)</td>
<td>9. Gross weight or other quantity</td>
<td>10. Number and date of invoices</td>
</tr>
<tr>
<td colspan="3">11. Certifcation
It is hereby certified, on the basis of control carried out, that the declaration by the exporter is correct.

……………………………………………………..
Place and date, signature and stamp of certifying authority</td>
<td colspan="3">12. Declaration by the exporter
The undersigned hereby declares that above details and statements are correct; that all goods were produced in
………………... ……………………... ...
(country)
and that they comply with the original requirements specified for those goods in the generalized system of preferences for goods exported to
………………… …………... ...

…………………………………………………....
Place and date, signature and stamp of certifying authority</td>
</tr>
</table>

项目六　报检单据制作业务

项目预期目标

在项目实施过程中，通过对报检单的制作和学习，熟悉了报检的流程，掌握了报检单、换证凭条和出境货物通关单的制作方法。逐渐培养学生的报检、制单、归类等国际商务单证基本职业能力，亦培养独立操作业务和与商检部门有效沟通的能力。

表 6-1　　项目预期目标

目标类型	报检单填制
知识目标	熟悉报检流程
	掌握报检单的缮制方法
	掌握商品检验的基本知识
能力目标	能区分出境货物通关单和换证凭条
	根据商业发票和装箱单缮制报检单
职业素质目标	独立业务操作能力
	具有与商检部门的沟通衔接能力

项目实施条件

1. 向学生提供报检单样单，指出报检单的必要项目和非必要项目
2. 学生进行角色扮演，能根据实际需要申领出境货物通关单或者出境货物换证凭条
3. 学生能够在实训室根据提供的业务资料网上申报并缮制报检单
4. 指导教师熟悉我国的对外贸易管制政策，具备扎实的外贸业务基础

开篇业务引入

由于 L-12017 号信用证的出口产品为日用陶瓷，商品编码为 69111010.00，其监管条件为 B，即需要办理出境货物通关单，据此，长沙鹏兴进出口有限公司业务员李望在 2012 年 8 月 18 日，根据商业发票、装箱单和其他相关信息制作报检单，向湖南省出入境检验检疫局办理报检手续，申领出境货物换证凭条，准备寄往深圳大鹏海关办理货物出口报关手续。该项目任务具体由鹏兴瓷厂报检员赵斌负责。

子项目一　报检单据制作

商品出入境检验检疫是国际贸易中一个重要的环节，商品报检是检验检疫重要的工作内容，从事报检工作必须了解并掌握出入境检验检疫基础知识，从而更好地熟悉检验检疫规定和相关业务，为做好报检工作打下扎实的基础。

报检是指有关当事人根据法律、行政法规的规定，对外贸易合同的约定或证明履约的需要，向检验检疫机构申请检检验、检疫、鉴定，以获准出入境或取得销售使用的合法凭证及某种公证证明所必须履行的法定程序和手续。

出入境报检程序一般包括：准备单证、电子报检数据录入、现场递交单证、联系配合检验检疫、缴纳检验检疫费、签领检验检疫单证等几个环节。

中华人民共和国出入境检验检疫

出境货物报检单

报检单位（加盖公章）：　　　　　　　　　　　　*编　号

单位地址

报检单位登记号：　　　联系人：　　　电话：　　　报检日期：　　年　　月　　日

<table>
<tr><td rowspan="2">发货人</td><td colspan="5">（中文）</td></tr>
<tr><td colspan="5">（外文）</td></tr>
<tr><td rowspan="2">收货人</td><td colspan="5">（中文）</td></tr>
<tr><td colspan="5">（外文）</td></tr>
<tr><td>货物名称
（中/外文）</td><td>H.S.编码</td><td>产地</td><td>数/重量</td><td>货物总值</td><td>包装种类及数量</td></tr>
<tr><td></td><td></td><td></td><td></td><td></td><td></td></tr>
<tr><td>运输工具名称号码</td><td></td><td>贸易方式</td><td></td><td>货物存放地点</td><td></td></tr>
<tr><td>合同号</td><td></td><td>信用证号</td><td></td><td>用途</td><td></td></tr>
<tr><td>发货日期</td><td></td><td>输往国家
（地区）</td><td></td><td>许可证/审批号</td><td></td></tr>
<tr><td>启运地</td><td></td><td>到达口岸</td><td></td><td>预计工作日期</td><td>年　月　日</td></tr>
</table>

<table>
<tr><td>合同、信用证订立的检验检疫条款或特殊要求</td><td colspan="2">标 记 及 号 码</td><td colspan="3">随附单据（划“√”或补填）</td></tr>
<tr><td></td><td colspan="2"></td><td>()合同
()信用证
()发票
()换证凭单
()装箱单
()厂检单</td><td colspan="2">()包装性能结果单
()许可/审批文件
()出口货物报关单
()
()</td></tr>
<tr><td colspan="3">需要证单名称（划“√”或补填）</td><td colspan="3">*检验检疫费</td></tr>
<tr><td rowspan="3">()品质证书 __正__副
()重量证书 __正__副
()数量证书 __正__副
()兽医卫生证书 __正__副
()健康证书 __正__副
()卫生证书 __正__副
()动物卫生证书 __正__副</td><td colspan="2" rowspan="3">()植物检疫证书 __正__副
()熏蒸/消毒证书 __正__副
()出境货物换证凭单 __正__副
()出竞货物通关单</td><td colspan="2">总金额（人民币元）</td><td></td></tr>
<tr><td colspan="2">计费人</td><td></td></tr>
<tr><td colspan="2">收费人</td><td></td></tr>
<tr><td colspan="2" rowspan="3">报检人郑重声明：
1. 本人被授权报检。
2. 上列填写内容正确属实，货物无伪造或冒用他人的厂名、标志、认证标志，并承担货物质量责任。
签名：____________</td><td colspan="4">领 取 证 单</td></tr>
<tr><td colspan="2">日期</td><td colspan="2"></td></tr>
<tr><td colspan="2">签名</td><td colspan="2"></td></tr>
</table>

注：有“*”号栏由出入境检验检疫机关填写　　◆国家出入境检验检疫局制

出境货物报检单样本

一、出境货物报检单填制要求

出境货物报检单所列各栏必须填写完整、准确、清晰，没有内容填写的栏目应以斜杠“/”表示，不得留空。

1 栏 编号：是指检验检疫机构受理本批货物报检后，系统自动生成 15 位数的报检编号，该编号的前 6 位为检验检疫局机关代码，第 7 位为报检类代码（1 表示入境，2 代表出境），第 8、9 位为年份代码，第 10 至 15 位为流水号。

2 栏 报检单位：报检单位是指经检验检疫机构核准，在检验检疫机构备案或注册登记，有权从事报检业务的法人或其他组织。

填写内容：本栏目填写报检单位的中文名称，并加盖报检单位公章。

实例：醴陵市鹏兴瓷厂

3 栏 报检单位登记号：指报检单位在检验检疫机构备案或注册登记后取得的 10 位数代码。

填写内容：本栏目填 10 位数登记证号码。

实例：4300123456

4 栏 联系人：指本批货物的报检员

填写内容：填报报检人的姓名、电话

实例：赵斌，13907332687

5栏 报检日期：报检日期是指检验检疫机构接受出口货物的发货人或其代理人报检的日期。

实例：2012年8月18日

6栏 发货人（中/外文）：指外贸合同中的发货方

填写内容：应与本批货物贸易合同中卖方名称或信用证中受益人或者商业发票的出票人一致。本栏目分别用中英文填写。

实例：醴陵鹏兴陶瓷厂

LILING PENGXING CERAMIC FACTORY

7栏 收货人（中/外文）：指外贸合同中的收货方。

填写内容：应与本批出境货物贸易合同中或信用证中买方或者商业发票中的受票人一致。本栏目分别用中英文填写。

实例：中文名称填写"***"

英文名称填写：ELBY GIFTS INC.

8栏 货物名称（中/外文）：是指国际贸易买卖双方同意买卖的货物名称。

填写内容：应填写本批货物的品名及规格、型号或品牌号、成分。按贸易合同、信用证或者发票所列的货物名称填写。货物名称不得填写笼统的商品类，"陶瓷"、"玩具"等。货物名称必须填写具体的类别名称，如"日用陶瓷"、"塑料玩具"。不够位置填写的，可用附页的形式填报。

实例：日用陶瓷

CERAMIC CUP AND BOWLS.

9栏 H.S.编码：指进出口货物的税则号列并符合海关要求的附件号码组成的10位编号。

实例：69111010.00

10栏 产地：指本批货物生产地或加工制造地名称。

填写内容：填报出境货物生产地的省、市、县的中文名称

实例：湖南省醴陵市

11栏 数/重量：填写报检货物的数/重量，重量一般填写净重。如填写毛重，或以毛重作净重则需注明。

本栏目可以填报一个以上计量单位。如：第一计量单位："个"；第二计量单位："千克"。

实例：17 655千克 或者10 944套

12栏 货物总值：货物总值指出境货物的商业总值及币种。本栏应与合同或发票上所列的总值一致。

注意：本栏目不需要填写报价格术语。

实例：27 010.40美元

13栏 包装种类及数量：指货物实际运输外包装的种类及及数量。

实例：1 596纸箱

14 栏 运输工具名称号码：运输工具名称是指载运出境货物运输工具的名称和编号。本栏按货物实际装载的运输工具类别名称（如船、飞机、货柜车、火车等）及运输工具编号（船名、飞机航班号、车牌号码、火车车次）填写。报检时，未能确定运输工具编号的，可只填写运输工具类别。

实例：船舶或 COSCO SEATTLE/0078E

15 栏 贸易方式：① 一般贸易、② 来料加工、③ 进料加工、⑨ 其他等。

实例：一般贸易

16 栏 货物存放的地点：指本批货物存放的地点。

实例：醴陵市枣树乡乌石村

17 栏 合同号：指本批货物贸易合同编号。

实例：CB121039

18 栏 信用证号：指本批货物的信用证编号。

实例：L-12017

19 栏 用途：指本批出境货物用途，如种用或繁殖、食用、奶用、观赏或演艺、实验、药用、饲用、介质土、食品包装材料、食品加工设备、食品添加剂、食品容器、食品消毒剂、食品洗涤剂、其他等。对于选择“其他”的，应在报检单中手填具体用途。

实例：食品容器

20 栏 发货日期：按本批货物信用证或合同上所列的出境日期填写。

实例：2012.8.24

21 栏 输往国家（地区）：指贸易合同中买方（进口方）所在的国家或地区。

实例：加拿大

22 栏 许可证/审批号：对实施许可证制度或者审批制度管理的货物，报检时填写许可证编号或审批单编号。

实例：无

23 栏启运地：指装运本批货物离境的交通工具的启运口岸/地区城市名称。

实例：深圳

24 栏 到达口岸：指装运本批货物的交通工具最终抵达目的地停靠的口岸名称。

实例：鲁珀特港

25 栏 生产单位注册号：指生产/加工本批货物的单位在检验检疫机构的注册登记编号。

实例：4300123456

26 栏 集装箱规格、数量及号码：填写装载本批货物的集装箱规格（如 40 英尺、20 英尺等）以及分别对应的数量和集装箱号码。若集装箱太多，可用附单形式填报。

实例：1×40 英尺 FCL

27 栏 合同、信用证订立的检验检疫条款或特殊要求：指贸易合同或信用证中贸易双方对本批货物特别约定而订立的质量、卫生等条款和报检单位对本批货物检验检疫的特别要求。

实例：无

28 栏 标记及号码：按出境货物实际运输包装标记填写。如没有标记，填写 N/M。标记栏不够位置填写时，可用附页填写。

实例：N/M

29 栏 随附单据：按实际提供的单据，在对应的“□”打“ √ ”。对报检单上未标出的，须自行填写提供的单据名称。

实例：在合同、信用证、商业发票、装箱单、包装性能结果单前划“ √ ”，不能填写“***”。

30 栏 需要证单名称：按需要检验检疫机构出具的证单，在对应的“□”打“ √ ”，并对应注明所需证单的正副本的数量。对报检单上未标出的，如“通关单”等，须自行填写所需证单的名称和数量。

实例：在出境货物换证凭单前划“ √ ”

31 栏 报检人郑重声明：必须有报检人的亲笔签名。

实例：赵斌（手签）

32 栏 检验检疫费：检验检疫费是对本批货物进行检验检疫应收取的费用。本栏目由检验检疫机构计/收费人员填写，应填实际收取的检验检疫费的实际金额。

33 栏 领取证单：领取证单是指报检员在领取证单时填写领取证单的日期并签名。

本说明未尽事宜按国家质检总局发布的有关规定办理

子项目二　报检单典型业务演示

上接项目五，在完成备货及商业单据的制作后，鹏兴公司应当准备商品报检，在该项目中报检员赵斌应完成的工作任务包括：

任务 1：认真查看合同及信用证中对商品检验的条款。

任务 2：根据商业发票、装箱单等单证按要求缮制报检单。

1. 合同

CONTRACT

Contract No.: CB121039

Date: JUL. 5, 2012

THE SELLER:	PENGXING IMP&EXP COMPANY LILING PENGXING CERAMIC FACTOR WUSHI JIASHU LILING HUNAN, CHINA TEL: 86-731-23384199　FAX: 86-731-23384298
THE BUYER:	ELBY GIFTS INC. 879 INDUSTRIEL BOIS DES FILION

QUEBEC, J6Z 4T3, CANADA

TEL: 514-420-0282 FAX: 514-420-0322

This Contract is made by and between the Buyer and Seller, whereby the Buyer agrees to buy and the Seller agrees to sell the under mentioned goods on the terms and conditions stated below:

Description of Goods, Specifications,	Quantity (set)	Unit Price (U.S.D/set)	Amount (U.S.D)
Ceramic Cups and Bowls		C.I.F Prince	
V23-234	912	Rupert	3,693.60
V23-234F	912	4.05	3,693.60
V23-235	1,520	4.05	3,648.00
V23-236	1,512	2.40	3,175.20
V23-237	1,488	2.10	2,901.6
V23-2348	1,520	1.95	3,100.80
36-062	1,528	2.04	3,514.40
36-063	1,496	2.30	3,171.52
As per the P/I No.: CCB23-36		2.12	
Total	10,888		26,898.72

Say total: U.S DOLLARS TWENTY SIX THOUSAND EIGHT HUNDRED AND NINETY EIGHT AND CENTS SEVENTY TWO (USD 26,898.72) ONLY.

PACKING: 4 sets packed in a carton(V 23-234/V23-234F), 8 sets packed in a carton for others.

TRANSPORT DETAILS: the goods should shipped on or before: 5th Sep, 2012, from Shenzhen, China to Prince Rupert

Canada, transshipment and partial shipment are all allowed.

INSURANCE: To be effected by the Seller for 110% of invoice value covering all risks and S.R.C.C as per C.I.C of PICC dated 01/01/1981.

PAYMENT: By irrevocable documentary letter of credit at sight, reaching the seller not later than Aug 5,2012 and remain valid for negotiation in China for 15 days after shipment.

DOCUMENTS:

+ Signed commercial invoice one original and three copies.
+ Full set of clean on board ocean Bill of Lading made to order of issuing bank.
+ Packing List one original and two copies.
+ Insurance policy endorsed in blank.
+ GSP Form A certified by government authority.

INSPECTION: Quality/Quantity/Weight Discrepancy and Claim: In case the quality and/or quantity/weight are found by the Buyer not to conform with the contract after arrival of the goods at the final destination, the Buyer may lodge a claim against the seller supported by a survey report issued by an inspection organization agreed upon by both parties with the exception of those claims for which the insurance company and/or the shipping company are to be held responsible. Claim for quality discrepancy should be filed by the Buyer within 60 days after arrival of the goods at the final destination while for quantity/weight discrepancy claim should be filed by the Buyer within 30 days after arrival of the goods at the final destination.

FORCE MAJEURE: The Seller shall not be held responsible for failure or delay in delivery of the entire or portion of the goods under this contract in consequence of any Force Majeure incidents.

ARBITRATION: All disputes in connection with this Contract or the execution thereof shall be settled through friendly negotiations. If no settlement can be reached, the case shall then be submitted to the Foreign Trade Arbitration Commission of the China Council for the Promotion of International Trade, Beijing, for settlement by arbitration in accordance with the Commission's Provisional Rules of Procedure. The award rendered by the Commission shall be final and binding on both parties. The arbitration expenses shall be borne by the losing party unless otherwise award by the arbitration organization.

Signed by:

THE SELLER:	**THE BUYER:**
PENGXING IMP&EXP COMPANY	ELBY GIFTS INC.
LILING PENGXING CERAMIC FACTORY	
李 望	Camp Wolf

2. 商业发票

PENGXING IMP&EXP COMPANY

LILING PENGXING CERAMIC FACTORY

WUSHI JIASHU LILING HUNAN CHINA

TEL: 86-731-23384199 FAX: 86-731-23384298

COMMERCIAL INVOICE

To:	ELBY GIFTS INC. 879 INDUSTRIEL BOIS DES FILION QUEBEC, J6Z 4T3, CANADA	**Invoice No.:**	PX12IVN1039
		Invoice Date:	AUG. 16, 2012
		S/C No.:	S/C NO.: CB121039
		S/C Date:	JUL. 5, 2012
From:	SHENZHEN, CHINA	**To:**	PRINCE RUPERT, BC, CANADA
Letter of Credit No.:	DC HMN214479	**Issued By:**	HSBC BANK, MONTREAL CANADA

Marks and Numbers	Number and kind of package / Description of goods	Quantity	Unit Price U.S.D/set	Amount
	CERAMIC CUPS AND BOWLS		CIF PRINCE RUPERT, BC	
ELBY		CTN	U.S.D	U.S.D
S/C NO.:CB121039	V23-234	228	4.05	3,693.60
NO: 1-1589	V23-234F	228	4.05	3,693.60
	V23-235	190	2.40	3,648.00
	V23-236	189	2.10	3,175.20
	V23-237	186	1.95	2,901.60
	V23-238	190	2.04	3,100.80
	36-062	191	2.30	3,514.40
	36-063	187	2.12	3,171.52
	Total:	1,589 CTNS		U.S.D 26,898.72

Say Total: U.S DOLLARS TWENTY SIX THOUSAND EIGHT HUNDRED AND NINETY EIGHT AND CENTS SEVENTY TWO(USD26,898.72)ONLY

PENGXING IMP&EXP COMPANY

李 望

3. 装箱单

PENGXING IMP&EXP COMPANY

LILING PENGXING CERAMIC FACTORY

WUSHI JIASHU LILING HUNAN CHINA

TEL: 86-731-23384199 FAX: 86-731-23384298

PACKING LIST

To:	ELBY GIFTS INC.	**Date**	AUG. 16, 2012
	879 INDUSTRIEL BOIS DES FILION	**Invoice No.:**	PX12IVN1039
	QUEBEC, J6Z 4T3, CANADA		
From:	SHENZHEN, CHINA	**To:**	PRINCE RPERT, BC, CANADA

Item No.	Description of goods	Quantity		Sets/CTN			G.W/N.W		Dimension			Meas.
V23-234	CERAMIC CUPS AND BOWLS	912	SETS	228	CTNS	4	11.8	9.6	38.9*	29.0*	26.6	6.84
V23-234F	CERAMIC CUPS AND BOWLS	912	SETS	228	CTNS	4	11.8	9.6	38.9*	29.0*	26.6	6.84
V23-235	CERAMIC CUPS AND BOWLS	1,520	SETS	190	CTNS	8	15.0	12.8	48.6*	31.6*	43.6	12.72
V23-236	CERAMIC CUPS AND BOWLS	1,512	SETS	189	CTNS	8	10.6	8.4	50.4*	27.0*	.34.8	8.95
V23-237	CERAMIC CUPS AND BOWLS	1,488	SETS	186	CTNS	8	8.4	6.4	31.0*	28.2*	39.2	6.37
V23-238	CERAMIC CUPS AND BOWLS	1,520	SETS	190	CTNS	8	10.5	8.0	48.6	28.2*	39.2	10.21
36-062	CERAMIC CUPS AND BOWLS	1,528	SETS	191	CTNS	8	12.0	9.6	49.0*	28.9*	38.2	10.33
36-063	CERAMIC CUPS AND BOWLS	1,496	SETS	187	CTNS	8	8.4	6.4	34.4*	33.0*	27.6	5.86
	Total:	10,888	SETS	1,589	CTNS		17,654.4	14,138.0				68.13

ALL PACKED IN CARTONS

SAY TOTAL: ONE THOUSAND FIVE HUNDRED AND EIGHTY NINE (1,589CTNS) CARTONS ONLY

据此，报检员赵斌完成了报检单的填制：

中华人民共和国出入境检验检疫

出境货物报检单

报检单位（加盖公章）： 醴陵市鹏兴陶瓷厂 *编 号

单位地址

报检单位登记号： 4300123456 联系人： 赵斌 电话： 88232366 报检日期： 2012 年 8 月 18 日

发货人	（中文）	醴陵鹏兴陶瓷厂
	（外文）	LILING PENGXING CERAMIC FACTORY
收货人	（中文）	***
	（外文）	ELBY GIFTS INC.

货物名称(中/外文)	H.S.编码	产地	数/重量	货物总值	包装种类及数量
日用陶瓷 CERAMIC CUP AND BOWLS.	69111010.00	湖南省醴陵市	17 655 千克	27 010.40 美元	1 596 纸箱

运输工具名称号码	COSCO SEATTLE/0078E	贸易方式	一般贸易	货物存放地点	醴陵市枣树乡乌石村
合同号	CB121039	信用证号	L-12017	用途	食品容器
发货日期	2012.8.24	输往国家(地区)	加拿大	许可证/审批号	无
启运地	深圳	到达口岸	鲁珀特港	预计工作日期	年 月 日

合同、信用证订立的检验检疫条款或特殊要求	标 记 及 号 码	随附单据（划“√”或补填）	
无	N/M	(√)合同 (√)信用证 (√)发票 ()换证凭单 (√)装箱单 ()厂检单	(√)包装性能结果单 ()许可/审批文件 ()出口货物报关单 () ()

需要证单名称（划“√”或补填）		*检验检疫费	
()品质证书 __正__副 ()重量证书 __正__副 ()数量证书 __正__副 ()兽医卫生证书 __正__副 ()健康证书 __正__副 ()卫生证书 __正__副 ()动物卫生证书 __正__副	()植物检疫证书 __正__副 ()熏蒸/消毒证书 __正__副 (√)出境货物换证凭单 1正1副 ()出竞货物通关单	总金额（人民币元）	
		计费人	
		收费人	

报检人郑重声明：	领 取 证 单	
1. 本人被授权报检。 2. 上列填写内容正确属实，货物无伪造或冒用他人的厂名、标志、认证标志，并承担货物质量责任。 签名： __赵斌__	日期	
	签名	

注：有“*”号栏由出入境检验检疫机关填写 ◆国家出入境检验检疫局制

子项目三　报检单拓展业务操作

能力实训项目 1：缮制报检单并办理报检手续

上接项目，根据上海淼睿进出口有限公司第 C-11027 号信用证的要求，2013 年 9 月 16 日，单证员张小兰根据商业发票、装箱单以及相关信息缮制报检单。

1. 商业发票

Jiangsu I-Touch Business Service Ltd.
Add: Room117, Jinggang Edifice Zhangjiagang Free Trade Zone, Jiangsu Province, China
Tel: 0086-512-56363783　Fax: 0086-512-56366780

COMMERCIAL INVOICE

To: M/S. MEMORY STEEL CORPORATION73/A, LAL MOHAN SHAHA STREET (DHOLAIKHAL),　DHAKA-1100. BANGLANDESH.

Contract No.: C20130807	**No.: 67080-9**
L/C No.: 0684130117426	**Date: SEP. 13, 2013**
From: SHANGHAI, CHINA	**To: CHITTAGONG, BANGLANDESH**

Marks & Nos. No	**Description of Goods Size(mm)**	**Quantity (G.W/KG)**	**Unit Price (USD/KG)**	**Amount**
	STAINLESS STEEL SHEET		CFR CHITTAGONG	
N/M	201/2B SECONDARY GRADE			
	1.2×1,219×2,438	5,728.00	1.4000	7,806.40
	1.5×1,219×2,438	3,315.20	1.4000	4,547.20
	2.0×1,219×2,438	11,894.00	1.4000	16,282.00
	1,219MM OR MORE THICKNESS 1MM TO 3MM 3.0×1,219×2,438	4,663.70	1.4000	6,364.40
	TOTAL:	25,600.90		35,000.00

SAY U.S.DOLLARS THIRTY FIVE THOUSAND ONLY
WE HEREBY CERTIFY THAT ABOVE MERCHANDISE TO BE OF CHINA ORIGIN AND ARE BEING IMPORTED AGAINST IRC NO. BA-0171646,TI NO. 157-107-0121,VAT REGISTRATION NO.9141093671 AND L.C.A. NO. 101804 UNDER H.S. CODE NO. 721933.00, 721934.00

Jiangsu I-Touch Business Service Ltd.

彭 婷

2. 其他信息

（1）上海淼睿进出口有限公司报检注册登记代码：43000123456

（2）商品编码：6200.2100

据此，请完成报检单的填制：

中华人民共和国出入境检验检疫

出境货物报检单

报检单位（加盖公章）： *编 号

单位地址

报检单位登记号： 联系人： 电话： 报检日期： 年 月 日

发货人	（中文）					
	（外文）					
收货人	（中文）					
	（外文）					
货物名称 （中/外文）	H.S.编码	产地	数/重量	货物总值	包装种类及数量	

运输工具名称号码		贸易方式		货物存放地点	
合同号		信用证号		用途	

发货日期		输往国家（地区）		许可证/审批号	
启运地		到达口岸		预计工作日期	年 月 日

合同、信用证订立的检验检疫条款或特殊要求	标 记 及 号 码	随附单据（划“√”或补填）	
		()合同 ()信用证 ()发票 ()换证凭单 ()装箱单 ()厂检单	()包装性能结果单 ()许可/审批文件 ()出口货物报关单 () ()

需要证单名称（划“√”或补填）		*检验检疫费	
()品质证书 __正__副 ()重量证书 __正__副 ()数量证书 __正__副 ()兽医卫生证书 __正__副 ()健康证书 __正__副 ()卫生证书 __正__副 ()动物卫生证书 __正__副	()植物检疫证书 __正__副 ()熏蒸/消毒证书 __正__副 ()出境货物换证凭单 __正__副 ()出竞货物通关单	总金额（人民币元）	
		计费人	
		收费人	

报检人郑重声明：	领 取 证 单	
1. 本人被授权报检。 2. 上列填写内容正确属实，货物无伪造或冒用他人的厂名、标志、认证标志，并承担货物质量责任。 签名：________	日期	
	签名	

注：有“*”号栏由出入境检验检疫机关填写 ◆国家出入境检验检疫局制

能力实训项目 2： 缮制报检单并办理报建手续

根据深圳比高进出口有限公司第 NK2-136 号信用证的要求，2013 年 8 月 25 日，报检员梁敏根据商业发票、装箱单和相关信息缮制报检单并办理报检手续。

1. 商业发票

Prima Construction Materials Co., Ltd.
Add: 1401Room, 38building, Chuangye Gardern, Baoan District, Shenzhen China
Tel: 0086-755-32076630　　Fax: 0086-755-32076630

COMMERCIAL INVOICE

To: CONSTRUCTION MOUDULAR SPECIALIST
POSTAL: 13 HARVEY RD.,SHENTON PK, WA 6008 AUSTRALIA

Contract No.: CBF130724		**No.:PR-20130820**		
L/C No.: DC 13720		**Date: AUG. 22, 2013**		
From: SHENZHEN		**To: FREMENTLE**		
Marks&Nos. No.	**Description of Goods**	**Quantity**	**Unit Price**	**Amount**
	BAMBOO FLOORING		CIF FREMENTLE	
CMS FREMENTLE CBF130724 NO.:1-109	CARBONISED BAMBOO FLOORING	100SQM	$ 20.00	$2,000.00
	STRAND WOVEN BAMBOO FLOOR- ING DECKING	100SQM	$39.50	$3,950.00
TOTAL			EXW PRICE	$5,950.00
			LCL CHARGE	$ 450.00
			INSURANCE COST	$ 60.00
			FREIGHT	$ 380.00
			CIFVALUE	$6,480.00

Prima Construction Materials Co., Ltd.
黄　柯

2. 其他信息

（1）深圳比高进出口有限公司报检注册登记代码：4300123456

（2）商品编码：4409.2110.90

据此，请你完成报检单的填制：

中华人民共和国出入境检验检疫

出境货物报检单

报检单位（加盖公章）： *编　号

单位地址

报检单位登记号： 联系人： 电话： 报检日期： 年　月　日

发货人	（中文）	
	（外文）	
收货人	（中文）	
	（外文）	

货物名称（中/外文）	H.S.编码	产地	数/重量	货物总值	包装种类及数量

运输工具名称号码		贸易方式		货物存放地点	
合同号		信用证号		用途	
发货日期		输往国家（地区）		许可证/审批号	
启运地		到达口岸		预计工作日期	年　月　日

合同、信用证订立的检验检疫条款或特殊要求	标 记 及 号 码	随附单据（划“√”或补填）	
		( )合同 ( )信用证 ( )发票 ( )换证凭单 ( )装箱单 ( )厂检单	( )包装性能结果单 ( )许可/审批文件 ( )出口货物报关单 ( ) ( )

<table>
<tr><td colspan="2">需要证单名称（划“√”或补填）</td><td colspan="2">*检验检疫费</td></tr>
<tr><td rowspan="3">()品质证书 __正__副
()重量证书 __正__副
()数量证书 __正__副
()兽医卫生证书 __正__副
()健康证书 __正__副
()卫生证书 __正__副
()动物卫生证书 __正__副</td><td rowspan="3">()植物检疫证书 __正__副
()熏蒸/消毒证书 __正__副
()出境货物换证凭单 __正__副
()出竞货物通关单</td><td>总金额
（人民币元）</td><td></td></tr>
<tr><td>计费人</td><td></td></tr>
<tr><td>收费人</td><td></td></tr>
</table>

<table>
<tr><td rowspan="3">报检人郑重声明：
1. 本人被授权报检。
2. 上列填写内容正确属实，货物无伪造或冒用他人的厂名、标志、认证标志，并承担货物质量责任。
签名：____________</td><td colspan="2">领 取 证 单</td></tr>
<tr><td>日期</td><td></td></tr>
<tr><td>签名</td><td></td></tr>
</table>

注：有“*”号栏由出入境检验检疫机关填写　　◆国家出入境检验检疫局制

项目七　报关单据制作业务

项目预期目标

熟悉报关单各栏目规范填制要求，能熟练运用海关使用手册寻找海关代码、出口货物监管条件、出口货物应征税率；能准确填制出口货物报关单及其他通关所需的随附单据。

在项目实施过程中，通过对报关单填制、申报、配合查验、计算和缴纳税费、装运货等任务的分解，在分工与合作中逐渐培养学生通关基本能力，培养学生团队合作能力以及与海关等政府部门有效沟通的能力。

表 7-1　　预期项目目标

目标类型	报关单的填制
知识目标	熟悉中国人民共和国海关法及其他法律法规
	掌握出口货物报关程序
	掌握不同性质货物的通过程序
能力目标	能按照我国《海关法》规范填制报关单
	能办理货物的通关手续
职业素质目标	学生团队合作能力
	与政府部门沟通衔接能力

项目实施条件

1. 组织学生参观长沙海关以及长沙霞凝新港口岸、长沙保税物流中心
2. 学生能够在实训室对该项目进行分组讨论并实施
3. 学生能够登陆出口货物申报系统界面
4. 指导教师掌握扎实的国家对外贸易管制法、海关法及其他相关法律法规，具备扎实的外贸业务基础

开篇业务引入

根据第 L-12017 号信用证的要求，长沙鹏兴出口有限公司业务员李望在办理好订舱手续后，根据以下相关信息马上办理、制作和备齐出口货物报关单、报关委托书等单证，同时备齐报检委托书、出境货物换证凭单等单证，寄给深圳货运代理，委托其向大鹏海关申请办理出口报关手续。该项目任务具体由报关员李艳负责。

子项目一　报关单据制作

出口货物的收发人或其代理人向海关办理出口手续时，在货物出口的时候填写《中华人民共和国进口货物报关单》或《中华人民共和国出口货物报关单》，同时提供准许货物出口的有关证件和有关的、商业货运单据，以便海关审查货物的出口是否合法，确定关税的征收或减免事宜，编制海关统计。能否正确填制报关单将直接影响报关率、企业的经济利益和海关监管的各个工作环节。因此，正确填制报关单是海关对报关企业和报关员的基本要求，也是报关员必须履行的义务。

一、出口货物报关单的含义

出口货物报关单是指出口货物的收发货人或其代理人，按照海关规定的格式对出口货物的实际情况作出书面申明，以此要求海关对其货物按照适用的海关制度办理通关手续的法律文书。

中华人民共和国海关出口货物报关单

预录入编号：　　　　　　　　　　　　海关编号：

出口口岸	备案号	出口日期	申报日期	
经营单位	运输方式	运输工具名称	提运单号	
发货单位	贸易方式	征免性质	结汇方式	
许可证号	运抵国（地区）	指运港	境内货源地	
批准文号	成交方式	运费	保费	杂费
合同协议号	件数	包装种类	毛重（公斤）	净重（公斤）
集装箱号	随附单据	生产厂家		
标记唛码及备注				

<table>
<tr><td>项号</td><td>商品编号</td><td>商品名称、规格型号</td><td>数量及单位</td><td>最终目的国（地区）单价</td><td>总价</td><td>币制</td><td>征免</td></tr>
<tr><td colspan="8"></td></tr>
<tr><td colspan="8">税费征收情况</td></tr>
<tr><td colspan="2">录入员　　录入单位</td><td colspan="3" rowspan="2">兹声明以上申报无讹并承担法律责任

申报单位（签章）

填制日期</td><td colspan="3">海关审单批注及放行日期(签章)

审单　　审价</td></tr>
<tr><td colspan="2">报关员

单位地址

邮编　　电话</td><td colspan="3">征税　　统计

查验　　放行</td></tr>
</table>

二、出口货物报关单的填制

1栏 预录入编号

预录入编号是指预录入单位录入报关单的编号，由接受申报的海关决定编号规则，计算机自动打印。

2栏 海关编号

海关编号是指海关接受申报时给予报关单的顺序号。海关编号由各直属海关在接受申报时确定，并标识在报关单的每一联上。一般来说海关编号就是预录入编号，由计算机自动打印，无须填写。

3 栏 进口口岸/出口口岸

进口口岸/出口口岸指货物实际进出我国关境口岸海关的名称。具体填报要求如下：

本栏目应根据货物实际出口的口岸海关选择填报《关区代码表》中相应的口岸海关名称及代码。

实例：大鹏海关 5316

4 栏 备案号

备案号指出口企业在海关办理加工贸易合同备案或征、减、免税审批备案等手续时，海关给予“中华人民共和国海关加工贸易手册”、“中华人民共和国海关加工贸易设备登记手册”、电子账册及其分册，“中华人民共和国海关出口货物征免税证明”或其他有关备案审批文件的编号。

该栏目填报要求如下：

（1）一份报关单只允许填报一个备案号。

（2）无备案审批文件的报关单，本栏免填。

（3）加工贸易合同项下使用《加工贸易手册》的货物和凡涉及减免税备案审批的货物，应填报《加工贸易手册》编号和《征免税证明》编号。

（4）实行原产地证书联网管理的香港、澳门 CEPA 项下的进口货物，填报“Y”+“11 位的原产地证书编号”；未实行原产地证书联网管理的曼协规则和东盟规则项下的进口货物均不填报原产地证书编号。

实例：免填

5 栏 出口日期

出口日期是指载运所申报货物的运输工具办结出境手续的日期。本栏目免于填报，仅供海关打印出口货物报关单退税证明联用。

具体填报要求如下：

（1）本栏目为 8 位数，顺序为年（4 位）、月（2 位）、日（2 位），如：“2006.08.10”

（2）无实际出境的报关单填报向海关办理申报手续的日期，以海关接受申报的日期为准。

实例：免填

6 栏 申报日期

指海关接受出口货物收、发货人或受其委托的报关企业申请办理货物出口手续的日期。填报要求如下：

（1）本栏目为 8 位数字，顺序为年（4 位）、月（2 位）、日（2 位）。

（2）以电子数据报关单方式申报的，申报日期为海关计算机系统接受申报数据时记录的日期。以纸质报关单方式申报的，申报日期为海关接受纸质报关单并进行登记处理的日期。

（3）除特殊情况外，出口货物申报日期不得晚于出口日期。

实例：20120815

7 栏 经营单位

经营单位是指对外签订并执行出口贸易合同的中国境内企业、单位或个人。填报要求如下：

本栏目应填报经营单位中文名称及经营单位编码。经营单位编码是经营单位在海关办理注册登记手续时，海关给予的注册登记 10 位数的编码。

实例：醴陵鹏兴瓷厂　4315973005

8 栏 运输方式

实际运输方式专指用于载运货物实际运出关境的运输方式，主要包括江海运输、铁路运输、航空运输、汽车运输、邮递运输和其他运输（驮畜、电网、管道等）。

本栏目应根据实际运输方式按海关规定的《运输方式代码表》选择填报相应的运输方式。

实例：水路运输或者代码 2

9 栏 运输工具名称

运输工具名称指载运货物出境的运输工具的名称或运输工具编号。

一份报关单只允许填报一个运输工具的名称，且与运输部门向海关申报的载货清单所列相应内容一致。

本栏具体填报要求如下：

（1）水路运输填报船舶英文名称（来往港澳小型船舶为监管簿编号）或者船舶编号+“/”+航次号。例如：提单显示“Shipped by S/S：DONGFENG V.101”，即“DONGFENG”为船名，“101”为航次，本栏目填报为“DONGFENG/101”。

（2）汽车运输填报该跨境运输车辆的国内行驶车牌号+“/”+出境日期（8 位数字）。

（3）铁路运输填报车厢编号或交接单号+“/”+出境日期（8 位数字）。

（4）航空运输填报航班号。如“KZ0225”，前两位为航空公司代号。

（5）邮政运输填报邮政包裹单号+“/”+出境日期（8 位数字）。

（6）其他运输填报具体运输方式名称，如：管道、驮畜等。

实例：COSCO　SEATTLE/0078E

10 栏 提运单号

提运单号是指出口货物提单或运单的编号。本栏目填报的内容应与运输部门向海关申报的载货清单的相应内容一致。一份报关单只允许填报一个提运单号，一票货物对应多个提运单时，应分单填报。无实际出境的，免于填报。

填报要求如下：

（1）水路运输：填报出口提运单号，如果有分提运单的，填报出口提运单号+“*”+分提运单号。例如：1320135*P130

（2）汽车运输：免于填报

（3）铁路运输：填报铁路运单号。

（4）航空运输：填报总运单号+“-”（下划线）+分运单号，无分运单的填报总运单号。

（5）邮政运输：填报邮运包裹单号。

（6）无实际出境的，本栏免于填报。

实例：CSZC02080497

11 栏 发货单位

发货单位指出口货物在境内的生产或销售单位，如自行出口货物的单位和委托有出口经营权的企业出口货物的单位等。具体填报要求如下：

（1）备有海关注册编号或加工生产企业编号的收、发货单位，本栏目填报其经营单位的编码或加工生产企业编号；否则填报其中文名称。

（2）加工贸易报关单的收、发货单位应与《加工贸易手册》的货主单位一致。

（3）减免税货物报关单的收、发货单位应与《征免税证明》的申请单位一致。

实例：醴陵鹏兴瓷厂 4315973005

12 栏 贸易方式（监管方式）

贸易方式是专指以国际贸易中出口货物的交易方式为基础，结合海关对出口货物监督管理需要综合设定的对出口管理管理方式。本栏目填报要求为：

（1）一份报关单只允许填报一种贸易方式。

（2）根据实际情况，按照海关规定的《监管方式代码表》选择填报相应的贸易方式简称或代码。

实例：一般贸易或者代码 0110

13 栏 征免性质

征免性质是指海关根据《海关法》、《关税条例》及国家有关政策对出口货物实施的征、减、免税管理的性质类别。填报要求如下：

（1）一份报关单只允许填报一种征免性质。

（2）按照海关核发的征免税证明中批注的征免性质填报，或根据出口货物的实际情况，参照《征免性质代码表》选择填报相应的征免性质简称或代码。

（3）加工贸易货物应按海关核发的登记手册中批注的征免性质填报相应的征免性质简称或代码。

实例：一般征税或者代码 101

14 栏 征税比例/结汇方式

（1）征税比例

征税比例原用于“进料非对口”贸易方式下进口料件的进口报关单，现该栏不需填报。

（2）出口填报结汇方式

结汇方式是指出口货物的发货人或其代理人收结外汇的方式。

按海关规定的《结汇方式代码表》选择填报相应结汇方式的名称或缩写或代码。

实例：信用证或者代码 6

15 栏 许可证号

许可证号应填写由商务主管部门及其授权发证机关签发的出口货物许可证的编号。填报要求：

（1）许可证管理商品必须填报，非许可证管理商品本栏留空。

（2）一张报关单只允许填报一个许可证号。

实例：免填

16 栏 起运国（地区）/运抵国（地区）

起运国指进口货物起始发出的国家(地区);运抵国是指出口货物直接运抵的国家(地区)。填报要求:

（1）本栏目应按海关规定的《国别（地区）代码表》选择填报相应的起运国（地区）货运抵国（地区）中文名称或代码。

（2）无实际出境的，本栏目填报“中国”(代码 142)。

（3）对发生运输中转的货物，如中转地未发生任何商业性交易，则起、抵地不变，如中转地发生商业性交易，则中转地作为起运/运抵国（地区）填报。

实例：加拿大或者国别代码 501

17 栏 指运港

指运港是指出口货物运往境外的最终目的港。本栏目应根据实际情况按海关规定的《港口航线代码表》选择填报相应的港口中文名称或代码，具体填报要求如下：

（1）对于直接运抵货物，以货物实际装货的港口为装货港，货物直接运抵的港口为运抵港。

（2）对于发生运输中转的货物，中转港为装货港，指运港不受中转影响。

（3）对于无实际出境的货物，本栏目填报“中国境内”(代码“0142”)

实例：鲁珀特港

18 栏 境内货源地

境内货源地指出口货物在境内的生产地或原始发货地（包括供货地点）。填报要求如下:

按《国内地区代码表》选择填报国内地区名称或代码，代码含义与经营单位代码前5位的定义相同。

实例：醴陵其他或者 43159

19 栏 批准文号

本栏免填

20 栏 成交方式

成交方式是指在出口贸易中出口商品的价格构成和买卖双方各自应承担的责任、费用和风险，以及货物所有权转移的界限。本栏目填报要求如下：

（1）本栏目应根据实际成交价格条款按海关规定的《成交方式代码表》填报相应的成交方式代码。

（2）无实际出境的，出口填报 FOB 或其代码。

实例：FOB

21 栏 运费

运费是指出口货物从始发地至目的地的国际运输所需要的各种费用。该栏请根据贸易术语进行填制。如术语为 F 组，该栏免填。

可按运费单价、总价或运费率三种方式之一填报，同时注明运费标记，并按海关规定的《货币代码表》选择填报相应的币种代码。

运费标记“1”表示运费率，“2”表示每吨货物的运费单价，“3”表示运费总价。

本栏目不同的运费标记填报如下：

a. 运费率：直接填报运费率的数值，如 5%的运费率填报为“5”。

b. 运费单价：填报运费币值代码+“/”+运费单价的数值+“/”+运费单价标记，如：30 美元的运费单价填报为“502/30/2”。

c. 运费总价：填报运费币值代码+“/”+运费总价的数值+“/”+运费总价标记，如：3 000 美元的运费总价填报为“502/3000/3”。

（1）运保费合并计算的，运保费填报在运费栏目中。

实例：免填

22 栏 保费

保费是指出口货物在国际运输过程中，由被保险人付给保险人的保险费用。该栏请根据贸易术语进行填制。如术语为 F 组或 CFR，该栏免填。

（1）可按保险费总价或保险费率两种方式之一填报，同时注明保险费标记，并按海关规定的《货币代码表》选择填报相应的币种代码。

保险费标记“1”表示保险费率，“3”表示保险费总价。

填纸质报关单时，本栏目不同的保费标记填报如下：

a. 保费率：直接填报保费率的数值，如：5‰的保险费率填报为“0.5”。

b. 保费总价：填报保费币值代码+“/”+保费总价的数值+“/”+保费总价标记，如：500 美元保险费总价填报为“502/500/3”。

（2）运保费合并计算的，运保费填报在运费栏目中。

实例：免填

23 栏 杂费

杂费是指成交价格以外的、按照《中华人民共和国出口关税条例》相关规定应计入完税价格或应从完税价格中扣除的费用。

本栏目不同的杂费标记填报如下：

a. 杂费率：直接填报杂费率的数值，如：应计入完税价格的 1.5%的杂费率填报为“1.5”；应从完税价格中扣除的 1%的回扣率填报为“-1”。

b. 杂费总价：填报杂费币值代码+“/”+杂费总价的数值+“/”+杂费总价标记，如：应计入完税价格的 500 英镑杂费总价填报为“303/500/3”。

（1）无杂费时，免填。

实例：免填

24 栏 合同协议号

本栏目应填报出口货物合同（协议）的全部字头和号码。

实例：PX12SC1039

25 栏 件数

件数是指有外包装的单件出口货物的实际件数。填报要求：

（1）本栏目应填报有外包装的出口货物的实际件数。

（2）本栏目不得填报为零，裸装与散装货物应填报为“1”。

（3）有关单据仅列明托盘件数，或者既列明托盘件数，又列明单件包装件数的，填报托盘数。如：“3PALLET/S.T.C. 150CARTONS”本栏目填报“3”。

（4）有关单据既列明集装箱个数，又列明托盘件数、单件包装件数的，按以上要求填报；如果只列明集装箱个数，未列明托盘件数、单件包装件数的，填报集装箱数。

实例：1596

26 栏 包装种类

指出口货物在运输过程中外表所呈现的状态。填报要求：

（1）本栏目应填报出口货物的实际外包装的名称。

（2）如果有多种包装材料，统报为“其他”。件数是各种包装的合计数。

实例：纸箱

27 栏 毛重

指货物及其包装材料的重量之和。填报要求如下：

本栏目填报出口货物实际毛重，计量单位为公斤，不足一公斤的填报为“1”。

实例：17655

28 栏 净重

指货物的毛重减去外包装材料后的重量，即商品本身的实际重量。填报要求：

本栏目填报出口货物的实际净重，计量单位为公斤，不足一公斤的填报为“1”。

实例：14138

29 栏 集装箱号

集装箱号是在每个集装箱箱体两侧标示的全球唯一的编号。填报要求：

（1）在填制纸质报关单时，按照“集装箱号”+“/”+“规格”+“/”+“自重”方式填报。如“COSU8491952/20/2275”。多个集装箱的，第一个集装箱号填报在本栏目，其余填报在“标记唛码及备注”栏内。

（2）非集装箱货物，填报为“0”。

实例：CBHU8150082/40/4150

30 栏 随附单据

指随出口货物报关单一并向海关递交的单证或文件。包括发票、装箱单、提单、运单等基本单证，监管证件、征免税证明、外汇核销单等特殊单证和合同、信用证等预备单证。填报要求：

（1）基本单证和运输单证号码不在本栏目填报，“随附单据”栏仅填报除出口许可证之外的监管证件的代码及编号。

（2）本栏目应按海关规定的《监管证件名称代码表》选择填报相应证件的代码；编号应填报监管证件编号，格式为：监管证件代码+“：”监管证件编号。

（3）所申报货物涉及多个监管证件的，第一个监管证件代码和编号在本栏目填报，其余填报在“标记唛码及备注”栏。

实例：470600212065706000

31 栏 用途/生产厂家

用途是指进口货物在境内应用的范围；生产厂家是指出口货物的境内生产企业的名称。填报要求如下：

（1）进口货物填报用途，应根据进口货物的实际用途按海关规定的《用途代码表》选择填报相应的用途代码，如“企业自用”填报“04”。

（2）生产厂家指出口货物的境内生产企业。本栏目供必要时填报。

实例：免填

32栏 标记唛码及备注

标记唛码是运输标记的俗称，出口货物报关单上的标记唛码专指货物的运输标记。如该业务无唛头则免填。其填报要求如下：

（1）标记唛码中除图形以外的文字、数字。

（2）填报关联备案号。与本报关单有关联关系的，同时在业务管理规范方面又要求填报的备案号，如加工贸易结转货物及凭《征免税证明》转内销货物，其对应的备案号应填报在本栏，格式为：“转至（自）************手册”。

（4）填报关联报关单号。与本报关单有关联关系的，同时在业务管理规范方面又要求填报的报关单号，应填报在本栏。

（5）所申报货物涉及多个监管证件的，除第一个监管证件外的其余监管证件和代码。

实例：免填

33栏 项号

项号是指申报货物在报关单中的商品排列序号。其填报要求如下：

（1）一张纸质报关单最多可打印5项商品，纸质报关单表体共有5栏，可另外附带3张纸质报关单，合计一个报关单编号下的一份报关单最多可打印20项商品。

（2）本栏目分两行填报及打印。第一行打印报关单中的商品排列序号。第二行专用于加工贸易和特定减免税货物等已备案的货物，填报和打印该项货物在《加工贸易手册》中的项号和对应的《征免税证明》上的商品项号。

如一张加工贸易料件进口报关单上某项商品的项号是上“03”、下“027”，说明其位列报关单申报商品第3项，且对应加工贸易登记手册备案料件第27项。

实例：01、02、03、04、05

34 商品编号

指按海关规定的商品名称与编码制度或者按《中华人民共和国海关出口税则》确定的出口货物的商品编号进行填报。

实例：69111010.00

35栏 商品名称、规格型号

商品名称是指出口货物规范的中文名称。商品的规格型号是指反映商品性能、品质和规格的一系列指标，如品牌、等级、成分、含量、纯度、大小、长短、粗细等。其填报要求如下：

（1）本栏目分两行填报。第一行填报出口货物规范的中文商品名称，必要时可加注原文；第二行填报规格型号。

（2）商品名称及规格型号应据实填报，并与所提供的商业发票相符。

（3）商品名称应当规范，规格型号应当足够详细，以能满足海关归类、审价及许可证件管理要求为准。根据商品属性，本栏目填报内容包括：品名、牌名、规格、型号、成份、含量、等级、用途、功能等。

（4）一份报关单最多允许填报 20 项商品。

实例：

1. 日用瓷：钵加盖加勺

瓷制/餐具/VERDICI 牌/21 888 件 4.5'

2. 日用瓷：杯

瓷制/餐具/VERDICI 牌/18 240 件 11/12/180Z

3. 日用瓷：杯碟

瓷制/餐具/VERDICI 牌/12 160 件 3.50Z

4. 日用瓷：杯加勺

瓷制/餐具/VALENTINO 牌/1 216 件 120Z

5. 日用瓷：杯碟加勺

瓷制/餐具 VALENTINO 牌/18 240 件 3.50Z

36 栏 数量及单位

数量及单位是指出口商品的实际数量及计量单位。本栏目分三行填报，具体填报要求如下：

（1）出口货物必须按海关法定计量单位填报，法定第一计量单位及数量填报在本栏目第一行。

（2）凡海关列明第二计量单位的，必须报明该商品第二计量单位及数量，填报在本栏目第二行。无第二计量单位的，本栏目第二行为空。

（3）以成交计量单位申报的，须填报与海关法定计量单位转化后的数量，同时须将成交计量单位及数量应当填报在第三行。如成交计量单位与海关法定计量单位一致时，本栏目留空。

实例：

第一行：4 377.60 千克　　第三行：4 377.60 千克

第一行：5 548 千克　　第三行：5 548 千克

第一行：1 216 千克　　第三行：1 216 千克

第一行：1 824 千克　　第三行：1 824 千克

第一行：1 216 千克　　第三行：1 216 千克

37 栏 最终目的国（地区）

最终目的国（地区）指已知的出口货物的最终实际消费、使用或进一步加工制造国家（地区）。本栏目应按海关规定的《国别（地区）代码表》选择填报相应的国家（地区）名称或代码。

实例：加拿大或者代码 501

38 栏 单价

单价是指商品的一个计量单位以某一种货币表示的价格。一个完整的单价包括计价货币、单位价格金额、计量单位、价格术语四个部分，如果含佣金和折扣，也应注明。填报要求如下：

（1）本栏目应填报同一项号下出口货物实际成交的商品单位价格。单价如果不是整数，小数点后保留 4 位。如原始单据显示单价条款为：USD31.68 PER DOZEN CIF LONDON，则本栏填报“31.68”。

（2）无实际成交价格的，本栏目填报货值。

实例：

01：1.687 5　02：1.791 8　03：2.437 5　04:：1.916 7　05：2.650 0

39 栏 总价

总价是指出口货物实际成交的商品总值。填报要求如下：

（1）本栏目应填报同一项号下出口货物实际成交的商品总价。总价如果不是整数，小数点后保留 4 位。如原始单据显示：“TOTAL AMOUNT：USD56,234.16”，则本栏填报“56,234.16”。

（2）无实际成交价格的，本栏目填报货值。

实例：

01：7 387.20　02：9 940.80　03：2 964.00　04：3 496.00　05：3 222.40

40 栏 币制

指出口货物实际成交价格的币种。填报要求如下：

（1）本栏目应根据实际成交情况按海关规定的《货币代码表》选择填报相应的货币名称或代码或符号。

（2）《货币代码表》中无实际成交币种的，需转换后填报。

实例：美元（502）

41 栏 征免

征免指海关对出口货物进行征税、减税、免税或特案处理的实际操作方式。本栏目应按照海关核发的《征免税证明》或有关政策规定，对报关单所列每项商品选择填报海关规定的《征减免税方式代码表》中相应的征减免税方式的名称。

实例：照章征税或者代码 1

42 栏 税费征收情况

本栏目供海关批注出口货物税费征收及减免情况。

43 栏 录入员

本栏目用于记录预录入操作人员的姓名并打印。

44 栏 录入单位

本栏目用于记录并打印电子数据报关单的录入单位名称。

45 栏 填制日期

指报关单的填制日期，填报要求如下：

电子数据报关单的填制日期由计算机自动打印。栏目为 8 位数字，顺序为年（4 位）、月（2 位）、日（2 位）。

46栏 申报单位

申报单位是指经海关注册登记，有权向海关办理报关手续，并对其申报内容的真实性、有效性、合法性直接向海关负责的中国境内企业或单位，其填报要求如下：

（1）自理报关的，应填报出口货物的经营单位中文名称及编码。

（2）委托代理报关的，应填报经海关批准的报关企业中文名称及编码。

（3）本栏目还应加盖申报单位公章，报关员签名，以及填制日期。

47栏 海关审单批注栏

本栏目指供海关内部作业时签注的总栏目，由海关关员手工填写在预录入报关单上。其中“放行”栏填写海关对接受申报的出口货物做出放行决定的日期。

子项目二 报关单典型业务演示

上接项目六，鹏兴公司在完成货物报检后应凭合同、商业发票及通关单等单据办理货物报关手续。在外贸业务中，考虑到实际装运时货物数量可能变动，业务员一般只在报关委托书上盖章，而不填写详细内容，详细内容由报关员报关时填写。报关委托书正反两面都印有内容，现需要单证员李望完成的工作任务包括：

任务1：认真审核商业发票、装箱单和订舱单等单证

任务2：填制报关委托书及报关单

代理报关委托书

编号：□□□□□□□□□□□□□：

我单位现(A逐票√、B长期)委托贵公司代理等通关事宜。（A、填单申报√ B、辅助查验 C、垫缴税款 D、办理海关证明联√ E、审批手册 F、核销手册 G、申办减免税手续 H、其他 ）详见《委托报关协议》。 我单位保证遵守《海关法》和国家有关法规，保证所提供的情况真实、完整、单货相符。否则，愿承担相关法律责任。

本委托书有效期自签字之日起至 2012 年 9月 12 日止。

委托方（盖章）：醴陵鹏兴瓷厂

法定代表人或其授权签署《代理报关委托书》的人（签字）

年 月 日

委托报关协议

<table>
<tr><td colspan="5">为明确委托报关具体事项和各自责任，双方经平等协商签定协议如下：</td></tr>
<tr><td>委托方</td><td>醴陵鹏兴瓷厂</td><td>被委托方</td><td colspan="2">深圳市康海国际货运代理有限公司</td></tr>
<tr><td>主要货物名称</td><td>日用陶瓷</td><td>*报关单编码</td><td colspan="2">No.</td></tr>
<tr><td>HS 编码</td><td>69111010.00</td><td>收到单证日期</td><td colspan="2">2012 年 8 月 12 日</td></tr>
<tr><td>货物总价</td><td>U.S.D 6,480.00</td><td rowspan="4">收到单证情况</td><td>合同□ √</td><td>发票□ √</td></tr>
<tr><td>出口日期</td><td>2012 年 8 月 15 日</td><td>装箱清单□ √</td><td>提（运）单□ √</td></tr>
<tr><td>提单号</td><td>CSZC02080497</td><td>加工贸易手册□</td><td>许可证件□</td></tr>
<tr><td>贸易方式</td><td>一般贸易</td><td></td><td>其他</td></tr>
<tr><td>原产地/货源地</td><td>中国</td><td>报关收费</td><td colspan="2">人民币： 240.00 元</td></tr>
<tr><td>其他要求：</td><td></td><td>承诺说明：</td><td colspan="2"></td></tr>
<tr><td colspan="2">背面所列通用条款是本协议不可分割的一部分，对本协议的签署构成了对背面通用条款的同意。</td><td colspan="3">背面所列通用条款是本协议不可分割的一部分，对本协议的签署构成了对背面通用条款的同意。</td></tr>
<tr><td colspan="2">委托方业务签章：</td><td colspan="3">被委托方业务签章：</td></tr>
<tr><td colspan="2">经办人签章：李望
联系电话：
2012 年 8 月 12 日</td><td colspan="3">经办报关员签章：
联系电话：
2012 年 8 月 12 日</td></tr>
</table>

（白联：海关留存、黄联：被委托方留存、红联：委托方留存）　　中国报关协会监制

中华人民共和国海关出口货物报关单

预录入编号： 海关编号：

出口口岸 大鹏海关 5316	备案号	出口日期	申报日期 20120815

经营单位 醴陵鹏兴陶瓷厂 4315973005	运输方式 2 水路运输	运输工具名称 COSCO SEATTLE/ 0078E	提运单号 CSZC02080497

发货单位 醴陵鹏兴瓷厂 4315973005	贸易方式（0110） 一般贸易	征免性质（） 一般征税 101	结汇方式 信用证

许可证号	运抵国（地区） 加拿大	指运港 鲁珀特港	境内货源地 醴陵其他

批准文号	成交方式 FOB	运费	保费	杂费

合同协议号 PX12SC1039	件数 1 596	包装种类 纸箱	毛重（公斤） 17 655	净重（公斤） 14 138

集装箱号 CBHU8150082/ 40/4150	随附单据 B：470600212065706	生产厂家

标记唛码及备注

项号	商品编号	商品名称、规格型号	数量及单位	最终目的国（地区）单价	总价	币制	征免
01	69111010.00	日用瓷：钵加盖加勺 瓷制/餐具/VERDICI 牌/21 888 件 4.5’	4 377.60 千克 4 377.60 千克	加拿大 1.687 5	7 378.20	美元	照章征税
02	69111010.00	日用瓷：杯 瓷制/餐具/VERDICI 牌/18 240 件 11/12/180Z	5 548 千克 5 548 千克	加拿大 1.791 8 （501）	9 940.80	美元	照章征税

03	69111010.00	日用瓷：杯碟 瓷制/餐具/VERDICI 牌/12 160 件 3.50Z	1 216 千克 1 216 千克	加拿大	2.437 5	2 964.00	美元	照章征税
04	69111010.00	日用瓷：杯加勺 瓷制/餐具 /VALENTINO 牌 /1 216 件 3.50Z	1 824 千克 1 824 千克	加拿大	1.916 7	3 496.00	美元	照章征税
05	69111010.00	日用瓷：杯碟加勺 瓷制/餐具 /VALENTINO 牌 /18 240 件 3.50Z	1 216 千克 1 216 千克	加拿大	2.650 0	3 222.40	美元	照章征税

税费征收情况		
录入员　　录入单位	兹声明以上申报无讹并承担法律责任	海关审单批注及放行日期（签章） 审单　　审价
报关员 单位地址	申报单位（签章）	征税　　统计
邮编　　电话	填制日期	查验　　放行

子项目三　报关单拓展业务操作

能力实训项目 1： 缮制报关单并办理报关手续

根据南昌智创公司 LC123 信用证的要求，出口门把手和水平仪到日本大阪，2008 年 6 月 13 日，单证员刘燕备齐商业发票和装箱单等资料，填写报关委托书以及出口货物报关单，向青岛海关办理出口报关手续。

1. 商业发票

NANCHANG ZHICHUANG CO., LTD.

No.2 Taiping St. Nanchang, China

Tel: 0086-532-8391926 Fax:0086-532-8391928

COMMERCIAL INVOICE

TO:	Taka Co., Ltd. 12-15,Aza shinbo, Ohzaz Yamaya, Osaka, Japan Tel: 0081-665-39-3123 Fax: 0081-665-29-3133	**INVOICE NO.:**	LJ08071
		INVOICE DATE:	Jun. 10, 2008
		S/C NO.:	2008072
		S/C DATE:	May 9, 2008

FROM: Nanchang, China **TO:** Osaka, Japan

Marks and Numbers	Number and kind of package Description of goods	Quantity	Unit Price	Amount
			FOB Qingdao	
	(1) Door Handle			
	Article No.DH5010	4,500 pairs	USD8.80/pair	USD39,600.00
N/M	Article No.DH5020	4,500 pairs	USD8.50/pair	USD38,250.00
	PACKED IN 450 CARTONS OF 20 EACH			
	(2) Spirit Level			
	Article No.19161	8,820 pcs	USD2.00/pc	USD17,640.00
	Article No.19163	14,700 pcs	USD2.20/pc	USD32,340.00
	PACKED IN 392 CARTONS OF 60 EACH			
		Total:		**USD127,830.00**

SAY TOTAL: U.S. DOLLARS ONE HUNDRED TWENTY SEVEN THOUSAND EIGHT HUNDRED THIRTY ONLY

NANCHANG ZHICHUANG CO., LTD.

***

2. 装箱单

NANCHANG ZHICHUANG CO., LTD.

No.2 Taiping St. Nanchang, China

Tel: 0086-532-8391926 Fax:0086-532-8391928

PACKING LIST

TO:	Taka Co., Ltd. 12-15,Aza shinbo, Ohzaz Yamaya, Osaka, Japan Tel: 0081-665-39-3123 Fax: 0081-665-29-3133	**INVOICE NO.:**	LJ08071
		INVOICE DATE:	Jun. 10, 2008
		S/C NO.:	2008072
		S/C DATE:	May 9, 2008

FROM: Nanchang, China **TO:** Osaka, Japan

Marks and Numbers	Number and kind of package Description of goods	Quantity	PACKAGE	G.W	N.W	Meas.
	(1) Door Handle					
	Article No.DH5010	4,500 pairs	225CTNS	4,162.5KGS	3,937.5KGS	12.325M³
N/M	Article No.DH5020	4,500 pairs	225CTNS	4,050KGS	3,825KGS	12.325M³
	PACKED IN 450 CARTONS OF 20 EACH					
	(2) Spirit Level					
	Article No.19161	8,820 pcs	147CTNS	2,352KGS	2,205KGS	8.467M³
	Article No.19163	14,700 pcs	245CTNS	4,165KGS	3,920KGS	18.816M³
	PACKED IN 392 CARTONS OF 60 EACH					
	Total:		842CTNS	14,729.5KGS	13,887.5KGS	51.933M³

SAY TOTAL: EIGHT HUNDRED AND FORTY TWO CARTONS ONLY

3. 其他信息

（1）出境货物通关单编号：123456789000

（2）南昌智创公司经营代码：5201056356

（3）商品编码：门把手（金属制）83024100；水平仪：90153000

（4）运输工具：YONG YUE，VOY.NO. 067E

（5）原产地证明编号：CCPIT2008061111

据此，请完成报关单的填制：

中华人民共和国海关出口货物报关单

预录入编号：　　　　　　　　　　　　　　　　海关编号：

出口口岸	备案号	出口日期	申报日期	
经营单位	运输方式	运输工具名称	提运单号	
发货单位	贸易方式	征免性质	结汇方式	
许可证号	运抵国（地区）	指运港	境内货源地	
批准文号	成交方式	运费	保费	杂费
合同协议号	件数	包装种类	毛重（公斤）	净重（公斤）
集装箱号	随附单据	生产厂家		
标记唛码及备注				

项号	商品编号	商品名称、规格型号	数量及单位	最终目的国（地区）单价	总价	币制	征免

<table>
<tr><td colspan="3">税费征收情况</td></tr>
<tr><td>录入员　　录入单位</td><td rowspan="2">兹声明以上申报无讹并承担法律责任

申报单位（签章）

填制日期</td><td>海关审单批注及放行日期(签章)

审单　　审价</td></tr>
<tr><td>报关员

单位地址

邮编　　电话</td><td>征税　　统计

查验　　放行</td></tr>
</table>

能力实训项目 2：缮制报关单并办理报关手续

根据深圳普瑞玛出口有限公司出口竹地板，装船期是 2013 年 8 月 20 日，2013 年 8 月 10 日单证员李红备齐商业发票和装箱单等资料，填写报关委托书以及出口货物报关单，向上海海关办理出口报关业务。

1. 商业发票

Prima Construction Materials Co., Ltd.

Add: 1401Room, 38building, Chuangye Gardern, Baoan District, Shenzhen China

Tel: 0086-755-32076630 Fax: 0086-755-32076630

COMMERCIAL INVOICE

To: CONSTRUCTION MOUDULAR SPECIALIST
POSTAL: 13 HARVEY RD.,SHENTON PK, WA 6008 AUSTRALIA

Contract No.: CBF130724	**No.:PR-20130820**
L/C No.: DC 13720	**Date: AUG. 22, 2013**
From: SHENZHEN	**To: FREMENTLE**

Marks&Nos. No.	**Description of Goods**	**Quantity**	**Unit Price**	**Amount**
	BAMBOO FLOORING		CIF FREMENTLE	
CMS FREMENTLE CBF130724 NO.:1-109	CARBONISED BAMBOO FLOORING	100SQM	$ 20.00	$2,000.00
	STRAND WOVEN BAMBOO FLOORING DECKING	100SQM	$39.50	$3,950.00
TOTAL			EXW PRICE	$5,950.00
			LCL CHARGE	$ 450.00
			INSURANCE COST	$ 60.00
			FREIGHT	$ 380.00
			CIF VALUE	$6,480.00

Prima Construction Materials Co., Ltd.

黄 柯

2. 装箱单

PENGXING IMP&EXP COMPANY

LILING PENGXING CERAMIC FACTORY

WUSHI JIASHU LILING HUNAN CHINA

TEL: 86-731-23384199 FAX: 86-731-23384298

PACKING LIST

To: CONSTRUCTION MOUDULAR SPECIALIST
POSTAL: 13 HARVEY RD.,SHENTON PK, WA
6008 AUSTRALIA

Date AUG. 22, 2013

Invoice No.: PR-20130820

From: SHANGHAI, CHINA **To:** FREMENTLE, CANADA

Item No.	Description of goods	Quantity (CTN)	G.W (KGS)	N.W (KGS)	Meas. (CBM)
	BAMBOO FLOORING				
CMS FREMENTLE CBF13072 NO.:1-109	CARBONISED BAMBOO FLOORING	55CTNS	1,600KGS	1,519KGS	2CBM
	STRAND WOVEN BAMBOO FLOORING DECKING	54CTNS	1,528KGS	1,500KGS	2CBM

ALL PACKED IN CARTONS

SAY ONE HUNDRED AND NINE(109CTNS)CARTONS ONLY

Total: 109 CTNS 3,128KGS 3,019KGS 4CBM

3. 其他信息

（1）深圳普瑞玛出口有限公司经营单位代码：

（2）出口海运提单编号：LLLFMT3821018

（3）出境货物通关单编号：

（4）熏蒸证号码：330802212023407

（5）运输工具名称：MOL INTEGRITY，VOY.NO.102W

中华人民共和国海关出口货物报关单

预录入编号：　　　　　　　　　　　　　　海关编号：

出口口岸	备案号	出口日期	申报日期	
经营单位	运输方式	运输工具名称	提运单号	
发货单位	贸易方式	征免性质	结汇方式	
许可证号	运抵国（地区）	指运港	境内货源地	
批准文号	成交方式	运费	保费	杂费
合同协议号	件数	包装种类	毛重（公斤）	净重（公斤）
集装箱号	随附单据	生产厂家		
标记唛码及备注				

项号	商品编号	商品名称、规格型号	数量及单位	最终目的国（地区）单价	总价	币制	征免

<table>
<tr><td colspan="3">税费征收情况

</td></tr>
<tr><td>录入员　　　录入单位</td><td rowspan="3">兹声明以上申报无讹并承担法律责任

申报单位（签章）

填制日期</td><td>海关审单批注及放行日期(签章)

审单　　　　审价</td></tr>
<tr><td rowspan="2">报关员

单位地址

邮编　　　　电话</td><td>征税　　　　统计</td></tr>
<tr><td>查验　　　　放行</td></tr>
</table>

能力实训项目 3：缮制报关单并办理报关手续

上接项目，根据江西出口有限公司第 DOCMTN55123 号信用证的要求，2005 年 10 月 20 日，报关员张小兰根据商业发票、装箱单以及相关信息缮制报关单，办理报关手续。

1. 商业发票

JIANGXI INTERNATIONAL IMP. & EXP. CORP.

8TH FLOOR FOREIGN TRADER BUILDING
200 ZHANQIAN ROAD, NANCHANG BUILDING

COMMERCIAL INVOICE

TO:	NICHIMEN CORPORATION	**INVOICE NO.:**	05AO-P001
	2-2 NAKANOSHINA 3-CHOME, KITA-KU	**INVOICE DATE:**	MAR. 10, 2005
	NAGOYA, 632-8620, JAPAN	**S/C NO.:**	J515
		S/C DATE:	
		L/C NO.:	DCMTN55123
		L/C DATE:	FEB. 12, 2005

From: SHANGHAI **to:** NAGOYA

Marks and Numbers	Number and Kind of Package Description of Goods	Quantity	Unit Price	Amount
			CIF NAGOYA	
J-515 NAGOYA PKG. NO. 1-166	100PCT COTTON GREIGE PRINT CLOTH ART. NO. 3042 FIRST QUALITY SIZE:30×30 68×68 50" EXPORT PACKING IN 166 SEAWORTHY BALES OF 1200 EACH THIS IS TO CERTIFY THAT THE GOODS IS CHINESE ORIGIN	199,200YDS	CIF NAGOYA USD 0.32/YD	USD63,744.00
	Total:	199,200YDS		USD63,744.00

SAY TOTAL: U.S. DOLLARS SIXTY THREE THOUSAND SEVEN HUNDRED AND FORTY FOUR ONLY

JIANGXI INTERNATIONAL IMP. & EXP. CORP.

XXX

2. 装箱单

JIANGXI INTERNATIONAL IMP. & EXP. CORP.

8TH FLOOR FOREIGN TRADER BUILDING
200 ZHANQIAN ROAD, NANCHANG BUILDING

PACKING LIST

TO:	NICHIMEN CORPORATION	**INVOICE NO.:**	05AO-P001
	2-2 NAKANOSHINA 3-CHOME, KITA-KU	**INVOICE DATE:**	MAR. 10, 2005
	NAGOYA, 632-8620, JAPAN	**S/C NO.:**	J515
		S/C DATE:	
		L/C NO.:	DCMTN55123
		L/C DATE:	FEB. 12, 2005

FROM: SHANGHAI **to:** NAGOYA

Marks and Numbers	Number and Kind of Package Description of Goods	Quantity	PACKAGE	G.W	N.W	Meas.
J-515 NAGOYA PKG. NO. 1-166	100PCT COTTON GREIGE PRINT CLOTH ART. NO. 3042 FIRST QUALITY SIZE:30×30 68×68 50" EXPORT PACKING IN 166 SEAWORTHY BALES OF 1200 EACH	199,200YDS	166 BALES	23,406 KGS	23,074 KGS	53.618 M^3
	Total:	199,200YDS	166 BALES	23,406 KGS	23,074 KGS	53.618 M^3

SAY TOTAL: ONE HUNDRED AND SIXTY SIX BALES ONLY

JIANGXI INTERNATIONAL IMP. & EXP. CORP.

XXX

3. 其他信息

（1）江西出口有限公司的经营单位代码：

（2）出口海运提单号码：MSCU42014737

（3）运输工具名称：MSC SARAH V.6A

（4）商品编码（HS 编码）：学生归类查找该出口商品的编码

（5）出境货物通关单编号：

据此，请你完成报关单的填制：

中华人民共和国海关出口货物报关单

预录入编号：　　　　　　　　　　　　　　　海关编号：

出口口岸	备案号		出口日期	申报日期
经营单位	运输方式	运输工具名称		提运单号
发货单位	贸易方式		征免性质	结汇方式
许可证号	运抵国（地区）		指运港	境内货源地

批准文号	成交方式	运费	保费	杂费
合同协议号	件数	包装种类	毛重（公斤）	净重（公斤）
集装箱号	随附单据			生产厂家

标记唛码及备注

项号	商品编号	商品名称、规格型号	数量及单位	最终目的国（地区）单价	总价	币制	征免

税费征收情况

录入员　　录入单位	兹声明以上申报无讹并承担法律责任	海关审单批注及放行日期(签章) 审单　　审价
报关员 单位地址 邮编　　电话	申报单位（签章） 填制日期	征税　　统计 查验　　放行

项目八　运输单据制作业务

项目预期目标

掌握海运提单的作用与分类，了解海运提单缮制中应注意事项；通过对信用证项下装运条款的认真解读，结合该项目提供的商业发票等相关单据，掌握海运提单的缮制。

表 8-1　　**项目预期目标**

<table>
<tr><td>目标类型</td><td>运输单据的缮制</td></tr>
<tr><td rowspan="2">知识目标</td><td>熟悉海运提单的作用、分类</td></tr>
<tr><td>了解运输单据的必要填写栏目</td></tr>
<tr><td>能力目标</td><td>能根据信用证及托运资料缮制运输单据</td></tr>
<tr><td rowspan="2">职业素质目标</td><td>海运业务操作能力</td></tr>
<tr><td>与工厂、货代的沟通协调能力</td></tr>
</table>

项目实施条件

1. 组织学生参观货代公司或港口堆场
2. 学生能够在实训室对该项目进行分组讨论并实施
3. 指导教师熟悉贸易政策，具备扎实的外贸业务基础

开篇业务引入

根据“DC HMN214479”号信用证的要求，中国湖南某外贸公司“LILING PENGXING CERAMIC FACTORY WUSHI JIASHU LILING HUNAN, CHINA”出口货物一批给加拿大进口商“ELBY GIFTS INC.879 INDUSTRIEL BOIS DES FILION,QUEBEC, J6Z 4T3, CANADA”。由 COSCO 中国远洋运输（集团）总公司承运该笔业务，公司业务员李某根据 L/C 规定：“FULL SET OF CLEAN MULTIMODAL TRANSPORT DOCUMENT PLUS 2 N/N COPIES, MADE TO THE ORDER OF HSBC BANK CANADA, SHOWING ON BOARD NOTATION, MARKED FREIGHT PREPAID, AND NOTIFY APPLICANT (STATING FULL NAME AND ADDRESS)”，以及双方签订的外销合同、已缮制好的商业发票出具海运提单，多式联运提单亦可接受。

子项目一　运输单据的制作

一、海运提单的定义

海运提单（Marine Bill of Lading，B/L）简称提单，是货物的承运人或其代理人收到货物后，签发给托运人证明货物表面状况良好的一种证件。提单是托运人凭以向银行办理议付、结汇的主要单据之一，并在运输费用的结算和对外索赔中具有重要作用。

二、海运提单的作用

1. 提单是承运人或其代理人签发的货物收据（Receipt for the goods）。证明承运人或其代理人已按提单所载内容收到货物。

2. 提单是一种货物所有权的凭证。提单代表货物，掌握了提单就掌握了货物。提单合法持有人有权凭提单在目的港向承运人提货。

3. 提单是托运人与承运人之间所订立的运输契约的证明（Evidence of contract of carriage）。承运人和托运人之间的有关运输条件，双方的权利和义务，责任与豁免都以提单作为合约凭证，它是处理承运人与货方运输方面的争议、纠纷的法律依据。

三、海运提单的种类

海运提单的种类很多，格式也不尽相同，但基本内容大致相同。以海运方式为主的几种不同提单如下：

1. 清洁已装船提单（Clean Shipped on Board B/L，Clean Shipped B/L）

提单上必须以文字表明货物已装船，且提单上还需记载已装船日期。提单签发时未加注任何货损或包装不良之类批注。

UCP600 规定：银行只接受清洁已装船运输单据。

2. 备运提单（Received for Shipment B/L）

B/L 上只说明货物已经收到，暂代存入码头仓库，准备装船。承运人先签发提单，待船到港后再装船。此种提单虽列有承运船名，该船是否如期到达船公司并不负责。所以，备运提单实际上等于货运收据，而不构成运输契约。目前集装箱使用的提单和联合运输提单多属于备运提单。为满足银行只接受已装船提单的要求，这类提单需加“已装船批注（Laden on Board Vessel）”。

3. 指示提单（Order B/L）

在提单收货人一栏带有“凭指示（To Order）”的字样。这种提单通过指示人的背书而转让、流通。银行一般接受指示提单作为议付的凭证。在实务中，指示提单被广泛采用。

4. 记名提单（Straight B/L）

提单收货人是指明特定的，提单收货人一栏填上具体的收货人。

记名提单又叫直交式提单，收货人可以不凭正本提单只需证明自己的收货人身份便可以提货，但不能转让提单。此类提单只在运送价值较高的货物或展品时使用。

5. 不记名提单（Open B/L）

提单的收货人一栏表示“货交持票人（To Bearer）”。这种提单无须证明收货人身份就可以提货，风险很大。提单一旦丢失，货物很容易被人提走。

6. 多式或联合运输提单（Multimodal or Combined Transport Bill of Lading，CTB/L）

国际多式联运（International Multimodal Transport）是一种利用集装箱进行联运的运输方式，它通过采用海、陆、空等两种以上的运输手段，完成国际间的货物运输，从而打破了过去海、铁、公、空等单一运输方式互不连贯的传统做法。

国际多式联运能集中发挥各种运输方式的优势，使国际货物运输既快捷又安全，同时它简化了手续，减少了中间环节，加快了货运速度，降低了运输成本，并提高了货运质量，为实现“门到门”运输创造了有利条件。

多式联运提单指货物由海上、内河、铁路、公路、航空等两种或多种运输方式进行联合运输而签的适用于全程运输的提单。

目前我国使用的多式联合运输提单往往具有如下功能：

（1）既适用于不同方式的联合运输一陆海陆联合运输、海空联运、海铁联运等。

例如，联运承运人的责任是从接收货物起至交付货物为止，其接收货物地点可能是集装箱码头、内陆堆场、工厂或仓库、集装箱货运站等，因此在联运提单上印有货物收妥或接管的地点（Place of Receipt）。由于多式联运提单是在多式联运经营人收到货物后签发的，收货地不同，经营人签发的地点、时间也不同，承担的责任也就不同。另外，在提单上还印有最终交付货物的内陆交货地（Place of Delivery）。

（2）在多式联运中有海运方式。

例如：提单中还印有装货港（Port of Loading）、卸货港（Port of Discharge）和船名（Ocean Vessel）。

因此，在多式联合运输提单上通常包括六个运输项目：

① Pre—carriage（前段运输可以是陆运一火车或卡车）

② Place of Receipt.（收货地点）

③ Port of Loading（装运港，海运）

④ Ocean Vessel（船名）

⑤ Port of Discharge（卸货港）

⑥ Place of Delivery（内陆交货地，陆运）

（3）多式联运提单还适于我国港口单一运输直达各国港口的集装箱运输

例如：联合运输提单上包括三个项目：

① Container No.（集装箱号）

② Seal No.（铅封号）

③ 注意集装箱运输应在这种提单上加注“已装船批注”：

a. 装船日期

b. 船名

c. 承运人签字。

四、海运提单正反面内容

各国海运提单的格式不一，但其内容大致有正面内容和背面条款组成。

1. 正面内容

（1）承运人或其代理人印定的文字声明。

表明提单（Bill of Lading）字样。

船公司名称（Name of the Shipping Company）。

承运人收到表面状况良好的货物。并已装船，将运往目的港卸货。

船方对在提单上所装货物的重量、数量、价值等内容不负责核对，概不知悉。

对托运人、收货人等在提单正面印定的条款表示接受。

承运人或其代理人为证明以上各个内容，签发正本提单，凭其中一份提货，其余各份即行失效。

（2）由托运人及承运人或其代理人填写的部分。包括：

提单号（B/L No.）

托运人（Shipper）

收货人（Consignee）与背书（Endorsement）

被通知人（Notify Party）

船名（Name of Vessel）

装运港（Port of Loading）

卸货港（Port of Discharge）

唛头（Marks & Numbers）

大小写件数和包装种类（Number and Kind of Packages In words）

货名（Description of Goods）

毛重（Gross Weight）

尺码（Measurements）

运费（Freight and Charges）

运费预付和到付地点（Prepaid at & Payable at）

正本提单份数（Number of Original Bs/L）

提单签发地点及日期（Place and Date of Issue）

承运人签字（Signed for the Carrier）

2. 背面条款

船公司通常在其背面印有承运人的责任、权利、义务的豁免，是托运人和承运人处理争议时的依据。承运人收到提单，如不表示异议，即被认为对此印定条款同意接受。

UPC600 第 20 条规定：载有承运条款和条件，或提示承运条款和条件参见别处（简式/背面空白的提单）。银行将不予审核承运条款和条件的内容。

BILL OF LADING

<table>
<tr><td colspan="2">1) SHIPPER</td><td colspan="4" rowspan="6">10) B/L NO.

COSCO
中国远洋运输（集团）
总公司

CHINA OCEAN
SHIPPING (GROUP) CO.

ORIGINAL
COMBINED TRANPORT BILL OF LADING</td></tr>
<tr><td colspan="2">2) CONSIGNEE</td></tr>
<tr><td colspan="2">3) NOTIFY PARTY</td></tr>
<tr><td>4) PLACE OF RECEIPT</td><td>5) OCEAN VESSEL</td></tr>
<tr><td>6) VOYAGE NO.</td><td>7) PORT OF LOADING</td></tr>
<tr><td>8) PORT OF DISCHARGE</td><td>9) PLACE OF DELIVERY</td></tr>
<tr><td colspan="6">11) MARKS 12) NOS.&KINDS OF PKGS 13) DESCRIPTION OF GOODS 14) G.W.(kg) 15) MEAS(m^3)</td></tr>
<tr><td colspan="6"></td></tr>
<tr><td colspan="6">16) TOTAL NUMBER OF CONTAINERS OR PACKAGES (IN WORDS)</td></tr>
<tr><td>FREIGHT & CHARGES</td><td>REVENUE TONS</td><td>RATE</td><td>PER</td><td>PREPAID</td><td>COLLECT</td></tr>
<tr><td>PREPAID AT</td><td colspan="2">PAYABLE AT</td><td colspan="3">17) PLACE AND DATE OF ISSUE</td></tr>
<tr><td>TOTAL PREPAID</td><td colspan="2">18) NUMBER OF ORIGINAL B(S)L</td><td colspan="3"></td></tr>
<tr><td colspan="3">LOADING ON BOARD THE VESSEL

19) DATE</td><td colspan="3">20) BY</td></tr>
</table>

海运提单样本

五、海运提单的缮制项目

1 栏 提单号（B/L No.）

（1）填写内容：

提单号码（B/L No）位于提单右上角。提单上必须注明承运人及代理人规定的提单号，以便核查，便于工作联系，否则提单无效。

（2）实例：

B/L No.：CDE567420

2 栏 托运人（Shipper）

（1）填写内容：

在信用证项下，托运人一般为受益人。以托收支付方式成交的，托收的委托人为托运人。

（2）实例：

Shipper：

HUNAN TEXTILE IMP & EXP CORP.

4E WUYI RD., CHANGSHA, CHINA

3 栏 收货人（Consignee）与背书（Endorsement）

收货人（Consignee）

（1）填写内容：

提单的收货人又称“抬头人”。提单的抬头决定了海运提单的性质和货权的归属。所以，信用证项下的提单必须严格按照信用证规定的提单条款缮制。

一般信用证支付方式多使用指示式抬头。这种抬头的特征是有“凭指示”（To Order）字样。指示式收货人将收货人以广义的形式表示出来，掩饰了具体的收货人的名称、地址，使单据可以背书转让、流通。

指示式的抬头人又分为两种：不记名指示式（To order）和记名指示式（To order of ×× Bank/shipper）。

不记名指示式（To order）

“To order”（凭指示或称空白抬头）没有具体的收货人名称。常见信用证规定为：“Full set of…B/L made out to order endorsed in blank/blank endorsed”字样。“信用证要求提单空白抬头、空白背书”。

（2）实例 1：

① 提单正面收货人一栏填：To order

② 背面由背书人签章并注明背书的日期：

B.T.I Co.（背书人签章）

Mar. 12，2004

③ 此种提单由托运人在提单背面进行背书后，即可转让。由被转让人持单向船公司提货。

（2）记名指示式抬头（To order of××Bank/Shipper）

“To order o××Bank/Shipper”（凭银行或托运人指示）。由银行或托运人背书转让。

记名指示中的记名人有权控制和转让提单。信用证一般规定为“...B/L made out to order of××Bank/Shipper endorsed in blank/blank endorsed”。

实例 2：

① 单正面收货人一栏填：To order of××Bank/Shipper

② 背面由银行或托运人签章并注明背书的日期：

××Bank/××Co.（银行或托运人签章）

Mar.12, 2004.

③ 此种提单由银行/托运人在提单背面进行背书后，即可转让。由被转让人持单向船公司提货。

背书（Endorsement）

（1）填写内容：

背书分为记名背书（Endorsement in full）和空白背书（Endorsement in blank）两种：

① 记名背书：在提单的背面先写上被背书人的名称，同时再由背书人签署并盖章，并注明背书的日期。例如：“...B/L made out to order deliver to/endorsed to A.B.C Co.”

② 不记名背书：

只在背面有托运人签章即可。

（2）实例：

a. 提单正面填：To order

b. 背面由背书人做记名背书，提单记名背书的指示文句中不用“Pay”而用“Deliver”。

Deliver to/Endorsed to A.B.C Co.

c. 背书人签章并注明背书的日期

J.M. L Co.（签章）

Mar.12.20

4 栏 被通知人（Notify Party）

（1）填写内容：

指货物到达目的港时船方发送到货通知的对象。其职责是及时地接受船方发出的到货通知，并将该通知转告真实的收货人。被通知人无权提货。“被通知人栏目”是对指示提单方法的一个补充，在提单抬头人不是收货人时，减少了船方通知提货、报关的麻烦。因此，在空白指示提单和银行及托运人指示提单时，此栏必须详细将被通知人的名称、地址写清楚，否则船方就无法与收货人联系，收货人也不能及时报关提货，甚至会因超过海关规定申报时间而被没收货物。此栏在信用证方式下按规定填写。有时为进口方或买方代理。

（2）实例 1:

信用证条款为“Full set of B/L... notify applicant”

应在此栏中将开证申请人的全称及地址填上。

实例 2：

信用证条款为“Full set of B/L…notify our forwarding agent：M.K Co. addressed to 60 Green RD., London U.K.”

应在此栏中将货代 M K Co. 的全称及地址填上。

5 栏 船名（Name of Vessel）

（1）填写内容：

按实际所装运的船只名称填写。

（2）实例：

Name of Vessel: S.S Taishan V.108

6 栏 装运港（Port of Loading）。

（1）填写内容：

填实际装运港口的具体名称，不能笼统填写“Chinese Port”字样。

（2）实例：

Port of Loading: Qingdao

7 栏 卸货港（Port of Discharge）

（1）填写内容：

填实际货物卸下的港口。如经转船，则应填上转运港字样。

（2）实例：

from Qingdao to Rotterdam w/t Hong Kong

注意事项：

A. 卸货港和装运港一样不能填笼统名称，如“European Main Ports（欧洲主要口岸）”，应填具体卸货港。

实例：Port of Discharge: Antwerp

如果在国际上有重名港口的，还要加注国名和地区名来区别。

B. 如来证列明几个卸货港的，如“Hamburg/Rotterdam”提单只能填一个具体卸货港的名称。

C. 货物经转（Transshipment），如：货物从青岛装运，在香港转船再运至德国汉堡，可有以下填法：

① 在提单中印有装货港（Port of Loading）、卸货港（Port of Discharge）和最终目的港（Final Destination）栏目，应分别在装货港栏内填“青岛（Qingdao）”，卸货港栏内填“香港（Hong Kong）”，在最终目的港栏内填“汉堡（Hamburg）”。

② 在提单中只有卸货港栏，没有最终目的港栏目，则在卸货港栏内填“汉堡（Hamburg）”，再加注转船港名称：如“Hamburg With Transshipment at Hong Kong 或 Hamburg W/T Hong Kong（在 Hong Kong 转船）”。

③ 如有印就的转船港（Port of Transshipment）栏目，则直接将“香港（Hong Kong）”填入转船港栏即可。有关转运事项，请参见“转船提单”。

（4）如果信用证中规定卸货港后有“In transit to×××”，则表明货物自卸货港卸货后，经转运或陆运至其他目的地或邻国，尤其在卖方不负责转口时，不能在卸货港栏内后加填转船港的港名，应另在货名栏下方的空白处或在唛头处加注“In transit to×××”。

实例：来证规定：“Marseilles in transit to Genoa”，具体做法是：

① 卸货港栏：Marseilles

② 货名栏下方的空白处或在唛头处加注：In transit to Genoa.

注意："In transit to×××"一般不能填在卸货港后。因为卖方只负责将货运至该卸货港，以后的转运由买方负责。

8 栏 唛头（Marks & Numbers）

（1）填写内容：

按发票缮制

（2）实例：

Marks & Numbers

N/M（没有唛头）

9 栏 大小写件数和包装种类（Number and Kind of Packages& In words）

（1）填写内容：

应填写数量和计量单位，与唛头中件号的累计数相符。大写是用英文打出包装及数量，必须大小写一致。

（2）实例：

小写（In figures)：240 cartons.

大写（In words)：（Say Two Hundred and Forty Cartons Only）

小写（In figures)：350 cases.

大写（In words)：（Say Three Hundred and Fifty Cases Only）

10 栏 货名（Description of Goods）

（1）填写内容：

提单列明的货名仅是信用证规定装运的货物名称，应与商业发票及其他单据一致。如信用证规定品名繁多，允许提单打出货物的统称表示商品的名称。

（2）实例：

Description of Goods

T-SHIRT

11 栏 毛重（Gross Weight）

（1）填写内容：

应与发票一致，一般以公斤为计算单位，毛重指包括包装材料在内的货物重量。如果一次装运的货物中有几种不同的包装材料或完全不同的货物，那么应先分别计算并将合计的毛重填在这一栏目中。

（2）实例：

Gross Weight

123.56KGS

12 栏 尺码（Measurements）

（1）填写内容：

与发票一致，小数点后保留三位数，以立方米为计算单位，应填一批货的尺码总数。总尺码不仅包括各件货物尺码之和，还应包括件与件之间堆放时的合理空间所占的体积。因此总尺码数等于各种货物的尺码之和。

（2）实例：

Measurements

6CBMS

13 栏 运费（Freight and Charges）

（1）填写内容：

除非信用证中明确规定提单中表明运费的计算与数额，否则提单中不填运费的数额为好。

（2）实例：

① 在以 CIF 或 CFR 成交的价格术语中，支付的运费为卖方，一般卖方在交货前把运费付清，计入 CIF 或 CFR 价格中。因此应根据信用证的规定，选择“Freight Prepaid（运费预付）”或“Freight Paid（运费已付）”。银行将接受以戳记或以其他方式清楚表明运费预付或已付的词语。

② 价格术语为 FOB 或 FAS 时，运费由买方支付，此时应填“Freight Collect（运费到付）”或“Payable at destination（运费在目的港支付）”。

14 栏 运费预付和到付地点（Prepaid at &Freight Payable at）

（1）填写内容：

在提单相应栏目中填实际运费预付和到付的地点。

（2）实例：

Prepaid at：Qingdao

Freight Payable at：New York

15 栏 正本提单份数（Number of Original Bs/L）

（1）填写内容：

按照 UCP600 规定，运输单据必须注明所出具的正本的份数。正本提单的份数按信用证的要求应在本栏中用大写（如 THREE，TWO）等注明。向银行提供信用证规定的全套正本提单的份数，可使收货人凭正本提单提货。UCP600 第 17 条 a 款规定：凡信用证规定的每一种单据必须至少提交一份正本。对正副本提单的要求，一般在信用证中有规定，出口商应按要求提供。

（2）实例：

“Full set of B/L in triplicate with two non-negotiable Bs/L”（三份正本两份副本）

注意事项：

① 注明“第一正本（First Original）”、“第二正本（Second Original）”、“第三正本（Third Original）”、“正本（Original）”、“第二份（Duplicate）”、“第三份（Triplicate）”等类似表述的运输单据都是正本。提单不一定非要注明“正本（Original）”字样才能被接受为正本提单。

② 提单有正本（original）和副本（non-negotiable B/L）之分。正本提单可交银行议付，并流通转让，副本则不行。每份正本提单的份数效力相同，凭其中一份提货后，其余各份失效。

16 栏 提单签发地点及日期（Place and Date of Issue）

（1）填写内容：

地点应为装运地点。日期应不迟于信用证或合同规定的最迟装运日期。该日期将视为装运日期。如果提交的是预先印就“已装运于船”的提单（a pre-printed “Shipped on board” bill of lading），提单的出具日期即视为装运日，除非提单带有加注日期的单独装船批注（a separate dated on board notation），此时，该装船批注的日期即视为装运日，而不论该批注日期是在提单签发日期之前还是之后。

（2）实例：

Place and Date of Issue

QINGDAO, SEPT. 25, 2013

17 栏 承运人签字（Signed for the Carrier）

（1）填写内容:

正本提单必须有承运人（carrier）或其代理人、船长（master）或其代理人的签字或印章方能生效。

根据 UCP600 规定：

① 承运人（船长、船东、多式运输营运人）的签署或证实时，须分别按实际情况标明其真实身份，代理需要表明被代理人身份。例如船长签署提单，则船长的签字必须表明“船长”身份。在此情况下，不必标明船长的姓名。

② 代理人代表承运人（船长、船东、多式运输营运人）签署时，必须标明他所代表的委托人名称及身份，即分别按实际情况注明代理人是代表某承运人/船长签署或证实。如果由代理人代表船长签署提单，在此情况下，不必标明船长的姓名。

（2）实例 1：

承运人签字

提单上部：COSCO

提单签署处：COSCO（签署）

As Carrier/Signed on behalf of COSCO

实例 2：代理人签字

提单上部：COSCO

提单签署处：Sinotrans（签署）

As agent for（on behalf of）the Carrier：COSCO

实例 3：船长签字

提单上部：Pacific Ocean Shipping Company

提单签署处：Johnson（签署）

As Master/Signed on behalf of Pacific Ocean Shipping Company

子项目二 海运提单及多式联运提单典型业务演示

上接项目二、项目三及项目七，业务员李望完成了装船前的所有工作并取得了相应单据，据此，在该项目中应完成的工作任务包括：

任务 1：认真审核信用证中的装运条款。

任务 2：认真审核商业发票。

任务 3：根据要求缮制海运提单。

1. 信用证部分条款

DC NO:	DC HMN214479
DATE OF ISSUE:	120620
APPLICABLE RULES:	UCP LATEST VERSION
EXPIRY DATE AND PLACE:	120903 IN COUNTRY OF BENEFICIARY
APPLICANT:	ELBY GIFTS INC.879 INDUSTRIEL BOIS DES FILION,QUEBEC, J6Z 4T3, CANADA
BENEFICIARY:	LILING PENGXING CERAMIC FACTORY WUSHI JIASHU LILING HUNAN, CHINA
AMOUNT:	USD27,010.40
PCT CR AMT TOLERANCE:	10/10
AVAILABLE WITH/BY:	ANY BANK BY NEGOTIATION
DRAFTS AT:	AT SIGHT FOR FULL INVOICE VALUE
DRAWEE:	ISSUING BANK
PARTIAL SHIPMENTS:	ALLOWED
TRANSSHIPMENT:	ALLOWED
LOADING PORT/DEPART AIRPORT:	SHENZHEN, CHINA
DISCHARGE PORT/DEST AIRPORT:	PRINCE RUPERT,BC
FINAL DEST/DELIVERY/TRNSP TO:	BOIS DES FILION, CANADA
LATEST DATE OF SHIPMENT:	120819
GOODS:	CERAMIC CUPS AND BOWLS AS PER SC NO.:CB121039 CIF PRINCE RUPERT,BC V23-234 U.S.D 4.05/SET V23-234F U.S.D 4.05/SET V23-235 U.S.D 2.40/SET V23-236 U.S.D 2.10/SET ALL PACKED IN CARTONS.
DOCUMENTS REQUIRED:	+ ORIGINAL SIGNED INVOICE PLUS THREE COPIES. + FULL SET OF CLEAN MULTIMODAL TRANSPORT DOCUMENT PLUS 2 N/N COPIES, MADE TO THE ORDER OF HSBC BANK CANADA, SHOWING ON BOARD NOTATION, MARKED

FREIGHT PREPAID, AND NOTIFY APPLICANT (STATING FULL NAME AND ADDRESS).

2. 商业发票

PENGXING IMP&EXP COMPANY

LILING PENGXING CERAMIC FACTORY

WUSHI JIASHU LILING HUNAN CHINA

TEL: 86-731-23384199 FAX: 86-731-23384298

COMMERCIAL INVOICE

To:	ELBY GIFTS INC. 879 INDUSTRIEL BOIS DES FILION QUEBEC, J6Z 4T3, CANADA	**Invoice No.:**	PX12. IVN1039
		Invoice Date:	AUG. 16, 2012
		S/C No.:	S/C NO.: CB121039
		S/C Date:	JUL. 5, 2012
From:	SHENZHEN, CHINA	**To:**	PRINCE RUPERT, BC, CANADA
Letter of Credit No.:	DC HMN214479	**Issued By:**	HSBC BANK, MONTREAL CANADA

Marks and Numbers	Number and kind of package Description of goods	Quantity	Unit Price U.S.D/set	Amount
	CERAMIC CUPS AND BOWLS		CIF PRINCE RUPERT, BC	
ELBY		CTN	U.S.D	U.S.D
S/C NO.:CB121039	V23-234	228	4.05	3,693.60
NO: 1-1589	V23-234F	228	4.05	3,693.60
	V23-235	190	2.40	3,648.00
	V23-236	189	2.10	3,175.20
	V23-237	186	1.95	2,901.60
	V23-2348	190	2.04	3,100.80
	36-062	191	2.30	3,514.40
	36-063	187	2.12	3,171.52
	Total:	1,589 CTNS		U.S.D 26,898.72

Say Total: U.S DOLLARS TWENTY SIX THOUSAND EIGHT HUNDRED AND NINETY EIGHT AND CENTS SEVENTY TWO(USD26,898.72)ONLY

PENGXING IMP&EXP COMPANY

李 望

3. 其他信息：
提单号：B/L No.　COSFMT3821018
车次及船名航次：TRAIN NO.:67589
COSCO SEATTLE V.0078E
提单签发日：AUG. 24, 2012
据此，李望缮制了一份海运提单：

1. Shipper Insert Name, Address and Phone LILING PENGXING CERAMIC FACTORY WUSHI JIASHU LILING HUNAN, CHINA		许可证号 B/L No. COSFMT3821018
2. Consignee Insert Name, Address and Phone TO THE ORDER OF HSBC BANK CANADA		中远集装箱运输有限公司 **COSCO CONTAINER LINES** TLX: 33057 COSCO CN FAX: +86(021) 6545 8984 **ORIGINAL**
3. Notify Party Insert Name, Address and Phone (It is agreed that no responsibility shall attach to the Carrier or his agents for failure to notify) ELBY GIFTS INC. 879 INDUSTRIEL BOIS DES FILION		**Port-to-Port or Combined Transport** **BILL OF LADING** RECEIVED in external apparent good order and condition except as otherwise noted. The total number of packages or units stuffed in the container, the description of the goods and the weights shown in this Bill of Lading are furnished by the Merchants, and which the carrier has no reasonable means of checking and is not a part of this Bill of Lading contract. The carrier has issued the number of Bills of Lading stated below, all of this tenor and date, one of the original Bills of Lading must be surrendered and endorsed or signed against the delivery of the shipment and whereupon any other original Bills of Lading shall be void. The Merchants agree to be bound by the terms and conditions of this Bill of Lading as if each had personally signed this Bill of Lading. SEE clause 4 on the back of this Bill of Lading (Terms continued on the back hereof, please read carefully). *Applicable Only When Document Used as a Combined Transport Bill of Lading.
4. Combined Transport * Pre-carriage by TRAIN NO.:67589	5. Combined Transport* Place of Receipt CHANGSHA	
6. Ocean Vessel Voy. No. COSCO SEATTLE V.0078E	7. Port of Loading YANTIAN,SHENZHEN, CHINA	
8. Port of Discharge PRINCE RUPERT, BC, CANADA	9. Combined Transport * Place of Delivery BOIS DES FILION, CANADA	

Marks & Nos. Container/Seal No.	No. of Containers or Packages	Description of Goods (If Dangerous Goods, See Clause 20)	Gross Weight Kgs	Measurement
N/M	1589CTNS CONTAINER NO.: CBHU8150082/ B45171/40'HQ	SHIPPER'S LOAD & COUNT & SEAL 1X40'HQ (F.C.L) S.T.C CY/CY ONE THOUSAND FIVE HUNDRED AND EIGHTY NINE(1589CTNS)CARTONS OF CERAMIC CUPS AND BOWLS FOB SHENZHEN, CHINA THIS SHIPMENT CONTAINS NO SOLID WOOD PACKING MATERIALS.	17,654.40 KGS	68.130 CBM
		Description of Contents for Shipper's Use Only (Not part of This B/L Contract)		

10. Total Number of containers and/or packages (in words) SAY ONE THOUSAND FIVE HUNDRED AND EIGHTY NINE CARTONS　ONLY.

11. Freight & Charges	Revenue Tons	Rate	Per	Prepaid	Collect
FREIGHT PREPAID	AS ARRANGED				

Ex. Rate	Prepaid at	Payable at	Place and date of issue SHENZHEN, CHINA AUG. 24, 2012
	Total Prepaid	No. of Original B(s)/L THREE	Signed for the Carrier, COSCO CONTAINER LINES COSCO AS CARRIER XXXX

子项目三　海运提单及多式联运提单拓展业务操作

能力实训项目 1：海运提单业务操作

2013 年 9 月 5 号，单证员黄柯通过审核“DC 130720”号信用证并根据商业发票及装运资料，缮制海运提单。

海运提单。

1. 信用证

SEQUENCE OF TOTAL	27:	1/1
FORM OF DC	40A:	IRREVOCABLE
DC NO.	20:	DC 130720
DATE OF ISSUE	31C:	130720
APPLICABLE RULES	40E:	UCP 600
EXPIRY DATE AND PLACE	31D:	130920 IN CHINA
APPLICANT	50:	CONSTRUCTION MOUDULAR SPECIALIST POSTAL: 13 HARVEY RD., SHENTON PK, WA 6008 AUSTRALIA
BENEFICIARY	59:	PRIMA CONSTRUCTION MATERIOLS CO., LTD 1401 ROOM, 38 BUILDING, CHUANGYE GARDEN BAOAN DISTRICT, SHENZHEN, CHINA
AMOUNT	32B:	USD6,840.00
AVAILABLE WITH/BY	41D:	ANY BANK BY NEGOTIATION
DRAFTS AT	42C:	AT 30DAYS AFTER SIGHT
DRAWEE	42A:	DRAWN ON US
PARTIAL SHIPMENTS	43P:	ALLOWED
TRANSHIPMENT	43T:	ALLOWED
LOADING PORT	44E:	CHINA MAIN PORT
DISCHARGE PORT	44F:	FREMENTLE, AUSTRALIA
LATEST DATE OF SHIPMENT	44C:	130905
DESCRIPTION OF GOODS	45A:	BAMBOO FLOORING ITEM 1 100 SQM U.S.D20.00/SQM ITEM 2 100 SQM U.S.D39.50/SQM ALL PACKING IN SEA WORTHY CARTONS CIF FREMENTLE AS PER PI NO.: BFF0610
DOCUMENTS REQUIRED	46A:	+ MANUALLY SIGNED COMMECIAL INVOICE 3 ORIGINALS PLUS THREE COPIES. + FULL SET(3/3) OF MARINE BILLS OF LADING, MADE OUT TO ORDER, MARKED FREIGHT PREPAID, AND NOTIFY APPLICANT (STATING FULL NAME AND ADDRESS). + INSURANCE POLICY OR CERTIFICATE IN TRIPLICATE, BLANK INDORSED, FOR THE INVOICE VALUE PLUS 10% COVERING

ICC(A) RISK AND ICC(STRIKE). FROM WAREHOUSE TO WAREHOUSE AND I.O.P, PAYABLE AT FREMENTLE IN U.S.D.
+ PACKING LIST 3 ORIGINALS AND 2 COPIES.
+CERTIFICATE OF ORIGIN IN CHINA ISSUED BY OFFICIAL AUTRORITY.
+ BENNIFICIALRY'S CERTIFICATE SHOWING THAT A SET OF ORIGINAL SHIPPING DOCUMENTS HAS BEEN MAIL TO THE APPLICANT BY EXPRESS AFTER 2 DAYS OF SHIOMENT.

2. 商业发票

Prima Construction Materials Co., Ltd.
Add: 1401Room, 38building, Chuangye Gardern, Baoan District, Shenzhen China
Tel: 0086-755-32076630 Fax: 0086-755-32076630

COMMERCIAL INVOICE

Contract No.: CBF130724		**No.:PR-20130820**		
L/C No.: DC 13720		**Date: AUG. 22, 2013**		
From: SHENZHEN		**To: FREMENTLE**		
Marks&Nos.	**Description of Goods**	**Quantity**	**Unit Price**	**Amount**
	BAMBOO FLOORING		CIF FREMENTLE	
CMS FREMENTLE CBF130724 NO.:1-109	CARBONISED BAMBOO FLOORING	100SQM	$ 20.00	$2,000.00
	STRAND WOVEN BAMBOO FLOORING DECKING	100SQM	$39.50	$3,950.00
TOTAL			EXW PRICE	$5,950.00
			LCL CHARGE	$ 450.00
			INSURANCE COST	$ 60.00
			FREIGHT	$ 380.00
			CIF VALUE	$6,480.00

3. 其他信息：
提单号：B/L No.　COSFMT470204
船名航次：MOL INTEGRITY/102W
提单签发日：SEP. 5, 2013
据此，请缮制海运提单：

Shipper		**BILL OF LADING** B/L No.: **COSCO** **中国远洋运输公司** **CHINA OCEAN SHIPPING COMPANY** **ORIGINAL**	
Consignee			
Notify Party			
*Pre-carriage by	*Place of Receipt		
Ocean Vessel Voy. No.	Port of Loading		
Port of Discharge	*Final Destination	Freight Payable at	Number Original Bs/L
Marks and Numbers	Number and Kind of Packages; Description	Gross Weight	Measurement m³
TOTAL PACKAGES (IN WORDS)			
Freight and Charges		Place and Date of Issue	
		Signed for the Carrier	

*Applicable only when document used as a Through Bill of Loading

能力实训项目 2：海运提单业务操作

2013 年 9 月 24 号，单证员彭婷通过审核“0684130117426”号信用证并根据商业发票及装运资料，完成海运提单的制作。

1. 信用证：

SEQUENCE OF TOTAL	27:	1/1
FORM OF DC.	40A:	IRREVOCABLE
DC. NO.	20:	0684130117426
DATE OF ISSUE	31C:	130825
APPLICABLE RULES	40E:	UCP LATEST VERSION
EXPIRY DATE AND PLACE	31D:	131024,CHINA
APPLICANT	50:	M/S. MEMORY STEEL CORPORATION 73/A, LAL MOHAN SHAHA STREET (DHOLAIKHAL), DHAKA-1100. BANGLADESH.
BENEFICIARY	59:	JIANGSU I-TOUCH BUSINESS SERVICE LTD, ROOM 117, JIANGSU EDIFICE ZHANGJIAGANG FREE TRADE ZONE, JIANGSU, CHINA TEL:86-512-56363783
AMOUNT	32B:	USD35,000.00
AVAILABLE WITH/BY	41D:	ANY BANK IN CHINA BY NEGOTIATION
DRAFTS AT	42C:	AT SIGHT FOR FULL INVOICE VALUE
DRAWEE	42A:	DRAWN ON US
PARTIAL SHIPMENTS	43P:	ALLOWED
TRANSSHIPMENT	43T:	ALLOWED
PORT OF LOADING	44A:	ANY SEA PORT, CHINA
PORT OF DISCHARGE	44B:	CHITTAGONG SEA PORT, BANGLADESH
LATEST DATE OF SHIPMENT	44C:	131009
DESCRIPTION OF GOODS	45A:	201/2B SECONDARY GRADE STAINLESS STEEL SHEET OF WIDTH 1219MM THICKNESS 1MM TO 3MM, QTY:25,000KGS AT THE RATE OF USD1.40/KG FOR TOTAL AMOUNT OF USD35,000.00 CFR CHITTAGONG, BANGLADESH. AS PER BENEFICIARY'S PROFORMA INVOICE NO.

		SK20130802-001 DATED AUG 2,2013
DOCUMENTS REQUIRED	46A:	+MANUALLY SIGNED COMMERCIAL INVOICE IN TRIPLICATE CERTIFYING MERCHANDISE TO BE OF CHINA ORIGIN AND INDICATING THAT THE GOODS ARE BEING IMPORTED AGAINST IRC NO.BA-0171646, TI NO.157-107-0121, VAT REGISTRATION NO. 9141093671. +FULL SET OF CLEAN 'SHIPPED ON BOARD' OCEAN BILL OF LADING SHOWING' FREIGHT PREPAID' MADE OUT TO ORDER OF SHIPPER AND BLANK INDORSED, NOTIFY APPLICANT. +PACKING LIST IN TRIPLICATE SHOWING GROSS WEIGHT, NET WEIGHT. +CERTIFICATE OF ORIGIN ISSUED AND LEGALED BY CCPIT

2. 商业发票

<table>
<tr><td colspan="2">Jiangsu I-Touch Business Service Ltd.
Add: Room117, Jinggang Edifice Zhangjiagang Free Trade Zone,
Jiangsu Province, China
Tel: 0086-512-56363783 Fax: 0086-512-56366780</td></tr>
<tr><td colspan="2">COMMERCIAL INVOICE
To: M/S. MEMORY STEEL CORPORATION73/A, LAL MOHAN SHAHA STREET (DHOLAIKHAL), DHAKA-1100. BANGLANDESH</td></tr>
<tr><td>Contract No.: C20130807</td><td>No.: 67080-9</td></tr>
<tr><td>L/C No.: 0684130117426</td><td>Date: SEP. 13, 2013</td></tr>
<tr><td>From: SHANGHAI, CHINA</td><td>To: CHITTAGONG, BANGLANDESH</td></tr>
</table>

Marks	Description of Goods Size(mm)	Quantity (G.W/KG)	Unit Price (USD/KG)	Amount
	STAINLESS STEEL SHEET		CFR CHITTAGONG	
N/M	201/2B SECONDARY GRADE			
	1.2×1,219×2,438	5,728.00	1.4000	7,806.40
	1.5×1,219×2,438	3,315.20	1.4000	4,547.20
	2.0×1,219×2,438	11,894.0	1.4000	16,282.00
	1,219MM OR MORE THICKNESS 1MM TO 3MM			
	3.0×1,219×2,438	4,663.70	1.4000	6,364.40
	TOTAL:	25,600.90		35,000.00

SAY U.S.DOLLARS THIRTY FIVE THOUSAND ONLY

WE HEREBY CERTIFY THAT ABOVE MERCHANDISE TO BE OF CHINA ORIGIN AND ARE BEING IMPORTED AGAINST IRC NO. BA-0171646,TI NO. 157-107-0121,VAT REGISTRATION NO.9141093671 AND L.C.A. NO. 101804 UNDER H.S. CODE NO. 721933.00, 721934.00

Jiangsu I-Touch Business Service Ltd.

彭　婷

3. 其他信息

提单号：B/L No. EGL01206

船名航次：XINGHE V.182

提单签发日：SEP 24, 2013

据此，请缮制海运提单：

Shipper		**BILL OF LADING** B/L No.:
Consignee		**COSCO**
Notify Party		**中国远洋运输公司**
*Pre-carriage by	*Place of Receipt	**CHINA OCEAN SHIPPING COMPANY**
Ocean Vessel Voy. No.	Port of Loading	**ORIGINAL**

Port of Discharge	*Final Destination	Freight Payable at	Number Original Bs/L

Marks and Numbers	Number and Kind of Packages; Description	Gross Weight	Measurement m^3

TOTAL PACKAGES
(IN WORDS)

Freight and Charges

Place and Date of Issue
Signed for the Carrier

*Applicable only when document used as a Through Bill of Loading

项目九 汇票制作业务

项目预期目标

通过对信用证项下汇票条款的认真解读，介绍汇票的概念和汇票的种类，熟悉汇票的当事人及其关系，掌握汇票的内容。了解汇票在流通过程中的使用环节，具备缮制汇票的能力。

在项目实施过程中，通过学习汇票的缮制，了解汇票在国际结算中的重要性，逐渐培养审核、制单、归类等国际商务单证基本职业能力，亦培养独立操作业务和与银行等部门有效沟通的能力。

表 9-1　　项目预期目标

目标类型	汇票的缮制
知识目标	熟悉汇票的内容和汇票的票据行为
	了解汇票在流通过程中使用环节
	掌握信用证结算和托收方式下汇票的制作
能力目标	能区分不同种类的汇票
	根据合同和信用证准确缮制汇票
职业素质目标	独立业务操作能力
	与银行沟通衔接能力

项目实施条件

1. 向学生提供商业汇票样单，指出汇票的必要项目和非必要项目
2. 学生进行角色扮演展示汇票在流通过程中的使用环节
3. 学生能够在实训室根据提供的业务资料使用计算机缮制汇票
4. 指导教师掌握相关的国际贸易法律，具备扎实的外贸业务基础

开篇业务引入

根据第 L-12017 号信用证的要求，长沙鹏兴进出口有限公司已于 2012 年 8 月 24 日完成装运取得了所有的单据后，缮制汇票通过银行向付款人收款。该项目任务具体由单证员李望负责。2012 年 8 月 26 日，单证员李望根据发票、装运资料和 L/C 相关内容缮制汇票。

子项目一　汇票的制作

一、汇票的概念

汇票简称BILL或DRAFT或BILL OF EXCHANGE。它是一人（即：出票人DRAWER）向另一人（即：DRAWEE受票人/付款人）签发的，要求该受票人立即或在一定时间或一个固定时期支付一定金额给某人或其指定人或来人（持票人HOLDER）无条件书面支付命令。

国际贸易中使用的汇票是出口商凭以向进口商要求付款的收款工具，也是付款的重要凭证。由于该汇票由出口商签发，属商业汇票，收汇方式为逆汇。商业汇票通常签发一套，一式两份，具有同等的法律效力，个别标明：:(1), FIRST OF EXCHANGE(2)，付款人仅凭其中一份付一次款，先见到哪份付哪份，即“付一不付二”或“付二不付一”。在国际贸易实务中，托收或信用证方式都有可能使用汇票。在信用证方式下，除延期付款信用证不需要汇票外，其他情况下都可能使用，凡信用证中有“BY PAYMENT”字样的，就需要附有汇票。而托收方式下汇票则必不可少。

二、汇票的种类

1. 按有无附有货运单据，可分为光票和跟单汇票

光票（CLEAN BILL）：光票是不附带货运单据的汇票。光票的流通完全依靠当事人的信用，即完全看出票人、付款人或背书人的资信。在国际贸易中，对少量货运，或收取保险费、运费等其他费用，可采用光票向对方收款。

跟单汇票（DOCUMENTARY BILL）：跟单汇票是附带货运单据的汇票，以承兑或付款作为交付单据的条件。除了有当事人的信用外，还有货物的保证。因此，在国际贸易中，这种汇票使用较为广泛。

2. 按付款时间，可分为即期汇票和远期汇票

即期汇票（SIGHT BILL）：提示或见票时立即付款的汇票。

远期汇票（TIME BILL OR USANCE BILL）：在一定期限或特定日期付款的汇票。

3. 按出票人不同，可分为商业汇票和银行汇票

商业汇票（TRADE BILL）：商业汇票是指出票人是商号、企业或个人。在国际贸易结算中，出口商用逆汇法，向国外进口商收取货款进口签发的汇票，即属商业汇票。

银行汇票（BANKER’S BILL）：银行汇票的出票人是银行。在国际结算中，银行汇票签发后，一般交汇款人，由汇款人寄交国外收款人向指定的付款银行取款。银行汇票一般为光票，不随附货运单据。

4. 按承兑人的不同，分为商业承兑汇票和银行承兑汇票

商业承兑汇票（TRADER’S ACCEPTANCE BILL）：由工商企业或个人承兑的远期汇票。商业承兑汇票建立在商业信用的基础之上，出票人是工商企业或个人。

银行承兑汇票（BANKER’S ACCEPTANCE BILL）：由银行承兑的远期汇票。它是建

立在银行信用基础上的，出票人是出口商，银行对汇票承兑后成为了汇票主债务人，则出票人成为次债务人。

凭 信用证 第 号

Drawn under ________ L/C No. ________

日期 按 息 付款

Dated ________ Payable with interest @ ________ % per annum

号码 汇票金额 中国，上海 年 月 日

No.: ________ Exchange for ________ Shanghai, China ________

见票 日后（本汇票之副本未付）

At ________ Sight of this FIRST of Exchange(Second of Exchangc bcing unpaid)

Pay to the order of ________ 或其指定人

付金额

The sum of ________

To:

图 9-1 汇票空白样本

三、具体业务操作

（一）跟单 L/C 下汇票的缮制

1 栏 出票依据（Draw under…L/C No.…Dated ）

信用证项下的汇票需要列明出票条款即出票依据（Drawn under Clause）。出票条款是表明汇票的起源。

（1）填写内容：包括三个方面。

Drawn under 开证行名称、城市名、国名

L/C No. 信用证号码

Dated 开证日期

（2）实例：

Drawn under Bank of America, New York

L/C No. BOANY00158

Dated Feb.16, 2014

2 栏 利息（Interest）

信用证项下的汇票制作模板中一般会列出利息。通常填写的是合同或者信用证规定的利息率。一般情况下由银行填写。

3 栏 号码（No.）

（1）填写内容：填写发票号码。让该业务中的发票和汇票建立关联。

（2）实例：

No. HNCS001

4 栏 汇票金额（Exchange for（小写金额）/The sum of（大写金额））

（1）填写内容：1. 参照 L/C 的汇票条款分别填写小写金额和大写金额。

如果 L/C 规定：full invoice value 则填发票全额，V 汇=V 发。

如果发票金额含佣金、折扣,则取净价填写（即不含佣金和折扣）

CIF C5	USD 10,000.00	
LESSC5	USD 500.00	
	USD 9,500.00	V 汇<V 发

L/C 规定汇票金额按发票金额的一定百分比支付，例如议付金额按发票金额的 95%支付。　　V 汇= V 发×95%

2. 小写金额填货币代号和阿拉伯数字，小数点保留两位，第三位小数四舍五入，不得涂改。

3. 大写金额则填写在“The sum of”后面，用大写英语文字表示，并在文字金额后面加上“ONLY”，以防止涂改。大小写必须保持一致。

① 计价货币的英文全称 ② 大写汇票金额 ③ 辅币，如 CENTS ④ 前“SAY”+大写金额+后“ONLY”（整）。

（2）实例：Exchange for USD28,500.00

The sum of SAY U.S.DOLLARS TWENTY EIGHT THOUSAND FIVE HUNDRED ONLY.

5 栏 出票地点及日期

（1）填写内容：地点一般就印制在汇票上，无需填写。日期由银行填写。

日期：一般参照提单日期填写，不要早于提单日期，但又不能超过信用证规定的交单期和有效期。提单日期≤汇票日期≤交单期和有效期

（2）实例：Shanghai　Jan. 5, 2014

6 栏 付款期限（at…sight of…）

（1）填写内容：根据 L/C 上汇票条款所规定的付款期限填写,一般分为即期付款和远期付款两类。

（2）实例：

即期付款：At***sight of/At …sight of/At- - -sight of

远期付款：见票后若干天付款：at 60 DAYS AFTER sight of 见票后 60 天

出票后若干天付款：at 60 DAYS DATE SIGHT

提单后若干天付款：at 60 DAYS sight AFTER DATE OF B/L

7 栏 受款人（又称汇票抬头 Pay to the order of…）

（1）填写内容:信用证项下,如办理议付，则填写议付行名称或填写受益人指定银行。限制议付的 L/C,该栏只能填限制议付银行的名称。

（2）实例:

pay to the order of BANK OF CHINA, HUNAN BRANCH

8 栏　付款人（又称受票人 To…）

（1）填写内容:《UCP600》规定信用证业务下汇票付款人应为开证行或其指定银行。

（2）实例:

To: BANK OF MONTREL, MONTREL,CANADA

9 栏　出票人（Drawer）

（1）填写内容:一般是在汇票右下角打上受益人公司的名称及业务员姓名,多采用加盖受益人公司印章并手签的方式。

（2）实例:

HUNAN PROVINCIAL IMP&EXP CORP.

陈明

AUTHORIIED SIGNATURE

（二）托收项下汇票的缮制

托收项下汇票的缮制与信用证项下汇票的缮制大致相同，其区别的具体内容如下：

1 栏　出票依据（Draw under…L/C NO.…Dated ）

（1）填写内容：托收项下的汇票只需在 Draw under 后填写 For collection，其他不填。

（2）实例:

Drawn under　For collection

2 栏　付款期限（at…sight of…）

（1）填写内容：支付方式一般为 D/P 或者 D/A，填写在 AT 的前面，付款期限应填写在 AT 与 SIGHT 的中间。

（2）实例:

D/P At *** Sight　　即期付款交单

D/P At 60 DAYS Sight　60 天付款交单

3 栏　受款人（又称汇票抬头 Pay to the order of…）

（1）填写内容：收款人应填出口商。但实践中绝大多数都是填由出口商所委托的某家银行即托收行。

（2）实例：

Pay to the order of HSBC, SHANGHAI BRANCH

4 栏　付款人（又称受票人 To…）

（1）填写内容：托收项下汇票的付款人（Drawee）同样是在汇票的左下角“To”后面填写，填写的是进出口合同中的进口方名称和详细地址。

（2）实例：

TO: ABC TRADING CO., LTD.

LOS ANGELES, U.S.A

子项目二　信用证汇票及托收

汇票典型业务演示

上接项目八，在取得装运单据后，单证员李望在此项目中应完成的工作任务包括：

任务 1：认真审核信用证中的汇票条款。

任务 2：根据信用证、发票和装运资料等按要求缮制汇票。

提单上标注的装船日期为 AUG. 24, 2012

信用证如下：

SEQUENCE OF TOTAL	27:	1/1
FORM OF DC	40A:	IRREVOCABLE
DC NO	20:	DC HMN214479
DATE OF ISSUE	31C:	120720
APPLICABLE RULES	40E:	UCP LATEST VERSION
EXPIRY DATE AND PLACE	31D:	120919 IN COUNTRY OF BENEFICIARY
APPLICANT	50:	ELBY GIFTS INC.879 INDUSTRIEL BOIS DES FILION,QUEBEC, J6Z 4T3, CANADA
BENEFICIARY	59:	LILING PENGXING CERAMIC FACTORY WUSHI JIASHU LILING HUNAN, CHINA
AMOUNT	32B:	USD27,010.40
PCT 0R AMT TOLERANCE	39A:	10/10
AVAILABLE WITH/BY	41D:	ANY BANK BY NEGOTIATION
DRAFTS AT	42C:	AT SIGHT FOR FULL INVOICE VALUE
DRAWEE	42A:	ISSUING BANK
PARTIAL SHIPMENTS	43P:	ALLOWED
TRANSHIPMENT	43T:	ALLOWED
PORT OF LOADING	44E:	SHENZHEN, CHINA
PORT OF DISCHARGE	44F:	PRINCE RUPERT,BC
LATEST DATE OF SHIPMENT	44D:	120905
DESCRIPTION OF GOODS OR SERVICES	45A:	CERAMIC CUPS AND BOWLS AS PER S/C NO.:CB121039 CIF PRINCE RUPERT, BC ALL PACKED IN CARTONS.
DOCUMENTS REQUIRED	46A:	+ ORIGINAL SIGNED INVOICE PLUS THREE COPIES. + FULL SET OF CLEAN MULTIMODAL TRAN-

SPORT DOCUMENT PLUS 2 N/N COPIES, MADE TO THE ORDER OF HSBC BANK CANADA, SHOWING ON BOARD NOTATION, MARKED FREIGHT PREPAID, AND NOTIFY APPLICANT (STATING FULL NAME AND ADDRESS).

+ INSURANCE POLICY OR CERTIFICATE BLANK INDORSED, FOR THE INVOICE VALUE PLUS 10% COVERING ALL RISKS AND S.R.CC. FROM WAREHOUSE TO WARE-HOUSE.

+ ORIGINAL PACKING LIST PLUS 2 COPIES

+ GSP CERTIFICATE OF ORIGIN FORM A, IN ONE ORIGINAL PLUS 2 COPIES, INDICATING COUNTRY OF ORIGIN, COUNTERCHOPPED BY GOVERNMENT AUTHORITIES OR EXP-ORTER'S STATMENT OF ORIGIN

+ SHIPPING NOTE INCLUDING SHIPPING MARKS, CTN NO., B/L NO., QUANTITY, VESSEL'S NAME, VOYAGE NO., SHOULD BE SENT TO THE ISSUING BANK ON THE DATE OF SHIPMENT.

ADDITIONAL CONDITIONS 47A: + BENEFICIARY'S DETAILS:

CTC: MILLER LEE

TEL: 86-731-2338-4199

FAX: 86-731-2338-4298

FOLLOWING CHARGES ARE FOR BENEFICIARY'S ACCOUNT:

1) REIMBURSEMENT/REMITTANCE CHARGES

2) DISCREPANCY FEE OF USD/CAD/EUR100 PLUS ALL RELEVANT CABLE CHARGES WILL BE DEDUCTED FROM EACH PRESENTATION OF DISCREPANT

DOCUMENTS UNDER THIS DC.

CHARGES 71B: ALL BANKING CHARGES OUTSIDE COUN-TRY OF ISSUE FOR ACCOUNT OF BENEFI-CIARY/EXPORTER

PERIOD OF PRESENTATION 48: WITHIN 15 DAYS AFTER THE DATE OF SHIPMENT BUT WITHIN THE VALIDITY OF

		THE CREDIT
CONFIRMATION INSTRUCTIONS	49:	WITHOUT
INFO TO PRESENTING BK	78:	+ UPON RECEIPT OF DOCUMENTS CONFORMING TO THE TERMS OF THIS CREDIT WE UNDERTAKE TO REIMBURSE YOU IN THE CURRENCY OF THIS CREDIT IN ACCORDANCE WITH YOUR INSTRUCTIONS, LESS CABLE CHARGES, + FORWARD DOCUMENTS IN ONE LOT BY COURIER AT BENEFICIARY'S EXPENSES TO HSBC BANK CANADA, TRADE AND SUPPLY CHAIN, 5100 SHERBROOKE STREET EAST, SUITE 190, MONTREAL,QUEBEC,H1V 3R9 CANADA. + THE AMOUNT OF EACH DRAWING MUST BE ENDORSED ON THE REVERSE OF THIS DC BY THE NEGOTIATING/PRESENTING BANK.

发票如下：

PENGXING IMP&EXP COMPANY

LILING PENGXING CERAMIC FACTORY

WUSHI JIASHU LILING HUNAN CHINA

TEL: 86-731-23384199 FAX: 86-731-23384298

COMMERCIAL INVOICE

TO:	ELBY GIFTS INC. 879 INDUSTRIEL BOIS DES FILION QUEBEC, J6Z 4T3, CANADA	**INVOICE NO.:**	PX12IVN1039
		INVOICE DATE:	AUG. 16, 2012
		S/C NO.:	S/C NO.: CB121039
		S/C DATE:	JUL. 5, 2012
FROM:	SHENZHEN, CHINA	**TO:**	PRINCE RPERT, BC, CANADA
Letter of Credit No.:	DC HMN214479	**Issued By:**	HSBC BANK, MONTREAL CANADA

Marks and Numbers	Number and kind of package Description of goods	Quantity	Unit Price	Amount
	CERAMIC CUPS AND BOWLS		CIF PRINCE RUPERT, BC	
ELBY		CTN	U.S.D	U.S.D
S/C NO.:CB121039	V23-234	228	4.05	3,693.60
NO: 1-1589	V23-234F	228	4.05	3,693.60
	V23-235	190	2.40	3,648.00
	V23-236	189	2.10	3,175.20
	V23-237	186	1.95	2,901.60
	V23-2348	190	2.04	3,100.80
	36-062	191	2.30	3,514.40
	36-063	187	2.12	3,171.52
	Total:	1,589 CTNS		U.S.D 26,898.72

SAY TOTAL: U.S DOLLARS TWENTY SIX THOUSAND EIGHT HUNDRED AND NINETY EIGHT AND CENTS SEVENTY TWO(USD26,898.72)ONLY

PENGXING IMP&EXP COMPANY
李 望

由于汇票条款中出现了溢短装条款"PCT 0R AMT TOLERANCE:10/10"，必须根据商业发票确定交货数量 1589CTNS 和金额 USD26,898.72，据此，单证员李望缮制了一份汇票。

凭　信用证　　　　　　　　　　　　第　　　　号
Drawn under HSBC BANK CANADA　　　　L/C No. DC HMN214479
日期　　　　　　　　　　按　　　　息　　　　付款
Dated JULY 20, 2012 Payable with interest @________% per annum
号码　　　　　　汇票金额　　　　　　中国，长沙　年　月　日
No.: PX12IVN1039 Exchange for USD26,898.72 Changsha, China AUG.26,2012
见票　　　　　　　　　　　　　日后（本汇票之副本未付）
At *** Sight of this FIRST of Exchange(Second of Exchange being unpaid)
Pay to the order of BANK OF CHINA, HUNAN BRANCH 或其指定人付金额
The sum of U.S. DOLLARS TWENTY SIX THOUSAND EIGHT HUNDRED NINETY EIGHT AND CENTS SEVENTY TWO ONLY.
To: HSBC BANK CANADA
TRADE AND SUPPLY CHAIN, 5100 SHERBROOKE STREET EAST,
SUITE 190, MONTREAL,QUEBEC,H1V 3R9 CANADA.

LILING PENGXING CERAMIC FACTORY
李　望

子项目三 信用证汇票及托收汇票拓展业务操作

能力实训项目 1：信用证下汇票的缮制

上接项目八，根据 JIANGSU I-TOUCH BUSINESS SERVICE LTD 第 0684130117426 号信用证的要求，2013 年 9 月 24 日，单证员彭婷装船完毕后根据信用证、商业发票和提单缮制汇票。

1. 信用证

SEQUENCE OF TOTAL	27:	1/1
FORM OF DC.	40A:	IRREVOCABLE
DC. NO.	20:	0684130117426
DATE OF ISSUE	31C:	130825
APPLICABLE RULES	40E:	UCP LATEST VERSION
EXPIRY DATE AND PLACE	31D:	131024,CHINA
APPLICANT	50:	M/S. MEMORY STEEL CORPORATION 73/A, LAL MOHAN SHAHA STREET (DHOLAIKHAL), DHAKA-1100. BANGLADESH.
BENEFICIARY	59:	JIANGSU I-TOUCH BUSINESS SERVICE LTD, ROOM 117, JIANGSU EDIFICE ZHANGJIAGANG FREE TRADE ZONE, JIANGSU, CHINA TEL:86-512-56363783
AMOUNT	32B:	USD35,000.00
AVAILABLE WITH/BY	41D:	ANY BANK IN CHINA BY NEGOTIATION
DRAFTS AT	42C:	AT SIGHT FOR FULL INVOICE VALUE
DRAWEE	42A:	DRAWN ON US
PARTIAL SHIPMENTS	43P:	ALLOWED
TRANSSHIPMENT	43T:	ALLOWED
PORT OF LOADING	44A:	ANY SEA PORT, CHINA
PORT OF DISCHARGE	44B:	CHITTAGONG SEA PORT, BANGLADESH
LATEST DATE OF SHIPMENT	44C:	131009
DESCRIPTION OF GOODS	45A:	201/2B SECONDARY GRADE STAINLESS

STEEL SHEET OF WIDTH 1219MM THICKNESS 1MM TO 3MM, QTY:25,000KGS AT THE RATE OF USD1.40/KG

FOR TOTAL AMOUNT OF USD35,000.00 CFR CHITTAGONG, BANGLADESH. AS PER BENEFICIARY'S PROFORMA INVOICE NO. SK20130802-001 DATED AUG 2,2013

DOCUMENTS REQUIRED 46A: +MANUALLY SIGNED COMMERCIAL INVOICE IN TRIPLICATE CERTIFYING MERCHANDISE TO BE OF CHINA ORIGIN AND INDICATING THAT THE GOODS ARE BEING IMPORTED AGAINST IRC NO.BA-0171646, TI NO.157-107-0121, VAT REGISTRATION NO.9141093671.

+FULL SET OF CLEAN 'SHIPPED ON BOARD' OCEAN BILL OF LADING SHOWING' FREIGHT PREPAID' MADE OUT TO ORDER AND BLANK INDORSED, NOTIFY APPLICANT.

+PACKING LIST IN TRIPLICATE SHOWING GROSS WEIGHT, NET WEIGHT.

+CERTIFICATE OF ORIGIN ISSUED AND LEGALED BY CCPIT

+ BENEFICIARY'S DECLARATION SHOULD CERTIFY THAT THE COUNTRY OF ORIGIN HAS BEEN PRINTED ON GOODS PACKING BAG.

+BENEFICIARY SHOULD SEND A FAX OR BY COURIER TO L/C OPENING BANK WITHIN FIVE DAYS FROM THE OF SHIPMENT, ADVISING THE DATE OF SHIPMENT, VESSEL'S NAME, AMOUNT OF BILL AND L/C NO. AND A COPY OF THIS FAX SHOULD ACCOMPANY THE SHIPPING DOCUMENTS.

+SHIPMENT BY ISRAELI LINER IS PROHIBITED AND A CERTIFICATE TO THIS EFFECT ISSUED BY THE SHIPPING COMPANY MUST ACCOMPANY THE ORIGINAL DOCUMENTS.

CHARGES	71B:	ALL FOREIGN BANK CHARGES ARE FOR THE ACCOUNT OF THE BENEFICIARY.
PERIOD OF PRESENTATION	48:	15 DAYS FROM SHIPMENT DATE BUT WITHIN VALIDITY OF THE CREDIT

2. 其他信息

发票号码：67080-9

提单日期：SEP. 13，2013

凭　　　　　　　　　　　　信用证　　　第　　　号

Drawn under ________________ L/C No. ________________

日期　　　　　　　　　　　按　　　息　　　付款

Dated ________________ Payable with interest @ ________ % per annum

号码　　　　汇 票 金 额　　　　中 国，上海　　年 月 日

No.: ________________ Exchange for ________ Shanghai, China ________________

见票　　　　　　　　　　　日后（本 汇 票 之 副 本 未 付）

At ________________ Sight of this FIRST of Exchange(Second of Exchange being unpaid)

Pay to the order of ________________ 或其指定人

付金额

The sum of ________________

To:

For:

能力实训项目 2：托收下汇票的缮制

上接项目八，根据合同的要求，2013 年 10 月 18 日，单证员王丹装船完毕后根据合同、商业发票和提单相关信息缮制汇票。

1. 合同信息

合同卖方：GUANGDONG JIAMEI TRADING CO., LTD.

合同买方：G.KLEEYE GMBH, GERMANY

支付方式：D/P AT SIGHT

托收银行：BANK OF CONSTUCTION, GUANGZHOU BRANCH

合同金额：EUR70,800.00

2. 其他信息

发票号码：GDJM2013045

提单日期：OCT. 17, 2013

凭 信用证 第 号

Drawn under ______________ L/C No. ______________

日期 按 息 付款

Dated ______________ Payable with interest @ ________ % per annum

号码 汇 票 金 额 中 国，上海 年 月 日

No.: ______________ Exchange for ________ Shanghai, China ______________

见票 日后（本 汇 票 之 副 本 未 付）

At ______________ Sight of this FIRST of Exchange(Second of Exchange being unpaid)

Pay to the order of ______________ 或其指定人

付金额

The sum of

To:

For:

项目十　其他单据制作业务

项目预期目标

通过对信用证项下装运通知条款、受益人证明条款及船公司证明条款的认真解读，结合该项目提供的商业发票等相关单据，并介绍几种主要的附属单据背景知识，使同学们了解附属单据的使用场合及制作要领。

在项目实施过程中，通过对三种单据制作任务的分解，在分工与合作中逐渐培养审核、制单、归类等国际商务单证基本职业能力，亦培养独立操作业务和与其他业务或政府部门有效沟通的能力。

表 10-1　　项目预期目标

目标类型	其他单据的制作
知识目标	熟悉货运单据与其他单据的衔接
	掌握几种重要的其他单据的制作
能力目标	能根据贸易术语及信用证要求有效制作其他单据
	能备齐全套单据
职业素质目标	独立业务操作能力
	与国外客户及船公司的沟通衔接能力

项目实施条件

1. 学生能够在实训室对该项目进行分组讨论并实施
2. 指导教师具备扎实的外贸业务基础

开篇业务引入

根据第 DC HMN214479 号信用证的要求，长沙鹏兴进出口有限公司在完成货物的装运并取得提单后还需出具装运通知及受益人证明，同时信用证还要求一份船公司证明作为议付单据，这类单据统称为其他单据或附属单据。该项目任务具体由单证员李望负责。2012 年 8 月 25 日，单证员李望根据 L/C 规定：“+ SHIPPING NOTE INCLUDING SHIPPING MARKS, CTN NO., B/L NO., QUANTITY, VESSEL’S NAME, VOYAGE NO., SHOULD BE SENT TO THE ISSUING BANK ON THE DATE OF SHIPMENT.” 等条款，以及缮制好的商业发票及装运资料等，制作三种其他单据。

子项目一　其他单据的制作

一、其他单据的含义及使用场合

在国际贸易中，卖方应在发货完毕后按合同或信用证要求提供相关单据，这是卖方在国际贸易中应该履行的基础业务之一，同时也是卖方安全收汇的前提之一。卖方除应在提供基本结汇单证如商业发票、运输单据等外，在某些特定的情况下，往往还要根据买方、进口国海关的要求，提供如装箱单、受益人证明、装运通知、船公司证明等一些常见的辅助性结汇单据，这些单据对于出口商安全结汇都是必不可少的。

二、其他单据的主要范围

（一）受益人证明（Beneficiary‘s Certificate）

受益人证明亦称受益人声明（Beneficiary‘s Statement/Declaration），是由受益人签发的证实某件事实的单据，它是信用证支付方式下买方要求的常见单据之一。

1. 受益人证明的种类

（1）寄单证明（Beneficiary‘s Certificate for Dispatch of Documents）。

（2）寄样证明（Beneficiary‘s Certificate for Dispatch of Shipment Sample）。

（3）包装和标签证明。

2. 受益人证明的基本内容

受益人证明的内容一般包括：单据名称、出证日期与地点、抬头人、事由、证明文句、受益人名称及签章等，具体如下：

（1）单据名称。这种单据的名称因所证明的事项不同而略异，可能是寄单证明、寄样证明（船样、样卡和码样等）、取样证明、证明货物产地、品质、唛头、包装和标签情况、电抄形式的装运通知、证明产品生产过程、证明商品也已检验、环保人方面的证明（非童工、非狱工制造）等。

（2）出证日期和地点。单据一般都应在规定的时间内做出，并列明出证地点。

（3）证明上通常会显示发票号、合同号或信用证号以表明与其他单据的关系。

（4）受益人证明应明确列明抬头人。

（5）证明的内容严格与合同或信用证规定相符。

（6）因属于证明性质，按有关规定证明人（受益人）必须签字。

3. 受益人证明的应用

（1）买方为了某种原因如转口货物等，要求在限定时间内先直接邮寄必要的单据以便及时提货、通关或再另转口。买方为了确保卖方能按时寄单，在信用证条款中明确此要求并由受益人出具已寄送单据的证明，此即为寄单证明。

（2）买方为预先取得装运的货样，要求寄样的寄样证明。

（3）要求受益人在限定时间内将装运情况通知买方而出具的证明。

（4）买方要求单据由买方所属国的领事签证，但出口所在地又无该国领事而出具的证明。

（5）要求卖方执行某些行为而出具相应的证明。

（二）装运通知（Shipping Advice/Note）

装运通知或称装船证明（Shipping Statement 或 Shipping Declaration），即按信用证或合同规定出口方在订妥舱位或货物装船后向买方发出的通知，以便对方办理保险或准备提货、租仓等。其目的在于让进口商做好筹措资金、付款和接货准备，如成交条件FOB/FCA、CFR/CPT等还需要向进口国保险公司发出该通知以便其为进口商办理货物保险手续，出口装船通知应按合同或信用证规定的时间发出，通知客人发货的细节，包括船名、航班次、开船日、预计抵港日、货物及数量、金额、包装件数、唛头、目的港代理人等。接收通知的一般是进口方，也有的是进口方指定的保险公司。该通知副本（Copy of Telex/Fax）常作为向银行交单议付的单据之一，在进口方派船接货的交易条件下，进口商实现使船、货衔接也会向出口方发出有关通知。

装船通知一般英文信函的格式制作，也可根据业务需要自拟，但内容一定要符合信用证的规定，一般只提供一份正本，以电报的形式通知，副本则随其他单据交银行议付。

装运通知的内容主要包括：收件人名称和地址；合同号和信用证号、货名、数量、金额；船名、航次；开航日期；提单号码及出单日期等。

注意：出单日期不能超过信用证规定的日期，如装船后2天内（within two days after shipping）。如果信用证规定IMMEDIATELY AFTER SHIPMENT（装船后立即通知），应视为在提单后3天之内。

（三）船公司证明（Certificate of Shipping Co.,）

船公司证明为几类单据的统称，根据实际业务的需要通常有以下几种：

1. 船龄证明（Certificate of Age of Vessel/Certificate of Vessel's Age）

有些国家/地区来证规定装载货物的船舶的船龄不得超过15年，受益人必须要求船代或船公司出具载货船只的船龄证明书（Certificate to evidence the ship is not over 15 years old 或 is under 15 years of age），这样的要求主要目的在于禁止使用老龄船，保护货物运输安全。

2. 船籍证明（Certificate of Registry）

它用于证明船舶所属国籍，指的是证明船舶的国籍、船籍港及船舶所有权等得一种书面文书。一般的船籍证书的有效期为10年，自登记之日算起。有效期满，船舶所有人持原船籍证书到原登记机关换发新的船级证书。根据我国《海商法》及船舶登记规则的规定，船舶经登记并取得船舶国籍证书后，才有权悬挂我国国旗在海上航行。由此可见，船籍证书属于法律登记性质，船舶不得具有双重国籍。进口商要求出口商提供船籍证明一般是因为一些政治原因，如巴基斯坦银行开来的信用证会要求出口商提供载货船舶的船籍不属于印度的证明，阿拉伯国家银行开来的信用证会要求出口商提供载货船舶的船籍不属于以色列的证明。

3. 船级证明（Confirmation of Class）

有的信用证规定提供不同国家的船级社证明，对这样的要求我们通常应予以满足。

世界上比较著名的船级社，有英国劳合级社（LD）、德国劳埃德船级社（GL）、挪威船级社（DNV）、法国船级局（BV）、日本海事协会（NK）、美国航运局（ABS）、中国船级社（China Classification Society）等。中国船级社是中华人民共和国交通部所属的船舶检验局。船级证书除了记载船舶的主要技术性能外，还绘制出相应的船级符号，各国船级社对船级符号的规定不同。中国船级社的船级符号为ZC。劳合社的船级符号为LR，标志100A1,100A表示该船的船体和机器设备是根据劳氏规范和规定建造的，I表示船舶的装备如船锚、锚链和绳索等处于良好和有效的状态。

4. 黑名单证明（Black List Certificate）

证明运送货物的船舶不在黑名单之列和保险公司不在黑名单之列，由船舶公司和保险公司出具。典型的是阿拉伯国家所要求的抵制以色列证明（CERTIFICATE OF BOYCOTT ISRAEL）。其通常规定为：THE VESSEL CARRYING THE GOODS IS NOT ISRAELI AND WILL NOT CALL ON ANY ISRAELI PORTS WHILE CARRYING THE GOODS AND THAT THE VESSEL IS NOT BANNED ENTRY TO THE PORT OF THE ARAB STATES FOR ANY REASONS WHATEVER UNDER LAW AND THE LAWS AND REGULATIONS OF SUCH SATES ALLOWED.（船上所装货物为非以色列原产，船不经停任何以色列港口，船只可依法自由进入阿拉伯国家法律和规则所容许进出的港口。）

（四）运输和航行证明

1. 航程证明（Certificate of Itinerary）

它主要说明航程中船舶停靠的港口，一些阿拉伯国家开来的信用证中，往往要求在提单上随附声明一份，明确船籍、船名、船东及途中所经港口顺序，出口方须按要求签发此类证明并按证明中所述行驶、操作船舶。

2. 转船证明书（Certificate of Transshipment）

出口方出具转船证明书，说明出口货物将在中途转船且已联系妥当，并由托运人负责将有关转船事项通知收货人。

3. 货装具名船舶证明

如信用证要求："A CERTIFICATE FROM THE SHIPPING COMPANY OR ITS AGENT STATING THAT GOODS ARE SHIPPED BY COSCO"，意思是要求出口方提供由船公司或其代理出具的货装中国远洋集装箱运输有限公司的证明。

4. 船长收据（Captain's Receipt）

船长收据是指船长收到随船带交给收货人单据时的收单证明。船长收据的内容一般是：收到单据的种类、分数，并声明在船舶到达目的港后交给指定人。有的信用证规定，样品或单据副本交载货船只的船长代交进口商，并提供船长收据，若委托船长带去而未取得船长收据将影响出口商收汇，常见于近洋运输。如今随着航空快递业的发展，现在船长收据已基本不用。此外，船证还包括进港证明、运费已交收据、港口费用单（Port Charges Documents）、装卸准备就绪通知书和装卸时间事实记录等，由于政治原因，巴基斯坦和印度不允许悬挂对方国旗的船舶靠岸，巴基斯坦港口还不接受来自南非、韩国、以色列和中国台湾的船舶，若要求出具相应证明的，出口方必须提供。

5. 关于 SMC、DOC 和 SOLAS

这几个缩略语近年来常出现在信用证的要求中，SMC（Safety Management Certificate 船舶安全管理证书）和 DOC（Documents of Compliance 安全符合证书，也有人称其为船/港保安符合证书）是按照国际安全管理规则（ISM）的规定，载货船舶应在船上拥有的必要证书。我国海事局按 ISM 的规章发给船公司 DOC，船舶则可获 SMC，如果船公司没有相应证书则无法按信用证要求来出具此类证明。信用证中的一般要求是："THE CARRYING VESSEL SHOULD COMPLY WITH PROVISIONS OF THE (ISM) CODE WHICH NECESSITATES THAT SUCH VESSEL MUST HAVE ON BOARD, COPIES OF THE TWO (WMC AND DOC) VALID CERTIFICATES AND COPIES OF SUCH CERTIFICATE MUST BE PRESENTED WITH THE ORIGINAL DOCUMENTS." 也可体现为"Certificate issued, signed and stamped by the owner/carrier/master of the carrying vessel holds valid ISM certificate and ISPS (International Shipping and Port Security Safety Code,《国际船舶和港口设施保安规则》)"；SOLAS 指的是《1974 年国际海上人命安全公约》（简称 SOLAS 公约），公约规定，船舶应持有"安全管理证书"正本，其船名与国籍证书一致，所载公司名称与"符合证明"中的公司名称一致。

三、几种主要的附属单据制作

（一）受益人证明的缮制

1. 单据名称（Name of Documents）

单据名称位于单据正上方，可根据信用证要求确定具体名称。一般标明"Beneficiary's Certificate（受益人证明）"、"Beneficiary's Statement（受益人声明）或 Beneficiary's Declaration（受益人申明）"等。

2. 出证日期与地点（Date and Place of Issue）

按照实际签发日期与地点填写。地点一般即受益人所在地点；日期一般与提单日期相同或者稍晚，但不能迟于交单期和证效期。

3. 抬头人（To）

按信用证的要求填写开证申请人的名称，如无特别规定，也可填写笼统的抬头，如"TO WHOM IT MAY CONCERN"或"DAER SIRS"。

4. 交易参考号号码（Ref No.）

一般填写信用证号，非信用证支付方式下则填写发票号或合同号。有些信用证规定除汇票和发票外，其他单据都不能显示信用证号码，则不可填写信用证号码。

5. 证明内容（Content of Certificate）

此项内容必须与信用证要求的内容严格相符。通常以"We hereby certify that…"、"This is to certify that …"等常见句型开头，然后按照信用证中的受益人证明条款要求照抄，但有时根据实际情况也应作相应修改，如信用证要求受益人寄单据则提供寄单证明；若信用证要求受益人寄货样则提供寄样证明。

6. 受益人名称及签章（Signature）

该栏一般填写卖方或受益人（如出口公司）的名称，由法人代表或经办人签字盖章。

受益人证明一般不分正副本。若来证要求正本，可在单据名称的正下方打上“Origin”字样。证明的右下方必须由受益人即出口公司签章，才能生效。

（二）装运通知的缮制

1. 单据名称（Name of Documents）

主要体现为：Shipping/Shipment Advice，Advice of shipment 等，也有人将其称为 Shipping Statement/Declaration/Note，简称（S/A,S/N）如果信用证有具体要求，应严格按照信用证要求缮制。

2. 抬头（To）

该栏一般为提货人，即信用证开证申请人或合同的买方，有时在 CFR 术语下要求将装运通知同时寄给进口方及保险公司以保证业务衔接，此时则需做成两个抬头，并注明详细地址、如电话或传真号。

3. 合同号或信用证号（Contract No./L/C No.）

如信用证项下应注明信用证号及合同号；非信用证方式则注明合同或订单号。

4. 品名（Description of Goods）

一般只需列明品名品牌即可。

5. 数量（Quantity）

填写货物的外包装数量及包装单位，如有规定也可以同时填写内包装数量。

6. 船名及航次号（Vessel’s Name & Voyage No.）

应填写载货船只的船名及航次。

7. 预计开航日（ETD）

如果知道确切的开航日期，则应填写实际开航日，否则填写提单签发日。

8. 预计到港日期（ETA）

填写船舶预计到达目的港的时间，以便对方做好提货准备。

9. 提单号（B/L No.）

填写签发的海运提单的提单号码。

10. 日期（Date）

填写缮制装运通知的日期，该日期应严格按照信用证规定的日期填写，否则单证不符。常见的有以下三种表达方式：以小时为准（Within 24/48 Hours）；装船后立即通知（Immediately after shipment ），此时应视为提单后 3 天内发出；以天为准（Within 2 Days After Shipment Date），假如提单日为 4 月 10 日，则装运通知最晚不能超过 11 日午夜 12 点发出。

11. 签署（Signature）

此处一般可以不签署，若信用证要求，一般缮制卖方或受益人的名称。

（三）船公司证明的缮制

1. 单据名称（Name of Documents）

该栏应严格按照信用证要求填制相应的单据名称。

2. 抬头（To）

一般都笼统缮制“TO WHOM IT MAY CONCERN”（致启者）。

3. 出证地址和日期（Date And Place of Issue）

一般应为提单的签发地址和日期。

4. 船名及航次号（Vessel's Name & Voyage No.）

填写承担本次运输的船名及航次号。

5. 提单号（B/L No.）

填写本次运输的海运提单的提单号。

6. 证明内容（Content of Certificate）

严格按照信用证条款的要求，根据实际情况缮制，如证明船籍、船龄或船级等内容，格式与受益人证明类似。

7. 签章（Signature）

该类单据必须签章，且签章人与提单签发人一致，一般为船公司或多式联运经营人及其代理等。

子项目二　装运通知等典型业务演示

上接项目八，根据信用证要求，受益人在取得货运单据之后应立即制作装运通知及受益人证明并在规定时间内发出，据此，鹏兴公司单证员李望在此项目中的工作任务包括：

任务 1：认真审核信用证中的装运通知及受益人证明条款；

任务 2：准备制作单据要用的相关装运资料；

任务 3：制作装运通知并及时发送；

任务 4：制作受益人证明。

1. 信用证

SEQUENCE OF TOTAL	27:	1/1
FORM OF DC	40A:	IRREVOCABLE
DC NO	20:	DC HMN214479
DATE OF ISSUE	31C:	120720
APPLICABLE RULES	40E:	UCP LATEST VERSION
EXPIRY DATE AND PLACE	31D:	120919 IN COUNTRY OF BENEFICIARY
APPLICANT	50:	ELBY GIFTS INC.879 INDUSTRIEL BOIS DES FILION,QUEBEC, J6Z 4T3, CANADA
BENEFICIARY	59:	LILING PENGXING CERAMIC FACTORY WUSHI JIASHU LILING HUNAN, CHINA
AMOUNT	32B:	USD27,010.40
PCT CR AMT TOLERANCE	39A:	10/10
AVAILABLE WITH/BY	41D:	ANY BANK BY NEGOTIATION
DRAFTS AT	42C:	AT SIGHT FOR FULL INVOICE VALUE

DRAWEE	42A:	ISSUING BANK
PARTIAL SHIPMENTS	43P:	ALLOWED
TRANSHIPMENT	43T:	ALLOWED
PORT OF LOADING	44E:	SHENZHEN, CHINA
PORT OF DISCHARGE	44F:	PRINCE RUPERT,BC
LATEST DATE OF SHIPMENT	44D:	120905
DESCRIPTION OF GOODS OR SERVICES	45A:	CERAMIC CUPS AND BOWLS AS PER S/C NO.:CB121039 CIF PRINCE RUPERT,BC ALL PACKED IN CARTONS.
DOCUMENTS REQUIRED	46A:	+ ORIGINAL SIGNED INVOICE PLUS THREE COPIES. + FULL SET OF CLEAN MULTIMODAL TRANSPORT DOCUMENT PLUS 2 N/N COPIES, MADE TO THE ORDER OF HSBC BANK CANADA, SHOWING ON BOARD NOTATION, MARKED FREIGHT PREPAID, AND NOTIFY APPLICANT(STATING FULL NAME AND ADDRESS). + INSURANCE POLICY OR CERTIFICATE BLANK INDORSED, FOR THE INVOICE VALUE PLUS 10% COVERING ALL RISKS AND S.R.CC. FROM WAREHOUSE TO WAREHOUSE. + ORIGINAL PACKING LIST PLUS 2 COPIES + GSP CERTIFICATE OF ORIGIN FORM A, IN ONE ORIGINAL PLUS 2 COPIES, INDICATING COUNTRY OF ORIGIN, COUNTERCHOPPED BY GOVERNMENT AUTHORITIES OR EXPORTER'S STATMENT OF ORIGIN + SHIPPING NOTE INCLUDING SHIPPING MARKS, CTN NO., B/L NO., QUANTITY, VESSEL'S NAME, VOYAGE NO., SHOULD BE SENT TO THE ISSUING BANK ON THE DATE OF SHIPMENT. +BENEFICIARY SHOULD CERTIFY THAT ALL OF THE DOCUMENTS ARE TRUE AND CORRECT, THEN PRESENT TO THE BANK ACCOMPANIED WITH OTHER NEGOTIABLE DOCUMENTS

CHARGES	71B:	ALL BANKING CHARGES OUTSIDE COUNTRY OF ISSUE　FOR ACCOUNT OF BENEFICIARY/ EXPORTER
PERIOD OF PRESENTATION	48:	WITHIN 15 DAYS AFTER THE DATE OF SHIPMENT BUT WITHIN THE VALIDITY OF THE CREDIT
CONFIRMATION INSTRUCTIONS	49:	WITHOUT

2. 海运提单

1. Shipper Insert Name, Address and Phone

LILING PENGXING CERAMIC FACTORY
WUSHI JIASHU LILING HUNAN, CHINA

许可证号

B/L No.
COSFMT3821018

2. Consignee Insert Name, Address and Phone

TO THE ORDER OF HSBC
BANK CANADA

中远集装箱运输有限公司
COSCO CONTAINER LINES

TLX: 33057 COSCO CN
FAX: +86(021) 6545 8984
ORIGINAL

3. Notify Party Insert Name, Address and Phone
(It is agreed that no responsibility shall attach to the Carrier or his agents for failure to notify)

ELBY GIFTS INC.
879 INDUSTRIEL
BOIS DES FILION

4. Combined Transport * Pre-carriage by TRAIN NO.:67589	5. Combined Transport* Place of Receipt CHANGSHA
6. Ocean Vessel Voy. No. COSCO SEATTLE V.0078E	7. Port of Loading YANTIAN,SHENZHEN, CHINA
8. Port of Discharge PRINCE RUPERT, BC, CANADA	9. Combined Transport * Place of Delivery BOIS DES FILION, CANADA

Port-to-Port or Combined Transport
BILL OF LADING

RECEIVED in external apparent good order and condition except as otherwise noted. The total number of packages or units stuffed in the container, the description of the goods and the weights shown in this Bill of Lading are furnished by the Merchants, and which the carrier has no reasonable means of checking and is not a part of this Bill of Lading contract. The carrier has issued the number of Bills of Lading stated below, all of this tenor and date, one of the original Bills of Lading must be surrendered and endorsed or signed against the delivery of the shipment and whereupon any other original Bills of Lading shall be void. The Merchants agree to be bound by the terms and conditions of this Bill of Lading as if each had personally signed this Bill of Lading.
SEE clause 4 on the back of this Bill of Lading (Terms continued on the back hereof, please read carefully).
*Applicable Only When Document Used as a Combined Transport Bill of Lading.

Marks & Nos. Container/Seal No.	No. of Containers or Packages	Description of Goods (If Dangerous Goods, See Clause 20)	Gross Weight Kgs	Measurement
N/M	1589CTNS CONTAINER NO.: CBHU8150082/ B45171/40'HQ	SHIPPER'S LOAD & COUNT & SEAL 1X40'HQ (F.C.L) S.T.C CY/CY ONE THOUSAND FIVE HUNDRED AND EIGHTY NINE(1589CTNS)CARTONS OF CERAMIC CUPS AND BOWLS FOB SHENZHEN, CHINA THIS SHIPMENT CONTAINS NO SOLID WOOD PACKING MATERIALS.	17,654.40 KGS	68.130 CBM
		Description of Contents for Shipper's Use Only (Not part of This B/L Contract)		

10. Total Number of containers and/or packages (in words) SAY ONE THOUSAND FIVE HUNDRED AND EIGHTY NINE CARTONS ONLY.

11. Freight & Charges	Revenue Tons	Rate	Per	Prepaid	Collect
FREIGHT COLLECT	AS ARRANGED				

Ex. Rate	Prepaid at	Payable at	Place and date of issue SHENZHEN, CHINA AUG. 24, 2012
	Total Prepaid	No. of Original B(s)/L THREE	Signed for the Carrier, COSCO CONTAINER LINES COSCO AS CARRIER XXXX

据此，李望制作了装运通知及受益人证明：

PENGXING IMP&EXP COMPANY

LILING PENGXING CERAMIC FACTORY

WUSHI JIASHU LILING HUNAN CHINA

TEL: 86-731-23384199 FAX: 86-731-23384298

SHIPPING NOTE

To: ELBY GIFTS INC.
879 INDUSTRIEL BOIS DES FILION QUEBEC,
J6Z 4T3, CANADA

Date: AUG. 24, 2012

From: SHENZHEN, CHINA **To:** PRINCE RUPERT, BC, CANADA

DEAR SIRS,

WE HEREBY INFORM YOU THAT ALL OF THE CARGO UNDER THE L/C MENTIONED HAVE BEEN SHIPPED. THE DETAILS ARE AS FOLLOWS,

C/I NO. &DATE:	PX12IVN1039, AUG. 16, 2012
B/L NO. &DATE:	B/L NO.: AUG.24 2012, SHENZHEN, CHINA
VESSEL &VOY.:	COSCO SEATTLE V.0078E
QUANTITY:	1589 CARTONS
MARKS:	ELBY S/C NO.:CB121039 NO: 1-1589

PENGXING IMP&EXP COMPANY

李 望

PENGXING IMP&EXP COMPANY

LILING PENGXING CERAMIC FACTORY

WUSHI JIASHU LILING HUNAN CHINA

TEL: 86-731-23384199 FAX: 86-731-23384298

BENEFICIARY'S CERTIFICATE

To: ELBY GIFTS INC.
879 INDUSTRIEL BOIS DES FILION QUEBEC,
J6Z 4T3, CANADA

Date: AUG. 26, 2012

From: SHENZHEN, CHINA **To:** PRINCE RUPERT, BC, CANADA

DEAR SIRS,

WE HEREBY CERTIFY THAT ALL OF THE DOCUMENTS ARE TURE AND CORRECT.

PENGXING IMP&EXP COMPANY

李 望

子项目三 装运通知等拓展业务操作

能力实训项目 1: 根据上海淼睿进出口有限公司第 0684130117426 号信用证的要求，2013 年 9 月 24 日，单证员彭婷根据信用证的要求，备齐相关装运资料完成三个任务。

1. 信用证

SEQUENCE OF TOTAL	27:	1/1
FORM OF DC.	40A:	IRREVOCABLE
DC. NO.	20:	0684130117426
DATE OF ISSUE	31C:	130825
APPLICABLE RULES	40E:	UCP LATEST VERSION
EXPIRY DATE AND PLACE	31D:	131024,CHINA
APPLICANT	50:	M/S. MEMORY STEEL CORPORATION 73/A, LAL MOHAN SHAHA STREET (DHOLAIKHAL), DHAKA-1100. BANGLADESH.

BENEFICIARY	59:	JIANGSU I-TOUCH BUSINESS SERVICE LTD, ROOM 117, JIANGSU EDIFICE ZHANGJIAGANG FREE TRADE ZONE, JIANGSU, CHINA TEL:86-512-56363783
AMOUNT	32B:	USD35,000.00
AVAILABLE WITH/BY	41D:	ANY BANK IN CHINA BY NEGOTIATION
DRAFTS AT	42C:	AT SIGHT FOR FULL INVOICE VALUE
DRAWEE	42A:	DRAWN ON US
PARTIAL SHIPMENTS	43P:	ALLOWED
TRANSSHIPMENT	43T:	ALLOWED
PORT OF LOADING	44A:	ANY SEA PORT, CHINA
PORT OF DISCHARGE	44B:	CHITTAGONG SEA PORT, BANGLADESH
LATEST DATE OF SHIPMENT	44C:	131009
DESCRIPTION OF GOODS	45A:	201/2B SECONDARY GRADE STAINLESS STEEL SHEET OF WIDTH 1219MM THICKNESS 1MM TO 3MM, QTY:25,000KGS AT THE RATE OF USD1.40/KG FOR TOTAL AMOUNT OF USD35,000.00 CFR CHITTAGONG, BANGLADESH. AS PER BENEFICIARY'S PROFORMA INVOICE NO. SK20130802-001 DATED AUG 2,2013
DOCUMENTS REQUIRED	46A:	+MANUALLY SIGNED COMMERCIAL INVOICE IN TRIPLICATE CERTIFYING MERCHANDISE TO BE OF CHINA ORIGIN AND INDICATING THAT THE GOODS ARE BEING IMPORTED AGAINST IRC NO.BA-0171646, TI NO.157-107-0121, VAT REGISTRATION NO.9141093671. +FULL SET OF CLEAN "SHIPPED ON BOARD" OCEAN BILL OF LADING SHOWING "FREIGHT PREPAID" MADE OUT TO ORDER AND BLANK INDORSED, NOTIFY APPLICANT. +PACKING LIST IN TRIPLICATE SHOWING GROSS WEIGHT, NET WEIGHT. +CERTIFICATE OF ORIGIN ISSUED AND LEGALED BY CCPIT + BENEFICIARY'S DECLARATION SHOULD CERTIFY THAT THE COUNTRY OF ORIGIN

		HAS BEEN PRINTED ON GOODS PACKING BAG. +BENEFICIARY SHOULD SEND A FAX OR BY COUR-IER TO L/C OPENING BANK WITHIN FIVE DAYS FROM THE OF SHIPMENT, ADVISING THE DATE OF SHIPMENT, VESSEL'S NAME, AMOUNT OF BILL AND L/C NO. AND A COPY OF THIS FAX SHOULD ACCOMPANY THE SHIPPING DOCUMENTS. +SHIPMENT BY ISRAELI LINER IS PROHIBITED AND ACERTIFICATE TO THIS EFFECT ISSUED BY THE SHIPPING COMPANY MUST ACCOMPANY THE ORIGINAL DOCUMENTS.
ADDITIONAL CONDITIONS	47A:	ALL SHIPPING DOCUMENTS MUST SHOWING THE L/C NO. AND S/C NO.
PERIOD OF PRESENTATION	48:	15 DAYS FROM SHIPMENT DATE BUT WITHIN VALIDITY OF THE CREDIT

2. 商业发票

Jiangsu I-Touch Business Service Ltd.

Add: Room117, Jinggang Edifice Zhangjiagang Free Trade Zone, Jiangsu Province, China

Tel: 0086-512-56363783 Fax: 0086-512-56366780

COMMERCIAL INVOICE

To: M/S. MEMORY STEEL CORPORATION73/A, LAL MOHAN SHAHA STREET (DHOLAIKHAL), DHAKA-1100. BANGLANDESH

Contract No.: C20130807	**No.: 67080-9**
L/C No.: 0684130117426	**Date: SEP. 13, 2013**
From: SHANGHAI, CHINA	**To: CHITTAGONG, BANGLANDESH**

Marks	Description of Goods Size(mm)	Quantity (G.W/KG)	Unit Price (USD/KG)	Amount
	STAINLESS STEEL SHEET		CFR CHITTAGONG	
N/M	201/2B SECONDARY GRADE			
	1.2*1,219*2,438	5,728.00	1.400,0	7,806.40
	1.5*1,219*2,438	3,315.20	1.400,0	4,547.20
	2.0*1,219*2,438	11,894.0	1.400,0	16,282.00
	1,219MM OR MORE THICKNESS 1MM TO 3MM			
	3.0*1,219*2,438	4,663.70	1.400,0	6,364.40
	TOTAL:	25,600.90		35,000.00

SAY U.S.DOLLARS THIRTY FIVE THOUSAND ONLY

WE HEREBY CERTIFY THAT ABOVE MERCHANDISE TO BE OF CHINA ORIGIN AND ARE BEING IMPORTED AGAINST IRC NO. BA-0171646,TI NO. 157-107-0121,VAT REGISTRATION NO.9141093671 AND L.C.A. NO. 101804 UNDER H.S. CODE NO. 721933.00, 721934.00

Jiangsu I-Touch Business Service Ltd.

彭 婷

3. 装运资料

DATE OF SHIPMENT:2013-9-24

VESSEL VOYAGE: ZU.S.A. V.66W

根据上述资料完成下面几个实训项目：

任务 1：装运通知制作

任务 2：受益人证明制作

任务 3：船公司证明制作

项目十一　进口信用证业务

项目预期目标

信用证是当今国际贸易中的核心支付工具，也是我国进口业务中最主要的支付方式之一。在进口业务中，信用证申请书是企业自行缮制的一项重要文件，也是信用证的前身，进口商科学、缜密地设置相关条款并填写开证申请书，对于降低进口风险，有效履行合同非常关键。而当信用证受到受益人提出的改证申请后，也应当综合权衡，填写改证申请书并通过开证行办理改证手续。本项目通过介绍开证申请书和改证申请书的填制，引导学生熟悉开证和改证申请书的格式及内容，重点训练学生掌握开证和改证申请书的填制要点，并最终能独立完成开证和改证申请书的填写，掌握开证和改证手续的操作流程。

在项目实施过程中，有效训练学生对合同条款和信用证结构的理解和掌握，培养学生操作进口结汇业务的职业能力，亦培养其独立操作业务和与开证行有效沟通的能力。

表 11-1　　项目预期目标

目标类型	申请开立和修改信用证
知识目标	掌握开证申请书和改证申请书的填写要求
	熟悉申请开证和改证的业务操作流程
能力目标	能根据合同，正确填写开证申请书并办理申请开证手续
	能根据出口商的改证函或进口商的改证需求，填写改正申请书并办理申请改证手续
职业素质目标	独立业务操作能力
	与银行沟通衔接能力

项目实施条件

1. 教师演示工作项目和归纳技能要点
2. 学生能够在实训室对该项目进行分组讨论并实施

开篇业务引入

根据第 CB121039 号合同的要求，进口方 ELBY GIFTS INC.需要于 2012 年 8 月 5 日之前向出口方长沙鹏兴进出口有限公司开出不可撤销即期信用证，且该信用证的有效期为装运日后的 15 天。2012 年 7 月 15 日，进口方公司单证员根据第 CB121039 号合同，填写开证申请书并办理申请开证手续。在收到出口方的改证函后，结合自身改证需求，填写改证申请书并办理申请改证手续。

子项目一　开证申请书及信用证修改书的制作

一、开证申请书的使用

进出口双方在合同明确以信用证方式结算后，即由进口方向有关银行申请开立信用证。开证申请是进口信用证业务的第一个环节，进口方应在合同规定的时间或在规定的装船前一定时间内申请开证，并填制开证申请书。

开证申请书（Application Form）是进口方作为开证申请人委托开证行开出的以出口方为受益人的信用证申请文件，一般根据贸易合同中的商品条款、支付条款等主要条款填制，申请人填制后与合同副本一并提交银行，供银行参考、核对。但信用证一经开立则独立于合同，因而在填写开证申请书时应审慎查核合同的主要条款，并将其列入申请书中。开证行在接受开证申请并开出信用证后即成为第一性付款人，而开证申请书也成为开证申请人与开证行的合约，具有法律效力。目前常见的做法是由开证行事先将空白的开证申请书印就，再由开证申请人直接填制。

IRREVOCABLE DOCUMENTARY CREDIT APPLICATION

<table>
<tr><td colspan="2">To:</td><td>Date:</td></tr>
<tr><td colspan="2">□Issue by airmail　　□With brief advice by teletransmission
□Issue by express delivery
□Issue by teletransmission (which shall be the operative instrument)</td><td>Credit No.

Date and place of expiry</td></tr>
<tr><td colspan="2">Applicant</td><td>Beneficiary (Full name and address)</td></tr>
<tr><td colspan="2">Advising Bank</td><td>Amount</td></tr>
<tr><td>Partial shipments
□allowed　□not allowed</td><td>Transhipment
□allowed　□not allowed</td><td rowspan="2">Credit available with

By

□sight payment　□acceptance　□negotiation
□deferred payment at</td></tr>
<tr><td colspan="2">Loading on board/dispatch/taking in charge at/from</td></tr>
</table>

not later than For transportation to:	against the documents detailed herein □and beneficiary's draft(s) for ____ % of invoice
□FOB □CFR □CIF □or other terms	value at______________ sight drawn on

Documents required: (marked with X)

1. ( ) Signed commercial invoice in _____ copies indicating L/C No. and Contract No.

2. ( ) Full set of clean on board Bills of Lading made out To order and blank endorsed, marked "freight [ ] To collect/ [ ] prepaid [ ] showing freight amount" notifying ________________________________ .

( ) Airway bills/cargo receipt/copy of railway bills issued by ____________________________ showing "freight [ ] To collect/[ ] prepaid [ ] "indicating freight amount" and consigned To______________________.

3. ( ) Insurance Policy/Certificate in ______ copies for _______ % of the invoice value showing claims payable in ___________________in currency of the draft, blank endorsed, covering All Risks, War Risks and _____________ ___________________.

4. ( ) Packing List/Weight Memo in _____ copies indicating quantity, gross and net weights of each package.

5. ( ) Certificate of Quantity/Weight in ________ copies issued by _________________.

6. ( ) Certificate of Quality in ______ copies issued by [ ] manufacturer/[ ] public recognized surveyor _______.

7. ( ) Certificate of Origin in _______ copies .

8. ( ) Beneficiary's certified copy of fax/telex dispatched to the applicant within _______ days after shipment advising L/C No., name of vessel, date of shipment, name, quantity, weight and value of goods.

Other documents, if any

Description of goods:

Additional instructions:

1. ( ) All banking charges outside the opening bank are for beneficiary's account.

2. ( ) Documents must be presented within _______ days after date of issuance of the transport documents but within the validity of this credit.

3. ( ) Third party as shipper is not acceptable, Short Form/Blank back B/L is not acceptable.

4. ( ) Both quantity and credit amount ______ % more or less are allowed.

5. ( ) All documents must be sent to issuing bank by courier/speed post in one lot.

( ) Other terms, if any

开证申请书样本

二、申请开立信用证的流程

申请开立信用证的流程一般包括：填写开证申请书、开证申请人承诺书、提交有关合同的副本及附件、支付开证保证金、支付开证手续费等环节。

开证申请人承诺书

XX 银行：

我公司已办妥一切进口手续，现请贵行按我公司开证申请书内容（见背面英文）开出不可撤销跟单信用证，为此我公司承担有关责任如下：

一、我公司同意贵行依照国际商会第 500 号出版物《跟单信用证统一惯例》办理该信用证项下一切事宜，并同意承担由此产生的一切责任。

二、我公司保证按时向贵行支付该证项下的货款、手续费、利息及一切费用等（包括国外受益人拒绝承担的有关银行费用)所需的外汇和人民币资金。

三、我公司保证在贵行单到通知书中规定的期限之内通知贵行办理对外付款/承兑，否则贵行可认为我公司已接受单据，同意付款/承兑。

四、我公司保证在单证表面相符的条件下办理有关付款/承兑手续。如因单证有不符之处而拒绝付款/承兑，我公司保证在贵行单到通知书中规定的日期之前将全套单据如数退还贵行并附书面拒付理由，由贵行按国际惯例确定能否对外拒付。如贵行确定我公司所提拒付理由不成立，或虽然拒付理由成立，但我公司未能退回全套单据，或拒付单据退到贵行已超过单到通知书中规定的期限，贵行有权主动办理对外付款/承兑，并从我公司账户中扣款。

五、该信用证及其项下业务往来函电及单据如因邮、电或其他方式传递过程中发生遗失、延误、错漏，贵行当不负责。

六、该信用证如需修改，由我公司向贵行提出书面申请，由贵行根据具体情况确定能否办理修改。我公司确认所有修改当由信用证受益人接受时才能生效。

七、我公司在收到贵行开出的信用证、修改书副本后，保证及时与原申请书核对，如有不符之处，保证在接到副本之日起，两个工作日内通知贵行。如未通知，当视为正确无误。

八、如因申请书字迹不清或词意含混而引起的一切后果由我公司负责。

开证申请人
（签字盖章）
年　月　日

三、信用证修改书的使用

出口商在收到信用证后经审核发现证约不符或有些不能接受或无法办到的条款，可按合同规定并结合自身需要向进口商及开证行提出修改信用证，同时，进口商因一些形势或情况的变化，也可以对信用证提出修改。

（一）信用证修改的常见场合

1. 出口方（受益人）要求修改信用证

由于信用证内容与合同不符。

信用证中某些条款受益人无法办到，如软条款。

货源或船期等出现问题，要求展期。

2. 进口方（开证申请人）要求展期

受国际市场行情变化需临时改变交货期或调整货物价格。

由于进口国政策发生变化必须增加进口许可证等官方单据。

由于政治等方面原因导致进出口风险增加而要求加投战争险等。

3. 开证行印制信用证时出现的文字错误或传递上造成的错误必须修正。

（二）信用证修改的注意事项（根据 UCP 600 规定）

1. 需要修改的条款应一次性向对方提出，避免多次修改。

2. 任何条款的修改都必须取得当事人的同意后才能生效。对信用证修改内容的接受或拒绝有两种表示形式：

受益人明确作出接受或拒绝该信用证修改的通知；

受益人以实际行动表示接受或拒绝。如受益人虽没明确表示接受修改但单据是按修改后的条款制作并提示则认为实际接受修改。

3. 对于信用证修改书的条款要么全部接受，要么全部拒绝。部分接受视为拒绝接受修改。

4. 信用证的修改书必须由原通知行通知方可生效；当事人直接寄送视为无效修改。

编号 No.: ________

信用证修改申请书

APPLICATION FOR AMENDMENT
TO DOCUMENTARY CREDIT

致 To: 光大银行湖南省分行 银行 Bank

信用证编号 L/C No.: LCD6600201000165 开证日期 Issuing date: 101025

受益人 Beneficiary: AGILENT TECHNOLOGIES MALAYSIA (SALES) PTE LTD

有效期 Expiry date: 130215

装运期 latest shipment date: 130202

金额 Amount: USD235,000.00

请将上述信用证以□电讯□信函方式做如下修改：

Please amend the above credit by □ SWIFT or by □ AIRMAIL as follows:

最迟装运期展至 The latest shipment date extended To________（mm）/______（dd）/_____（yy）

有效期展至 The expiry date extended To_______（mm）/_______（dd）/_____（yy）

金额增加/减少 Increase/Decrease the amount by________到 To______________

其他 Other terms: Please amend 46A "+AIR WAYBILL SHOWING 'FREIGHT PREPAID' NOTIFYING APPLICANT INDICATING FREIGHT AMOUNT AND

CONSIGNED TO APPLICANT IN THREE ORIGINALS." To "+AIR WAYBILL SHOWING 'FREIGHT PREPAID' NOTIFYING APPLICANT INDICATING FREIGHT AMOUNT AND CONSIGNED TO APPLICANT IN 1 ORIGINAL & 2 COPIES."

银行费用 Banking charges by：受益人负担 Beneficiary，□申请人负担 Applicant。

信用证其他各项条款保持不变。

All other terms and conditions of the L/C remain unchanged.

除本申请书另有约定外，申请人和银行间的权利义务仍按原申请书（编号________）执行。

Except as otherwise expressly stated herein, the right(s) and obligation(s) between the Applicant and the Issuing bank are still subject to the application (No.________________).

申请人（公章）

(Stamp and) Signature of Applicant

____月（mm）____日（dd）____年（yy）

四、开证申请书的填制操作

1 栏 申请书抬头（TO）

（1）填写内容：

银行印制的申请书上事先都会印就开证银行的名称、地址，银行的 SWIFT CODE、TELEX NO 等也可同时显示。

（2）实例：

TO: HSBC BANK CANADA

2 栏 申请开证日期（DATE）

（1）填写内容：

在申请书右上角填写实际申请日期。

（2）实例：

Date: July 15, 2012

3 栏 信用证开立方式

（1）填写内容：

在相对应的方式前打"×"。开证方式多为电开（BY TELETRANSMISSION），也可以是信开（BY AIRMAIL）、快递（BY EXPRESS）或简电（WITH BRIEF ADVICE BY TELETRANSMISSION）开立。SWIFT 形式信用证即为电开本，在 ISSUE BY TELETRANSMISSION 前打"×"。如果信用证是保兑或可转让的，应在此加注有关字样。

注意：根据银行开证申请书填写操作习惯，在正确选择项前要打"×"，而不是打"√"。

（2）实例：

（×）ISSUE BY TELETRANSMISSION

4 栏 信用证号码（L/C NUMBER）

填写内容：此栏由银行填写。

5 栏 开证申请人（APPLICANT）

（1）填写内容：

本栏目填写开证申请人，即进口合同买方的全称及详细地址，有的要求注明联系电话、传真号码等。

（2）实例：

APPLICANT：ELBY GIFTS INC.879 INDUSTRIEL
BOIS DES FILION,QUEBEC, J6Z 4T3, CANADA

6 栏 受益人（BENEFICIARY）

（1）填写内容：

本栏目填写受益人，即进口合同卖方的全称及详细地址。

（2）实例：

BENEFICIARY：PENGXING IMP&EXP COMPANY
LILING PENGXING CERAMIC FACTORY
WUSHI JIASHU LILING HUNAN, CHINA

7 栏 通知行（ADVISING BANK）

（1）填写内容：

本栏目填写通知行名称、地址和 SWIFT 号码，若卖方没有提供，则由开证行指定。

（2）实例：

ADVISING BANK：BANK OF CHINA

8 栏 信用证金额（AMOUNT）

（1）填写内容：

本栏目填写信用证金额的大小写，即分别用数字和文字两种形式表示，并且表明币制。如果允许有一定比率的上下浮动，要在信用证中明确表示出来。

（2）实例：

AMOUNT：USD27,010.40

SAY: U.S.DOLLARS TWENTY SEVEN THOUSAND AND TEN CENTS FORTY ONLY.

9 栏 到期日期和地点（DATE AND PLACE OF EXPIRY）

（1）填写内容：

本栏目填写信用证的有效期及到期地点。到期地点一般情况下在受益人所在国，信用证有效期一般是最迟装运日期加交单期限。

（2）实例：

DATE AND PLACE OF EXPIRY: SEP.19, 2012 IN COUNTRY OF BENEFICIARY

10 栏 分批装运（PARTIAL SHIPMENT）、转运（TRANSHIPMENT）

（1）填写内容：

根据合同的实际规定打“×”进行选择。

（2）实例：

PARTIAL SHIPMENT：（×）ALLOWED

TRANSHIPMENT：（×）ALLOWED

11 栏 装运港/地（Loading on board/dispatch/taking in charge at/from）、目的港/地（For transportation To），最迟装运日期（DATE OF SHIPMENT）

（1）填写内容：

按实际情况填写，如允许有转运地/港，也应清楚标明，一般在目的港后加“VIA”和转运港/地。

（2）实例：

Loading on board/dispatch/taking in charge at/from：SHENZHEN, CHINA

not later than SEP.5, 2012

For transportation To：PRINCE RUPERT,BC

12 栏 指定银行和付款方式（CREDIT AVAILABLE WITH/BY）

（1）填写内容：

填写指定的银行，并选择对应的付款方式。在所提供的即期（SIGHT PAYMENT）、承兑（ACCEPTANCE）、议付（NEGOTIATION）和延期付款（DEFERRED PAYMENT）四种信用证有效兑付方式中选择与合同要求一致的类型。

（2）实例：

CREDIT AVAILABLE WITH HSBC BANK CANADA

BY (×) NEGOTIATION

13 栏 汇票条款（BENEFICIARY'S DRAFT）

（1）填写内容：

若需要出具汇票，则本栏目填写汇票金额。具体金额应根据合同规定填写为：发票金额的一定百分比；发票金额的 100%（全部货款都用信用证支付）；如部分信用证，部分托收时按信用证下的金额比例填写。

付款期限可根据实际填写即期或远期，如属远期则必须填写具体的天数。信用证条件下的付款人通常是开证行，也可能是开证行指定的另外一家银行。

（2）实例：

beneficiary's draft(s) for 100 % of invoice value

at ____****____ sight

drawn on ISSUING BANK

14 栏 所需单据条款（DOCUMENTS REQUIRED）

（1）填写内容：

根据合同的要求或实际需要选择所需提供的单据，在所需单据前面画“×”进行标识。

各银行提供的申请书中已印就的单据条款通常为十几条，从上至下一般为发票、运输单据（提单、空运单、铁路运输单据及运输备忘录等）、保险单、装箱单、质量证书、装运通知和受益人证明等，最后一条是 OTHER DOCUMENTS，IF ANY（其他单据），如要求提交超过上述所列范围的单据就可以在此栏填写，比如有的合同要求出具 CERTIFICATE OF BLACK LIST（黑名单证明）等。

申请人填制这部分内容时应依据合同规定，不能随意增加或减少。选中某单据后对该单据的具体要求（如一式几份、要否签字、正副本的份数、单据中应标明的内容等）也应如实填写，如申请书印制好的要求不完整应在其后予以补足。

（2）实例：

Documents required: (marked with X)
1. (X) Signed commercial invoice in ___3___ copies indicating L/C No. and Contract No.
2. (X) Full set of clean on board Bills of Lading made out To order and blank endorsed, marked “freight [X] To collect/[ ] prepaid [ ] showing freight amount” notifying ______APPLICANT______ .
( ) Airway bills/cargo receipt/copy of railway bills issued by ____________ showing “freight [ ] To collect/[ ] prepaid [ ] “indicating freight amount” and consigned To__________.
3. ( ) Insurance Policy/Certificate in _____ copies for _____ % of the invoice value showing claims payable in ____________ in currency of the draft, blank endorsed, covering currency of the draft, blank endorsed, covering All Risks, War Risks and ____________.
4. ( ) Packing List/Weight Memo in _____ copies indicating quantity, gross and net weights of each package.
5. ( ) Certificate of Quantity/Weight in _______ copies issued by ____________.

15 栏 商品描述（DESCRIPTION OF GOODS）

（1）填写内容：

所有内容（品名、规格、包装、单价、唛头）都必须与合同内容相一致，价格条款里附带“AS PER INCOTERMS 2010”、数量条款中规定“MORE OR LESS”或“ABOUT”、使用某种特定包装物等特殊要求必须清楚列明。

（2）实例：

DESCRIPTION OF GOODS：

CERAMIC CUPS AND BOWLS AS PER S/C NO.:CB121039 CIF PRINCE RUPERT,BC

ALL PACKED IN CARTONS.

16 栏 附加指示（ADDITIONAL INSTRUCTIONS）

（1）填写内容：

该栏通常体现为以下一些条款：

+ALL DOCUMENTS MUST INDICATE CONTRACT NUMBER（所有单据加列合同号码）。

+ALL BANKING CHARGES OUTSIDE THE OPENING BANK ARE FOR BENEFICIARY’S ACCOUNT（所有开证行以外的银行费用由受益人承担）。

+BOTH QUANTITY AND AMOUNT FOR EACH ITEM % MORE OR LESS ALLOWED（每项数量与金额允许 %增减）。

+THIRD PARTY AS SHIPPER IS NOT ACCEPTABLE（第三方作为托运人是不能接受的）。

+DOCUMENTS MUST BE PRESNTED WITHIN ××× DAYS AFTER THE DATE OF ISSUANCE OF THE TRANSPORT DOCUMENTS BUT WITHIN THE VALIDITY OF THIS CREDIT（单据必须在提单日后×××天送达银行并且不超过信用证有效期）。

+SHORT FORM/BLANK BACK/CLAUSED/CHARTER PARTY B/L IS UNACCEPTABLE

（银行不接受略式/不清洁/租船提单）。

+ALL DOCMENTS TO BE FORWARDED IN ONE COVER, UNLESS OTHERWISE STATED ABOVE（除非有相反规定，所有单据应一次提交）。

+PREPAID FREIGHT DRAWN IN EXCESS OF L/C AMOUNT IS ACCEPTABLE AGAINST PRESENTATION OF ORIGINAL CHARGES VOUCHER ISSUED BY SHIPPING CO./AIR LINE OR ITS AGENT（银行接受凭船公司/航空公司或其代理人签发的正本运费收据索要超过信用证金额的预付运费）。

+DOCUMENT ISSUED PRIOR TO THE DATE OF ISSUANCE OF CREDIT NOT ACCEPTABLE（不接受早于开证日出具的单据）。

如需要已印就的上述条款，可在条款前打“×”，对合同涉及但未印就的条款还可以做补充填写。

（2）实例：

Additional instructions:

1. (×) All banking charges outside the opening bank are for beneficiary's account.

2. (×) Documents must be presented within 15 days after date of issuance of the transport documents but within the validity of this credit.

3. ( ) Third party as shipper is not acceptable, Short Form/Blank back B/L is not acceptable.

17 栏 签章

填写内容：授权人名称、签章、电话、传真等内容。

五、改证申请书的填制操作

1 栏 申请书抬头（TO）

（1）填写内容：

开证银行的名称和地址，银行的 SWIFT CODE、TELEX NO 等也可同时显示。

（2）实例：

TO：HSBC BANK CANADA

2 栏 信用证号码（L/C No.）

（1）填写内容：

申请修改的信用证号码。

（2）实例：

L/C No.：DC HMN214479

3 栏 开证日期（Issuing date）

（1）填写内容：

申请修改的信用证开证日期。

（2）实例：

Issuing date：120720

4 栏 受益人（Beneficiary）

（1）填写内容：

申请修改的信用证的受益人。

（2）实例：

Beneficiary：PENGXING IMP&EXP COMPANY LILING PENGXING CERAMIC FACTORY WUSHI JIASHU LILING HUNAN, CHINA

5 栏 信用证的有效期（Expiry date）

（1）填写内容：

申请修改的信用证的有效期。

（2）实例：

Expiry date：120919

6 栏 最迟装运日（latest shipment date）

（1）填写内容：

申请修改的信用证的最迟装运日。

（2）实例：

latest shipment date：120905

7 栏 信用证金额（Amount）

（1）填写内容：

申请修改的信用证可使用的最高限额。

（2）实例：

Amount：USD27,010.40

8 栏 信用证修改书的传递方式

（1）填写内容：

本栏目可选择 SWIFT 系统或者航空挂号信（AIRMAIL）的方式，在对应的项目前选择。

（2）实例：

Please amend the above credit by □ SWIFT or by □ AIRMAIL as follows

9 栏 信用证申请修改的具体条款

（1）填写内容：

逐一列出需要修改的信用证条款。如：最迟装运日从×年×月×日延展至×年×月×日，信用证的有效期从×年×月×日延展至×年×月×日，信用证的金额从×增加至×等等。

（2）实例：

The latest shipment date extended To__09__（mm）/__15__（dd）/__2012__（yy） The expiry date extended To__09__（mm）/__29__（dd）/__2012__（yy） Increase the amount by__USD27,010.40__To__USD28,000.00__

Other terms：Please amend 43P "PARTIAL SHIPMENTS: NOT ALLOWED" To "PARTIAL SHIPMENTS: ALLOWED"

10 栏 改证申请人的签章（Signature of Applicant）

（1）填写内容：

改证申请人签章

（2）实例：

(Stamp and) Signature of Applicant Mary

11 栏 改证申请的日期（date）

（1）填写内容：

改正申请书的填制日期。

（2）实例：

07 （mm） 22 日（dd） 2012 年（yy）

子项目二 开证及改证典型业务演示

在双方签订销售合同并选用信用证方式结汇后，加拿大 ELBY GIFTS INC.公司的业务员在该项目中应完成的工作任务是：

1. 根据第 CB121039 号合同及第 DC HMN214479 号信用证填写开证申请书并向银行办理申请开证手续。

合同：

CONTRACT

Contract No.: CB121039

Date: JUL. 5, 2012

THE SELLER: PENGXING IMP&EXP COMPANY
LILING PENGXING CERAMIC FACTOR
WUSHI JIASHU LILING HUNAN, CHINA
TEL: 86-731-23384199 FAX: 86-731-23384298

THE BUYER: ELBY GIFTS INC.
879 INDUSTRIEL BOIS DES FILION
QUEBEC, J6Z 4T3, CANADA
TEL: 514-420-0282 FAX: 514-420-0322

This Contract is made by and between the Buyer and Seller, whereby the Buyer agrees To buy and the Seller agrees To sell the under mentioned goods on the terms and conditions stated below:

Description of Goods, Specifications,	Quantity (set)	Unit Price (U.S.D/set)	Amount (U.S.D)
Ceramic Cups and Bowls		C.I.F Prince	
V23-234	912	Rupert	3,693.60
V23-234F	912	4.05	3,693.60
V23-235	1,520	4.05	3,648.00
V23-236	1,512	2.40	3,175.20
V23-237	1,488	2.10	2,901.6
V23-2348	1,520	1.95	3,100.80
36-062	1,528	2.04	3,514.40
36-063	1,496	2.30	3,171.52
As per the P/I No.: CCB23-36		2.12	
Total	10,888		26,898.72

Say Total: U.S DOLLARS TWENTY SIX THOUSAND EIGHT HUNDRED AND NINETY EIGHT AND CENTS SEVENTY TWO(USD26,898.72)ONLY.

PACKING: 4 sets packed in a carTon(V 23-234/V23-234F), 8 sets packed in a carTon for others.

TRANSPORT DETAILS: the goods should be shipped on or before: 5th Sep, 2012, from Shenzhen, China To Prince Rupert Canada, transshipment and partial shipment are all allowed.

INSURANCE: To be effected by the Seller for 110% of invoice value covering all risks and S.R.C.C as per C.I.C of PICC dated 01/01/1981.

PAYMENT: By irrevocable documentary letter of credit at sight, reaching the seller not later than Aug 5,2012 and remain valid for negotiation in China for 15 days after shipment.

DOCUMENTS:

+ Signed commercial invoice one original and three copies.
+ Full set of clean on board ocean Bill of Lading made To order of issuing bank.
+ Packing List one original and two copies.
+ Insurance policy endorsed in blank.
+ GSP Form A certified by government authority.

INSPECTION: Quality/Quantity/Weight Discrepancy and Claim: In case the quality and/or quantity/weight are found by the Buyer not To conform with the contract after arrival of the goods at the final destination, the Buyer may lodge a claim against the seller supported by a survey report issued by an inspection organization agreed upon by both parties with the exception of those claims for which the insurance company and/or the shipping company are To be held responsible. Claim for quality discrepancy should be filed by the Buyer within 60 days after arrival of the goods at the final destination while for quantity/weight discrepancy claim should be filed by the Buyer within 30 days after arrival of the goods at the final destination.

FORCE MAJEURE: The Seller shall not be held responsible for failure or delay in delivery of the entire or portion of the goods under this contract in consequence of any Force Majeure incidents.

ARBITRATION: All disputes in connection with this Contract or the execution thereof shall be settled through friendly negotiations. If no settlement can be reached, the case shall then be submitted To the Foreign Trade Arbitration Commission of the China Council for the Promotion of International Trade, Beijing, for settlement by arbitration in accordance with the Commission's Provisional Rules of Procedure. The award rendered by the Commission shall be final and binding on both parties. The arbitration expenses shall be borne by the losing party unless otherwise award by the arbitration organization.

Signed by:

THE SELLER:	**THE BUYER:**
PENGXING IMP&EXP COMPANY	ELBY GIFTS INC.
LILING PENGXING CERAMIC FACTORY	
李 望	Camp Wolf

信用证：

SEQUENCE OF TOTAL	27:	1/1
FORM OF DC	40A:	IRREVOCABLE
DC NO	20:	DC HMN214479
DATE OF ISSUE	31C:	120720
APPLICABLE RULES	40E:	UCP LATEST VERSION
EXPIRY DATE AND PLACE	31D:	120919 IN COUNTRY OF BENEFICIARY
APPLICANT	50:	ELBY GIFTS INC.879 INDUSTRIEL BOIS DES FILION,QUEBEC, J6Z 4T3, CANADA
BENEFICIARY	59:	LILING PENGXING CERAMIC FACTORY WUSHI JIASHU LILING HUNAN, CHINA
AMOUNT	32B:	USD27,010.40
PCT CR AMT TOLERANCE	39A:	10/10
AVAILABLE WITH/BY	41D:	ANY BANK BY NEGOTIATION
DRAFTS AT	42C:	AT SIGHT FOR FULL INVOICE VALUE
DRAWEE	42A:	ISSUING BANK
PARTIAL SHIPMENTS	43P:	ALLOWED

TRANSHIPMENT	43T:	ALLOWED
PORT OF LOADING	44E:	SHENZHEN, CHINA
PORT OF DISCHARGE	44F:	PRINCE RUPERT,BC
LATEST DATE OF SHIPMENT	44D:	120905
DESCRIPTION OF GOODS OR SERVICES	45A:	CERAMIC CUPS AND BOWLS AS PER S/C NO.:CB121039 CIF PRINCE RUPERT,BC ALL PACKED IN CARTONS.
DOCUMENTS REQUIRED	46A:	+ ORIGINAL SIGNED INVOICE PLUS THREE COPIES. + FULL SET OF CLEAN MULTIMODAL TRANSPORT DOCUMENT PLUS 2 N/N COPIES, MADE TO THE ORDER OF HSBC BANK CANADA, SHOWING ON BOARD NOTATION, MARKED FREIGHT PREPAID, AND NOTIFY APPLICANT(STATING FULL NAME AND ADDRESS). + INSURANCE POLICY OR CERTIFICATE BLANK INDORSED, FOR THE INVOICE VALUE PLUS 10% COVERING ALL RISKS AND S.R.CC. FROM WAREHOUSE TO WAREHOUSE. + ORIGINAL PACKING LIST PLUS 2 COPIES + GSP CERTIFICATE OF ORIGIN FORM A, IN ONE ORIGINAL PLUS 2 COPIES, INDICATING COUNTRY OF ORIGIN, COUNTERCHOPPED BY GOVERNMENT AUTHORITIES OR EXPORTER'S STATMENT OF ORIGIN + SHIPPING NOTE INCLUDING SHIPPING MARKS, CTN NO., B/L NO., QUANTITY, VESSEL'S NAME, VOYAGE NO., SHOULD BE SENT TO THE ISSUING BANK ON THE DATE OF SHIPMENT.
ADDITIONAL CONDITIONS	47A:	+ BENEFICIARY'S DETAILS: CTC: MILLER LEE TEL: 86-731-2338-4199 FAX: 86-731-2338-4298

FOLLOWING CHARGES ARE FOR BENEFICIARY'S ACCOUNT:

		1) REIMBURSEMENT/REMITTANCE CHARGES 2) DISCREPANCY FEE OF USD/CAD/EUR100 PLUS ALL RELEVANT CABLE CHARGES WILL BE DEDUCTED FROM EACH PRESENTATION OF DISCREPANT DOCUMENTS UNDER THIS DC.
CHARGES	71B:	ALL BANKING CHARGES OUTSIDE COUNTRY OF ISSUE FOR ACCOUNT OF BENEFICIARY/EXPORTER
PERIOD OF PRESENTATION	48:	WITHIN 15 DAYS AFTER THE DATE OF SHIPMENT BUT WITHIN THE VALIDITY OF THE CREDIT
CONFIRMATION INSTRUCTIONS	49:	WITHOUT
INFO TO PRESENTING BK	78:	+ UPON RECEIPT OF DOCUMENTS CONFORMING TO THE TERMS OF THIS CREDIT WE UNDERTAKE TO REIMBURSE YOU IN THE CURRENCY OF THIS CREDIT IN ACCORDANCE WITH YOUR INSTRUCTIONS, LESS CABLE CHARGES, + FORWARD DOCUMENTS IN ONE LOT BY COURIER AT BENEFICIARY'S EXPENSES TO HSBC BANK CANADA, TRADE AND SUPPLY CHAIN, 5100 SHERBROOKE STREET EAST,SUITE 190, MONTREAL,QUEBEC,H1V 3R9 CANADA. + THE AMOUNT OF EACH DRAWING MUST BE ENDORSED ON THE REVERSE OF THIS DC BY THE NEGOTIATING/PRESENTING BANK.

IRREVOCABLE DOCUMENTARY CREDIT APPLICATION

To: HSBC BANK CANADA Date: Jul.15, 2012

☐Issue by airmail ☐With brief advice by teletransmission ☐Issue by express delivery (×)Issue by teletransmission (which shall be the operative instrument)	Credit No. Date and place of expiry Sep.19, 2012 IN COUNTRY OF BENEFICIARY
Applicant ELBY GIFTS INC.879 INDUSTRIEL BOIS DES FILION,QUEBEC, J6Z 4T3, CANADA	Beneficiary (Full name and address) PENGXING IMP&EXP COMPANY LILING PENGXING CERAMIC FACTORY WUSHI JIASHU LILING HUNAN, CHINA

<table>
<tr><td colspan="2">Advising Bank</td><td>Amount
USD27,010.40
SAY: U.S.DOLLARS TWENTY SEVEN THOUSAND AND TEN CENTS FORTY ONLY.</td></tr>
<tr><td>Partial shipments
(×)allowed　□not allowed</td><td>Transhipment
(×)allowed　□not allowed</td><td rowspan="3">Credit available with
ANY BANK
By

□sight payment　□acceptance　(×)negotiation
□deferred payment at against the documents detailed herein
(×)and beneficiary's draft(s) for <u>100</u> % of invoice value at <u>****</u> sight
drawn on ISSUING BANK</td></tr>
<tr><td colspan="2">Loading on board/dispatch/taking in charge at/from
SHENZHEN, CHINA
not later than　Sep.05, 2012
For transportation To:　PRINCE RUPERT,BC</td></tr>
<tr><td colspan="2">□FOB　□CFR　(×)CIF
□or other terms</td></tr>
</table>

Documents required: (marked with X)

1. (X) Signed commercial invoice in <u>4</u> copies indicating L/C No. and Contract No.

2. (X) Full set of clean on board Bills of Lading made out To order and blank endorsed, marked "freight [ ] To collect/ [X] prepaid [ ] showing freight amount" notifying <u>APPLICANT(STATING FULL NAME AND ADDRESS)</u> .

( ) Airway bills/cargo receipt/copy of railway bills issued by ______ showing "freight [ ] To collect/[ ] prepaid [ ] "indicating freight amount" and consigned To______.

3. (X) Insurance Policy/Certificate in <u>3</u> copies for <u>110</u> % of the invoice value showing claims payable in <u>CANADA</u> in currency of the draft, blank endorsed, covering All Risks and <u>S.R.CC.</u> .

4. (X) Packing List/Weight Memo in <u>3</u> copies indicating quantity, gross and weights of each package.

5. ( ) Certificate of Quantity/Weight in ______ copies issued by ______.

6. ( ) Certificate of Quality in ______ copies issued by [ ] manufacturer/[ ] public recognized surveyor ______.

7. (X) Certificate of Origin in <u>3</u> copies .

8. ( ) Beneficiary's certified copy of fax/telex dispatched To the applicant within ______ days after shipment advising L/C No., name of vessel, date of shipment, name, quantity, weight and value of goods.

(X)Other documents, if any

SHIPPING NOTE INCLUDING SHIPPING MARKS, CTN NO., B/L NO., QUANTITY, VESSEL'S NAME, VOYAGE NO., SHOULD BE SENT TO THE ISSUING BANK ON THE DATE OF SHIPMENT

Description of goods:

CERAMIC CUPS AND BOWLS AS PER S/C NO.:CB121039 CIF PRINCE RUPERT,BC
ALL PACKED IN CARTONS.

Additional instructions:

1. (X) All banking charges outside the opening bank are for beneficiary's account.

2. (X) Documents must be presented within <u>15</u> days after date of issuance of the transport documents but within the validity of this credit.

3. ( ) Third party as shipper is not acceptable, Short Form/Blank back B/L is not acceptable.

4. (X) Both quantity and credit amount <u>10</u> % more or less are allowed.

5. (X) All documents must be sent To issuing bank by courier/speed post in one lot.

( ) Other terms, if any

2. 根据长沙鹏兴公司的改证函填写改证申请书并办理申请改证手续。

改证函如下：

Dear sirs,

We here have received your L/C No. DC HMN214479 for Contract No. CB121039. After checking, we would request you to make the following amendments:

1) The latest date of shipment should be extended to Sep. 15, 2012.

2) The L/C's expiry date should extended to Sep. 29, 2012.

3) Increase the amount to U.S.D28,000.00

4) Partial shipment is allowed.

Yours truly

No.: ________

APPLICATION FOR AMENDMENT
TO DOCUMENTARY CREDIT

To: HSBC BANK CANADA

L/C No.: DC HMN214479　　Issuing date：120720

Beneficiary: PENGXING IMP&EXP COMPANY LILING PENGXING CERAMIC FACTORY WUSHI JIASHU LILING HUNAN, CHINA

Expiry date：120919

latest shipment date：120905

Amount：USD27,010.40

Please amend the above credit by □ SWIFT or by □ AIRMAIL as follows:

The latest shipment date extended To 09 （mm）/ 15 （dd）/ 2012 （yy）

The expiry date extended To 09 （mm）/ 29 （dd）/ 2012 （yy）

Increase the amount by USD27,010.40 To USD28,000.00

Other terms: Please amend 43P "PARTIAL SHIPMENTS: NOT ALLOWED" To "+ PARTIAL SHIPMENTS: ALLOWED"

Banking charges by: Beneficiary, □ Applicant.

All other terms and conditions of the L/C remain unchanged.

Except as otherwise expressly stated herein, the right(s) and obligation(s) between the Applicant and the Issuing bank are still subject To the application (No.________________).

(Stamp and) Signature of Applicant

07 （mm） 22 日（dd） 2012 年（yy）

子项目三　开证及改证拓展业务操作

能力实训项目 1：填写开证申请书

进口商 M/S. MEMORY STEEL CORPORATION 根据第 SSW0803 号合同及第 0684130117426 号信用证，2013 年 8 月 20 日，由业务员 John Lee 填写了开证申请书并办理申请开证手续。

合同：

SALES CONTRACT

Contract No.:SSW0803

Date: AUG. 15, 2013

THE SELLER: JIANGSU I-TOUCH BUSINESS SERVICE LTD,
ROOM 117, JIANGSU EDIFICE
ZHANGJIAGANG FREE TRADE ZONE,
JIANGSU, CHINA　TEL:86-512-56363783

THE BUYER: M/S. MEMORY STEEL CORPORATION
73/A, LAL MOHAN SHAHA STREET
(DHOLAIKHAL),　DHAKA-1100.
BANGLADESH.

This Contract is made by and between the Buyer and Seller, whereby the Buyer agrees to buy and the Seller agrees to sell the under mentioned goods on the terms and conditions stated below:

Description of　Goods, Specifications,	Quantity (set)	Unit Price (U.S.D/set)	Amount (U.S.D)
		C.F.R	CHITTAGONG
201/2B SECONDARY GRADE STAINLESS STEEL SHEET OF WIDTH 1,219MM OR MORE THICKNESS 1MM TO 3MM, QTY:25,000KGS AT THE RATE OF USD1.40/KG.　AS PER BENIFICIARY'S PROFORMA INVOIVE NO. SK20130802-001 DATED AUG 2,2013	1.2×1,219×2,438	1.40	7,806.40
	1.5×1,219×2,438	1.40	4,547.20
	2.0×1,219×2,438	1.40	16,282.00
	3.0×1,219×2,438	1.40	6,364.40
Total			35,000.00

Say Total: U.S DOLLARS THIRTY FIVE THOUSAND ONLY.

PACKING: Standard export packing on pallets.

TRANSPORT DETAILS: the goods should shipped before: 9th Oct, 2013, from any Chinese

port To Chittagong Bangladesh,
transshipment and partial shipment are allowed.

PAYMENT: By sight L/C and remain valid for negotiation in China for 15 days after shipment.

DOCUMENTS:

+ Signed commercial invoice in triplicate, certifying the goods are of Chinese origin and being imported against IRC No.BA-0171646,VAT Registration No.9141093671.

+ Full set (3/3) of clean on board ocean Bill of Lading made out To order of shipper and blank indorsed.

+ Packing List in triplicate.

+ Certificate of origin by CCPIT.

+Beneficiary's Declaration certifying that the country of origin has been printed on goods packing bag.

INSPECTION: Quality/Quantity/Weight Discrepancy and Claim: In case the quality and/or quantity/weight are found by the Buyer not To conform with the contract after arrival of the goods at the final destination, the Buyer may lodge a claim against the seller supported by a survey report issued by an inspection organization agreed upon by both parties with the exception of those claims for which the insurance company and/or the shipping company are To be held responsible. Claim for quality discrepancy should be filed by the Buyer within 60 days after arrival of the goods at the final destination while for quantity/weight discrepancy claim should be filed by the Buyer within 30 days after arrival of the goods at the final destination.

FORCE MAJEURE: The Seller shall not be held responsible for failure or delay in delivery of the entire or portion of the goods under this contract in consequence of any Force Majeure incidents.

ARBITRATION: All disputes in connection with this Contract or the execution thereof shall be settled through friendly negotiations. If no settlement can be reached, the case shall then be submitted To the Foreign Trade Arbitration Commission of the China Council for the Promotion of International Trade, Beijing, for settlement by arbitration in accordance with the Commission's Provisional Rules of Procedure. The award rendered by the Commission shall be final and binding on both parties. The arbitration expenses shall be borne by the losing party unless otherwise award by the arbitration organization.

Signed by:

THE SELLER:	THE BUYER:
JIANGSU I-TOUCH BUSINESS	M/S. MEMORY STEEL CORPORATION.
彭 婷	John Lee

信用证：

SEQUENCE OF TOTAL	27:	1/1
FORM OF DC.	40A:	IRREVOCABLE
DC. NO.	20:	0684130117426
DATE OF ISSUE	31C:	130825
APPLICABLE RULES	40E:	UCP LATEST VERSION
EXPIRY DATE AND PLACE	31D:	131024,CHINA
APPLICANT	50:	M/S. MEMORY STEEL CORPORATION 73/A, LAL MOHAN SHAHA STREET (DHOLAIKHAL), DHAKA-1100. BANGLADESH.
BENEFICIARY	59:	JIANGSU I-TOUCH BUSINESS SERVICE LTD, ROOM 117, JIANGSU EDIFICE ZHANGJIAGANG FREE TRADE ZONE, JIANGSU, CHINA TEL:86-512-56363783
AMOUNT	32B:	USD35,000.00
AVAILABLE WITH/BY	41D:	ANY BANK IN CHINA BY NEGOTIATION
DRAFTS AT	42C:	AT SIGHT FOR FULL INVOICE VALUE
DRAWEE	42A:	DRAWN ON US
PARTIAL SHIPMENTS	43P:	ALLOWED
TRANSSHIPMENT	43T:	ALLOWED
PORT OF LOADING	44A:	ANY SEA PORT, CHINA
PORT OF DISCHARGE	44B:	CHITTAGONG SEA PORT, BANGLADESH
LATEST DATE OF SHIPMENT	44C:	131009
DESCRIPTION OF GOODS	45A:	201/2B SECONDARY GRADE STAINLESS STEEL SHEET OF WIDTH 1219MM THICKNESS 1MM TO 3MM, QTY:25,000KGS AT THE RATE OF USD1.40/KG FOR TOTAL AMOUNT OF USD35,000.00 CFR CHITTAGONG, BANGLADESH. AS PER BENEFICIARY'S PROFORMA INVOICE NO. SK20130802-001 DATED AUG 2,2013
DOCUMENTS REQUIRED	46A:	+MANUALLY SIGNED COMMERCIAL INVOICE IN TRIPLICATE CERTIFYING MERCHANDISE TO BE OF CHINA ORIGIN AND INDICATING THAT THE GOODS ARE

		BEING IMPORTED AGAINST IRC NO.BA-0171646, TI NO.157-107-0121, VAT REGISTRATION NO.9141093671. +FULL SET OF CLEAN 'SHIPPED ON BOARD' OCEAN BILL OF LADING SHOWING' FREIGHT PREPAID' MADE OUT TO ORDER AND BLANK INDORSED, NOTIFY APPLICANT. +PACKING LIST IN TRIPLICATE SHOWING GROSS WEIGHT, NET WEIGHT. +CERTIFICATE OF ORIGIN ISSUED AND LEGALED BY CCPIT + BENEFICIARY'S DECLARATION SHOULD CERTIFY THAT THE COUNTRY OF ORIGIN HAS BEEN PRINTED ON GOODS PACKING BAG. +BENEFICIARY SHOULD SEND A FAX OR BY COURIER TO L/C OPENING BANK WITHIN FIVE DAYS FROM THE OF SHIPMENT, ADVISING THE DATE OF SHIPMENT, VESSEL'S NAME, AMOUNT OF BILL AND L/C NO. AND A COPY OF THIS FAX SHOULD ACCOMPANY THE SHIPPING DOCUMENTS. +SHIPMENT BY ISRAELI LINER IS PROHIBITED AND A CERTIFICATE TO THIS EFFECT ISSUED BY THE SHIPPING COMPANY MUST ACCOMPANY THE ORIGINAL DOCUMENTS.
CHARGES	71B:	ALL FOREIGN BANK CHARGES ARE FOR THE ACCOUNT OF THE BENEFICIARY.
PERIOD OF PRESENTATION	48:	15 DAYS FROM SHIPMENT DATE BUT WITHIN VALIDITY OF THE CREDIT

开证申请书

IRREVOCABLE DOCUMENTARY CREDIT APPLICATION

To: Date:

☐Issue by airmail ☐With brief advice by teletransmission ☐Issue by express delivery ☐Issue by teletransmission (which shall be the operative instrument)	Credit No. Date and place of expiry
Applicant	Beneficiary (Full name and address)
Advising Bank	Amount
Partial shipments ( )allowed ☐not allowed Transhipment ( )allowed ☐not allowed	Credit available with By
Loading on board/dispatch/taking in charge at/from not later than For transportation To:	☐sight payment ☐acceptance ☐negotiation ☐deferred payment at against the documents detailed herein ( ) and beneficiary's draft(s) for ____ % of invoice
☐FOB ☐CFR ☐CIF ☐or other terms	value at______________ sight drawn on

Documents required: (marked with X)

1. (   ) Signed commercial invoice in _____ copies indicating L/C No. and Contract No.

2. (   ) Full set of clean on board Bills of Lading made out To order and blank endorsed, marked "freight [   ] To collect/ [   ] prepaid [   ] showing freight amount" notifying ______________________________________.

(   ) Airway bills/cargo receipt/copy of railway bills issued by ________________________ showing "freight [   ] To collect/[   ] prepaid [   ] "indicating freight amount" and consigned To______________________.

3. (   ) Insurance Policy/Certificate in ______ copies for _______ % of the invoice value showing claims payable in ____________________in currency of the draft, blank endorsed, covering All Risks and ____________________.

4. (   ) Packing List/Weight Memo in _____ copies indicating quantity, gross and net weights of each package.

5. (   ) Certificate of Quantity/Weight in ________ copies issued by _______________.

6. (   ) Certificate of Quality in ______ copies issued by [   ] manufacturer/[   ] public recognized surveyor _______.

7. (   ) Certificate of Origin in _______ copies .

8. (   ) Beneficiary's certified copy of fax/telex dispatched To the applicant within _______ days after shipment advising L/C No., name of vessel, date of shipment, name, quantity, weight and value of goods.

(   ) Other documents, if any

Description of goods:

Additional instructions:

1. (　) All banking charges outside the opening bank are for beneficiary's account.

2. (　) Documents must be presented within ______ days after date of issuance of the transport documents but within the validity of this credit.

3. (　) Third party as shipper is not acceptable, Short Form/Blank back B/L is not acceptable.

4. (　) Both quantity and credit amount ______ % more or less are allowed.

5. (　) All documents must be sent to issuing bank by courier/speed post in one lot.

(　) Other terms, if any

能力实训项目 2：改证申请书及手续办理

进口商 M/S. MEMORY STEEL CORPORATION 业务员 John Lee 根据出口商的改证函和本公司的需求，于 2013 年 8 月 27 日填写改证申请书并办理申请改证手续。

Dear sirs,

We here have received your L/C No. DC HMN214479 for Contract No. CB121039. After checking, we would request you to make the following amendments:

1) The latest date of shipment should be extended to Oct 09,2013.

2) The L/C's expiry date should extended to Sep 24,2013, and should expiry in China.

3) Transshipment is allowed.

4) Our company correct name is JIANGSU I-TOUCH BUSINESS SERVICE LTD.

Yours truly

No.: ______

APPLICATION FOR AMENDMENT

TO DOCUMENTARY CREDIT

To:　L/C No.:　　　　　　Issuing date:

Beneficiary:

Expiry date:

latest shipment date:

Amount:

Please amend the above credit by □SWIFT or by □AIRMAIL as follows:

1.

2.

3.

……

Other terms: __________

Banking charges by: □Beneficiary, □ Applicant.

All other terms and conditions of the L/C remain unchanged.

Except as otherwise expressly stated herein, the right(s) and obligation(s) between the Applicant and the Issuing bank are still subject to the application (No.________________).

(Stamp and) Signature of Applicant

_____ (mm) _____ (dd) ____ (yy)

能力实训项目 3: 填写开证申请书

进口商 CONSTRUCTION MOUDULAR SPECIALIST 根据第 BFF0606 号合同及第 DC 130720 号信用证，2013 年 7 月 5 日，业务员 Rechard 填写了开证申请书并办理申请开证手续。

合同：

CONTRACT

No.: BFF0606

Date: JUL 1, 2013

THE SELLER: PRIMA CONSTRUCTION MATERIOLS CO., LTD.
1401 ROOM, 38 BUILDING, CHUANGYE GARDEN
BAOAN DISTRICT, SHENZHEN, CHINA

THE BUYER: CONSTRUCTION MOUDULAR SPECIALIST
POSTAL: 13 HARVEY RD.,
SHENTON PK, WA 6008 AUSTRALIA

This Contract is made by and between the Buyer and Seller, whereby the Buyer agrees to buy and the Seller agrees to sell the under mentioned goods on the terms and conditions stated below:

Description of Goods, Specifications,	Quantity (SQM)	Unit Price (U.S.D/SQM)	Amount (U.S.D)
BAMBOO FLOORING ITEM 1 ITEM 2 AS PER PI NO.: BFF0610	 100 100	CIF FREMENTLE 20.00 39.50	 2,000.00 3,950.00
Total	200		5,950.00

Say Total: U.S DOLLARS FIFTY NINE HUNDRED AND FIFTY (USD5,950) ONLY.

PACKING: ALL PACKING IN SEA WORTHY CARTONS.

TRANSPORT DETAILS: the goods should be shipped on or before: 5th Sep, 2012, from Shenzhen, China To Frementle Australia, transshipment and partial shipment are all allowed.

INSURANCE: To be effected by the Seller for 110% of invoice value covering ICC(A) risk and ICC(War Risk).

PAYMENT: By irrevocable documentary letter of credit at 30 days after sight, reaching the seller not later than Jul 30,2013 and remain valid for negotiation in China for 15 days after shipment.

DOCUMENTS:

+ Signed commercial invoice three originals and three copies.
+ Full set of clean on board ocean Bill of Lading made To order.
+ Packing List three originals and two copies.
+ Insurance policy endorsed in blank and in triplicate.
+Certificate of Origin in China issued by official authority.

信用证：

SEQUENCE OF TOTAL	27:	1/1
FORM OF DC	40A:	IRREVOCABLE
DC NO.	20:	DC 130720
DATE OF ISSUE	31C:	130720
APPLICABLE RULES	40E:	UCP 600
EXPIRY DATE AND PLACE	31D:	130920 IN CHINA
APPLICANT	50:	CONSTRUCTION MOUDULAR SPECIALIST POSTAL: 13 HARVEY RD., SHENTON PK, WA 6008 AUSTRALIA
BENEFICIARY	59:	PRIMA CONSTRUCTION MATERIOLS CO., LTD 1401 ROOM, 38 BUILDING, CHUANGYE GARDEN BAOAN DISTRICT, SHENZHEN, CHINA
AMOUNT	32B:	USD6,840.00
AVAILABLE WITH/BY	41D:	ANY BANK BY NEGOTIATION
DRAFTS AT	42C:	AT 30DAYS AFTER SIGHT
DRAWEE	42A:	DRAWN ON US
PARTIAL SHIPMENTS	43P:	ALLOWED
TRANSHIPMENT	43T:	ALLOWED
LOADING PORT	44E:	CHINA MAIN PORT

DISCHARGE PORT	44F:	FREMENTLE, AUSTRALIA
LATEST DATE OF SHIPMENT	44C:	130905
DESCRIPTION OF GOODS	45A:	BAMBOO FLOORING ITEM 1 100 SQM U.S.D20.00/SQM ITEM 2 100 SQM U.S.D39.50/SQM ALL PACKING IN SEA WORTHY CARTONS CIF FREMENTLE AS PER PI NO.: BFF0610
DOCUMENTS REQUIRED	46A:	+ MANUALLY SIGNED COMMECIAL INVOICE 3 ORIGINALS PLUS THREE COPIES. + FULL SET(3/3) OF MARINE BILLS OF LADING, MADE OUT TO ORDER, MARKED FREIGHT PREPAID, AND NOTIFY APPLICANT (STATING FULL NAME AND ADDRESS). + INSURANCE POLICY OR CERTIFICATE IN TRIPLICATE, BLANK INDORSED, FOR THE INVOICE VALUE PLUS 10% COVERING ICC(A) RISK AND ICC(STRIKE). FROM WAREHOUSE TO WAREHOUSE AND I.O.P, PAYABLE AT FREMENTLE IN U.S.D. + PACKING LIST 3 ORIGINALS AND 2 COPIES. +CERTIFICATE OF ORIGIN IN CHINA ISSUED BY OFFICIAL AUTRORITY. + BENNIFICIALRY'S CERTIFICATE SHOWING THAT A SET OF ORIGINAL SHIPPING DOCUMENTS HAS BEEN MAIL TO THE APPLICANT BY EXPRESS AFTER 2 DAYS OF SHIOMENT.
CHARGES	71B:	ALL BANKING CHARGES OUTSIDE COUNTRY OF ISSUE ARE FOR BENEFICIARY/'S ACCOUNT.
PERIOD OF PRESENTATION	48:	WITHIN 15 DAYS AFTER THE DATE OF SHIPMENT BUT WITHIN THE VALIDITY OF THE L/C
CONFIRMATION INSTRUCTIONS	49:	WITHOUT

开证申请书

IRREVOCABLE DOCUMENTARY CREDIT APPLICATION

To:

Date:

☐Issue by airmail ☐With brief advice by teletransmission ☐Issue by express delivery ☐Issue by teletransmission (which shall be the operative instrument)	Credit No. Date and place of expiry
Applicant	Beneficiary (Full name and address)
Advising Bank	Amount
Partial shipments ( )allowed ☐not allowed Transhipment ( )allowed ☐not allowed	Credit available with By
Loading on board/dispatch/taking in charge at/from not later than For transportation To:	☐sight payment ☐acceptance ☐negotiation ☐deferred payment at against the documents detailed herein
☐FOB ☐CFR ☐CIF ☐or other terms	( ) and beneficiary's draft(s) for ____ % of invoice value at______________ sight drawn on

Documents required: (marked with X)

1. ( ) Signed commercial invoice in _____ copies indicating L/C No. and Contract No.

2. ( ) Full set of clean on board Bills of Lading made out To order and blank endorsed, marked "freight [ ] To collect/[ ] prepaid [ ] showing freight amount" notifying ____.

( ) Airway bills/cargo receipt/copy of railway bills issued by ______________________________ showing "freight [ ] To collect/[ ] prepaid [ ] "indicating freight amount" and consigned To__________________________.

3. ( ) Insurance Policy/Certificate in ______ copies for _______ % of the invoice value showing claims payable in ____________________in currency of the draft, blank endorsed, covering All Risks and ______________________.

4. ( ) Packing List/Weight Memo in _____ copies indicating quantity, gross and net weights of each package.

5. ( ) Certificate of Quantity/Weight in ________ copies issued by ________________.

6. ( ) Certificate of Quality in ______ copies issued by [ ] manufacturer/[ ] public recognized surveyor _______.

7. ( ) Certificate of Origin in _______ copies .

8. ( ) Beneficiary's certified copy of fax/telex dispatched To the applicant within _______ days after shipment advising L/C No., name of vessel, date of shipment, name, quantity, weight and value of goods.

( ) Other documents, if any

Description of goods:

Additional instructions:

1. ( ) All banking charges outside the opening bank are for beneficiary's account.

2. ( ) Documents must be presented within _______ days after date of issuance of the transport documents but within the validity of this credit.

3. ( ) Third party as shipper is not acceptable, Short Form/Blank back B/L is not acceptable.

4. ( ) Both quantity and credit amount ______ % more or less are allowed.

5. ( ) All documents must be sent To issuing bank by courier/speed post in one lot.

( ) Other terms, if any

能力实训项目 4：改证申请书及手续办理

进口商 CONSTRUCTION MOUDULAR SPECIALIST 业务员 JACKY 根据出口商的改证函和本公司的需求，于 2013 年 7 月 13 日填写改证申请书并办理申请改证手续。

Dear sirs,

We here have received your L/C No. DC HMN214479 for Contract No. CB121039. After checking, we would request you to make the following amendments:

1) The L/C'S total amount is USD6,840.00

2) The L/C is at sight.

3) The freight is prepaid.

4) The PI NO. is BFF0610.

Yours truly

No.: ______

APPLICATION FOR AMENDMENT

TO DOCUMENTARY CREDIT

To: L/C No.: Issuing date:

Beneficiary:

Expiry date:

latest shipment date:

Amount:

Please amend the above credit by ☐SWIFT or by ☐AIRMAIL as follows:

1.

2.

3.

……

Other terms：______________

Banking charges by: ☐Beneficiary, ☐ Applicant.

All other terms and conditions of the L/C remain unchanged.

Except as otherwise expressly stated herein, the right(s) and obligation(s) between the Applicant and the Issuing bank are still subject to the application (No.__________________).

(Stamp and) Signature of Applicant

_____(mm) _____(dd) _____(yy)

项目十二　信用证项下单据审核与修改业务

项目预期目标

通过将制作好的全套单据与该出业务中的合同与信用证进行认真审核，在遵循UCP600条款的前提下，找出单据不符点，从而归纳审单原则和适当的不符点修改方法，今早交单结汇。

在项目实施过程中，通过对全套单据的审核与修改，在分工与合作中逐渐培养审核、修改和风险控制等国际商务单证基本职业能力，亦培养独立操作信用证业务的能力。

表 12-1　　项目预期目标

目标类型	信用证项下全套单据的审核与修改
知识目标	熟悉审单原则
	掌握常见的单据不符点类型
	掌握不符点修改方法
能力目标	能根据合同、信用证及国际惯例审核全套结汇单据
	能根据不符点对单据进行及时、有效地修改
职业素质目标	独立业务操作能力
	风险控制意识

项目实施条件

1. 学生能够利用制单软件审核并修改单据
2. 指导教师具备扎实的外贸业务基础且熟悉 UCP600

开篇业务引入

2012 年 8 月 27 日，长沙鹏兴进出口有限公司第 DC HMN214479 号信用证项下全套单据全部制作完毕，单证员李望拟根据合同、信用证以及 UCP600 等国际惯例对单据进行审核。

子项目一　信用证项下单据的审核

一、审单原则

在进出口业务中，国际商务单证员如果选用信用证方式结算，则在制单及审单时应时刻以“单证相符”三原则及 UCP600、ISBP 等国际惯例为根据，即：单证一致、单单一致、单货一致；如果选用托收或汇付方式结汇，则主要根据销售合同及相应的国际惯例制单审单，即：单约一致、单单一致、单货一致。

二、主要单据的 UCP 条款及审核要点介绍

（一）商业单据的审核及不符点列举

1. UCP600 中对商业发票的规定

第十八条 商业发票

a. 商业发票：

i. 必须在表面上看来系由受益人出具（第三十八条另有规定者除外）；

ii. 必须做成以申请人的名称为抬头（第三十八条（g）款另有规定者除外）；

iii. 必须将发票币别作成与信用证相同币种；

iv. 无须签字。

b. 按照指定行事的被指定银行、保兑行（如有）或开证行可以接受金额超过信用证所允许金额的商业发票，倘若有关银行已兑付或已议付的金额没有超过信用证所允许的金额，则该银行的决定对各有关方均具有约束力。

c. 商业发票中货物、服务或行为的描述必须与信用证中显示的内容相符。

2. 审核要点

（1）“形式发票”及“临时发票”不可接受

（2）商业发票的出票人及抬头是否分别于信用证中的受益人及开证申请人信息相符

（3）商业发票的日期不得早于合同，但可以与信用证同时

（4）正文部分的货物描述与信用证的货物描述严格相符，一般货描应包括品名品牌、规格、单价、参考号、贸易术语及包装条款等内容，请注意与信用证或合同认真核对。而其他单据（除装箱单外）的货物描述部分则可以使用统称，只要与商业发票不相冲突即可

（5）商业发票中每种规格货物的金额加总之后应与信用证金额要求及汇票金额一致，且大小写保持一致

（6）是否按信用证要求注明了证实问句。常见的证明问句有原产地证明问句、显示信用证号或注册号等，在发票条款中大多会以“CERTIFYING”、“INDICATING”、“SHOWING”、“MENTIONING”等词提示出现，该类问句如若未一起出现在发票中则视为实质性单证不符

（7）如果出现上下浮动幅度，且在金额、单价、数量前有“大约”等字样，则运行相应浮动上下10%但不得超过信用证金额，除非信用证另有规定

（8）正本发票是否需要签署

（9）是否提交正确的正、副本份数

值得一提的是，商业发票是全套单据的核心，也是制作最早的单据，因此它的审核需要格外严谨。

装箱单的审核要点与商业发票类似且出单日期为同一天，但一般不出现单价、金额及证实问句等，也无须签署，不过在审核商品的毛重、净重及体积等内容时要注意前后一致并予以加总。

（二）运输单据的审核及不符点列举

1. UCP600中对运输单据的规定

（1）如果提交的是提单则必须表面看来：

a. i. 显示承运人名称并由下列人员签署：承运人或承运人的具名代理或代表，或船长或船长的具名代理或代表。承运人、船长或代理的任何签字必须分别表明其承运人、船长或代理的身份。代理的签字必须显示其是否作为承运人或船长的代理或代表签署提单。

ii. 通过下述方式表明货物已在信用证规定的装运港装载上具名船只：预先印就的措词，或注明货物已装船日期的装船批注。提单的出具日期将被视为装运日期，除非提单包含注明装运日期的装船批注，在此情况下，装船批注中显示的日期将被视为装运日期。如果提单包含“预期船”字样或类似有关限定船只的词语时，装上具名船只必须由注明装运日期以及实际装运船只名称的装船批注来证实。

iii. 注明装运从信用证中规定的装货港至卸货港。如果提单未注明以信用证中规定的装货港作为装货港，或包含“预期”或类似有关限定装货港的标注者，则需要提供注明信用证中规定的装货港、装运日期以及船名的装船批注。即使提单上已注明印就的“已装船”或“已装具名船只”措辞，本规定仍然适用。

iv. 系仅有的一份正本提单，或者，如果出具了多份正本，应是提单中显示的全套正本份数。

v. 包含承运条件须参阅包含承运条件条款及条件的某一出处（简式或背面空白的提单）者，银行对此类承运条件的条款及条件内容不予审核。

vi. 未注明运输单据受租船合约约束。

b. 就本条款而言，转运意指在信用证规定的装货港到卸货港之间的海运过程中，将货物由一艘船卸下再装上另一艘船的运输。

c. i. 只要同一提单包括运输全程，则提单可以注明货物将被转运或可被转运。

ii. 银行可以接受注明将要发生或可能发生转运的提单。即使信用证禁止转运，只要提单上证实有关货物已由集装箱、拖车或子母船运输，银行仍可接受注明将要发生或可能发生转运的提单。

d. 对于提单中包含的声明承运人保留转运权利的条款，银行将不予置理。

（2）如果提交的多式联运单据则应注意：

显示承运人名称并由下列人员签署：承运人或承运人的具名代理或代表，或船长或船长的具名代理或代表。承运人、船长或代理的任何签字必须分别表明承运人、船长或代理的身份。代理的签字必须显示其是否作为承运人或船长的代理或代表签署提单。

运输单据的出具日期以及盖章或批注日期均将被视为发运、接受监管或装载以及装运日期。

转运意指货物在信用证中规定的发运、接受监管或装载地点到最终目的地的运输过程中，从一个运输工具卸下并重新装载到另一个运输工具上（无论是否为不同运输方式）的运输。

（3）如果提交的非转让海运单则应注意：

非转让海运单的出具日期将被视为装运日期，除非非转让海运单包含注明装运日期的装船批注，在此情况下，装船批注中显示的日期将被视为装运日期。

如果非转让海运单包含“预期船”字样或类似有关限定船只的词语，或未注明以信用证中规定的装货港作为装货港，或包含“预期”或类似有关限定装货港的标注者时，需要提供注明信用证中规定的装货港、装运日期以及实际装运船名的装船批注，即使非转让海运单上已注明印就的“已装船”或“已装具名船只”措词，本规定仍然适用。

（4）关于分批装运的规定：

在信用证没有明确是否分批的情况下应视为允许分批装运。UCP600 规定，使用同一运输工具并经由同次航程运输的数套运输单据在同一次提交时，只要显示相同目的地，将不视为部分发运，即使运输单据上标明的发运日期不通或装卸港、接管地或发送地点不同。如果交单由数套运输单据构成，其中最晚的一个发运日将被视为发运日。

2. 审核要点

（1）提交的运输单据种类必须符合信用证的要求。

（2）运输单据必须由符合规定的承运人或其代理签署。

（3）除非信用证另有规定，必须提交全套运输单据，且单据上必须以英文单词的形式显示正本份数。

（4）运输单据的托运人、收货人、被通知人及其他运输详情必须与信用证规定严格相符，有时信用证禁止提交以第三方为托运人的提单。

（5）运输单据中的货物描述在不与信用证规定冲突的前提下允许使用统称，并与其他单据一致。

（6）运输单据中的运费记载条款必须与贸易术语相符。如 CIF、CFR 术语应注明“FREIGHT PREPAID”（运费预付）或“FREIGHT PAID”（运费已付）；FOB 术语则应注明“FREIGHT COLLECT”（运费托收）。

（7）指示提单或空白提单应背书，但我国一般不接受空白提单。

（8）提单是否需要做已装船批注。

（三）保险单据的审核及不符点列举

（1）保险单据的份数必须符合信用证的规定。

（2）保险单据的签发日期不得晚于提单。

（3）保险单据的投保比例及投保险种必须与信用证规定一致。

（4）保险单据中的运输资料如船名航次、开航日期及运输路线等应与提单保持一致。

（5）保险单据中的货物描述和唛头等信息可以使用统称或简称，但不得与信用证的规定冲突，同时也要与其他单据保持一致。

（6）应提交符合信用证规定的保单类型。如来证要求提交保险单，则不能提交保险凭证，但如果要求提交保险凭证则可以用保险单代替。

（四）原产地证书的审核及不符点列举

（1）必须按信用证的要求提交规定的原产地证书种类，由于不同的原产地证书由不同的机构签发，因此切忌将证书类型混淆。

（2）原产地证书必须由发证机构签署或证明。

（3）原产地证书的日期不能迟于提单且一般晚于商业发票。

（4）原产地证书的正本一般只有一份，副本 1～2 份。

（五）其他单据的审核要点

该类单据的审核关键是要遵循信用证的要求，将来证当中要求列明或证明的内容一一罗列，有的信用证在附属条款当中额外要求所有单据均必须显示某些信息如开证行名称及信用证号，此时要特别注意在装运通知、受益人证明中予以列出，否则视为单证不符。

另外，当单据名称中含有“CERTIFICATE”、“DECLARATION”或“STATEMENT”等字样时，该单据必须签署。

（六）汇票的审核要点

（1）汇票的出票条款是否与信用证一致。

（2）汇票的出票人、持票人及付款人是否与信用证一致并符合 UCP600 规定。如信用证项下汇票的付款人必须是银行而非进口方，但托收汇票中则无此规定。

（3）汇票金额是否与信用证相符并保持大小写一致。

（4）汇票的出票时间不得早于提单，不得晚于证效期。

子项目二　开证及改证典型业务演示

上接项目十，鹏兴公司在备齐第 DC HMN214479 号信用证项下全套单据之后准备向中国银行湖南省分行交单议付，在此之前，单证员李望应完成下列工作任务：

任务 1：对照合同、信用证及相关国际惯例认真审核全套单据

任务 2：找出单据中的错误并及时修改

1. 信用证：

SEQUENCE OF TOTAL	27:	1/1
FORM OF DC	40A:	IRREVOCABLE
DC NO	20:	DC HMN214479
DATE OF ISSUE	31C:	120720
APPLICABLE RULES	40E:	UCP LATEST VERSION
EXPIRY DATE AND PLACE	31D:	120919 IN COUNTRY OF BENEFICIARY
APPLICANT	50:	ELBY GIFTS INC.879 INDUSTRIEL BOIS DES FILION,QUEBEC, J6Z 4T3, CANADA
BENEFICIARY	59:	LILING PENGXING CERAMIC FACTORY WUSHI JIASHU LILING HUNAN, CHINA
AMOUNT	32B:	USD27,010.40
PCT CR AMT TOLERANCE	39A:	10/10
AVAILABLE WITH/BY	41D:	ANY BANK BY NEGOTIATION
DRAFTS AT	42C:	AT SIGHT FOR FULL INVOICE VALUE
DRAWEE	42A:	ISSUING BANK
PARTIAL SHIPMENTS	43P:	ALLOWED
TRANSHIPMENT	43T:	ALLOWED
PORT OF LOADING	44E:	SHENZHEN, CHINA
PORT OF DISCHARGE	44F:	PRINCE RUPERT,BC
LATEST DATE OF SHIPMENT	44D:	120905
DESCRIPTION OF GOODS OR SERVICES	45A:	CERAMIC CUPS AND BOWLS AS PER S/C NO.:CB121039 CIF PRINCE RUPERT,BC ALL PACKED IN CARTONS.
DOCUMENTS REQUIRED	46A:	+ ORIGINAL SIGNED INVOICE PLUS THREE COPIES. + FULL SET OF CLEAN MULTIMODAL TRANSPORT DOCUMENT PLUS 2 N/N COPIES, MADE TO THE ORDER OF HSBC BANK CANADA, SHOWING ON BOARD NOTATION, MARKED FREIGHT PREPAID, AND NOTIFY APPLICANT(STATING FULL NAME AND ADDRESS). + INSURANCE POLICY OR CERTIFICATE BLANK INDORSED, FOR THE INVOICE VALUE PLUS 10% COVERING ALL RISKS AND S.R.CC. FROM WAREHOUSE TO WAREHOUSE. + ORIGINAL PACKING LIST PLUS 2 COPIES + GSP CERTIFICATE OF ORIGIN FORM A, IN

ONE ORIGINAL PLUS 2 COPIES, INDICATING COUNTRY OF ORIGIN, COUNTERCHOPPED BY GOVERNMENT AUTHORITIES OR EXPORTER'S STATMENT OF ORIGIN
+ SHIPPING NOTE INCLUDING SHIPPING MARKS, CTN NO., B/L NO., QUANTITY, VESSEL'S NAME, VOYAGE NO., SHOULD BE SENT TO THE ISSUING BANK ON THE DATE OF SHIPMENT.

ADDITIONAL CONDITIONS 47A: + BENEFICIARY'S DETAILS:
CTC: MILLER LEE
TEL: 86-731-2338-4199
FAX: 86-731-2338-4298
FOLLOWING CHARGES ARE FOR BENEFICIARY'S ACCOUNT:
1) REIMBURSEMENT/REMITTANCE CHARGES
2) DISCREPANCY FEE OF USD/CAD/EUR100 PLUS ALL RELEVANT CABLE CHARGES WILL BE DEDUCTED FROM EACH PRESENTATION OF DISCREPANT
DOCUMENTS UNDER THIS DC.

CHARGES 71B: ALL BANKING CHARGES OUTSIDE COUNTRY OF ISSUE FOR ACCOUNT OF BENEFICIARY/ EXPORTER

PERIOD OF PRESENTATION 48: WITHIN 15 DAYS AFTER THE DATE OF SHIPMENT BUT WITHIN THE VALIDITY OF THE CREDIT

CONFIRMATION INSTRUCTIONS 49: WITHOUT

INFO TO PRESENTING BK 78: + UPON RECEIPT OF DOCUMENTS CONFORMING TO THE TERMS OF THIS CREDIT WE UNDERTAKE TO REIMBURSE YOU IN THE CURRENCY OF THIS CREDIT IN ACCORDANCE WITH YOUR INSTRUCTIONS, LESS CABLE CHARGES,
+ FORWARD DOCUMENTS IN ONE LOT BY COURIER AT BENEFICIARY'S EXPENSES TO HSBC BANK CANADA, TRADE AND SUPPLY CHAIN, 5100 SHERBROOKE STREET EAST, SUITE 190, MONTREAL,QUEBEC,H1V 3R9 CANADA.
+ THE AMOUNT OF EACH DRAWING MUST

BE ENDORSED ON THE REVERSE OF THIS DC BY THE NEGOTIATING/PRESENTING BANK.

2. 合同：

CONTRACT

Contract No.: CB121039

Date: JUL. 5, 2012

THE SELLER: PENGXING IMP&EXP COMPANY
LILING PENGXING CERAMIC FACTOR
WUSHI JIASHU LILING HUNAN, CHINA
TEL: 86-731-23384199 FAX: 86-731-23384298

THE BUYER: ELBY GIFTS INC.
879 INDUSTRIEL BOIS DES FILION
QUEBEC, J6Z 4T3, CANADA
TEL: 514-420-0282 FAX: 514-420-0322

This Contract is made by and between the Buyer and Seller, whereby the Buyer agrees to buy and the Seller agrees to sell the under mentioned goods on the terms and conditions stated below:

Description of Goods, Specifications,	Quantity (set)	Unit Price (U.S.D/set)	Amount (U.S.D)
Ceramic Cups and Bowls		C.I.F Prince	
V23-234	912	Rupert	3,693.60
V23-234F	912	4.05	3,693.60
V23-235	1,520	4.05	3,648.00
V23-236	1,512	2.40	3,175.20
V23-237	1,488	2.10	2,901.6
V23-2348	1,520	1.95	3,100.80
36-062	1,528	2.04	3,514.40
36-063	1,496	2.30	3,171.52
As per the P/I No.: CCB23-36		2.12	
Total	10,888		26,898.72

Say total: U.S DOLLARS TWENTY SIX THOUSAND EIGHT HUNDRED AND NINETY EIGHT AND CENTS SEVENTY TWO(USD26,898.72)ONLY.

PACKING: 4 sets packed in a carton(V 23-234/V23-234F), 8 sets packed in a carton for others.

TRANSPORT DETAILS: the goods should be shipped on or before: 5th Sep, 2012, from Shenzhen, China to Prince Rupert Canada, transshipment and partial shipment are all allowed.

INSURANCE: To be effected by the Seller for 110% of invoice value covering all risks and

S.R.C.C as per C.I.C of PICC dated 01/01/1981.

PAYMENT: By irrevocable documentary letter of credit at sight, reaching the seller not later than Aug 5,2012 and remain valid for negotiation in China for 15 days after shipment.

DOCUMENTS:

+ Signed commercial invoice one original and three copies.
+ Full set of clean on board ocean Bill of Lading made to order of issuing bank.
+ Packing List one original and two copies.
+ Insurance policy endorsed in blank.
+ GSP Form A certified by government authority.

INSPECTION: Quality/Quantity/Weight Discrepancy and Claim: In case the quality and/or quantity/weight are found by the Buyer not to conform with the contract after arrival of the goods at the final destination, the Buyer may lodge a claim against the seller supported by a survey report issued by an inspection organization agreed upon by both parties with the exception of those claims for which the insurance company and/or the shipping company are to be held responsible. Claim for quality discrepancy should be filed by the Buyer within 60 days after arrival of the goods at the final destination while for quantity/weight discrepancy claim should be filed by the Buyer within 30 days after arrival of the goods at the final destination.

FORCE MAJEURE: The Seller shall not be held responsible for failure or delay in delivery of the entire or portion of the goods under this contract in consequence of any Force Majeure incidents.

ARBITRATION: All disputes in connection with this Contract or the execution thereof shall be settled through friendly negotiations. If no settlement can be reached, the case shall then be submitted to the Foreign Trade Arbitration Commission of the China Council for the Promotion of International Trade, Beijing, for settlement by arbitration in accordance with the Commission's Provisional Rules of Procedure. The award rendered by the Commission shall be final and binding on both parties. The arbitration expenses shall be borne by the losing party unless otherwise award by the arbitration organization.

Signed by:

THE SELLER:	THE BUYER:
PENGXING IMP&EXP COMPANY	ELBY GIFTS INC.
LILING PENGXING CERAMIC FACTORY	
李 望	Camp Wolf

3. 商业发票：

PENGXING IMP&EXP COMPANY

LILING PENGXING CERAMIC FACTORY

WUSHI JIASHU LILING HUNAN CHINA

TEL: 86-731-23384199 FAX: 86-731-23384298

COMMERCIAL INVOICE

To: ELBY GANTS INC.
879 INDUSTRIEL BOIS DES FILION
QUEBEC, J6Z 4T3, CANADA

Invoice No.: PX12IVN1039

Invoice Date: AUG. 16, 2012

S/C No.: S/C NO.: CB121039

S/C Date: JUL. 5, 2012

From: SHENZHEN, CHINA

To: PRINCE RPERT, BC, CANADA

Letter of Credit No.: DC HMN214479

Issued By: HSBC BANK, MONTREAL CANADA

Marks and Numbers	Number and Kind of Package Description of Goods	Quantity	Unit Price	Amount
ELBY	CERAMIC CUPS AND BOWLS	CFR PRINCE RUPERT, BC CTN		
S/C NO.:CB121039	V23-234	228	4.05	3,693.60
NO: 1-1589	V23-234F	228	4.05	3,693.60
	V23-235	190	2.40	3,648.00
	V23-236	189	2.10	3,175.20
	V23-237	186	1.95	2,901.60
	V23-2348	190	2.04	3,100.80
	36-062	191	2.30	3,514.40
	36-063	187	2.12	3,171.52
	Total:	1,589 CTNS		U.S.D 26,898.72

Say Total: U.S DOLLARS TWENTY SIX THOUSAND EIGHT HUNDRED AND NINETY EIGHT AND CENTS SEVENTY TWO(USD26,898.72)ONLY

PENGXING IMP&EXP COMPANY

李 望

4. 装箱单：

PENGXING IMP&EXP COMPANY

LILING PENGXING CERAMIC FACTORY

WUSHI JIASHU LILING HUNAN CHINA

TEL: 86-731-23384199　FAX: 86-731-23384298

PACKING LIST

To: ELBY GIFTS INC.
879 INDUSTRIEL BOIS DES FILION
QUEBEC, J6Z 4T3, CANADA

Date AUG. 16, 2012

Invoice No.: PX12IVN1039

From: SHENZHEN, CHINA　**To:** PRINCE RPERT, BC, CANADA

Item No.	Description of goods	Quantity		Sets/CTN			G.W/N.W		Dimension			Meas.
V23-234	CERAMIC CUPS AND BOWLS	912	SETS	228	CTNS	4	11.8	9.6	38.9*	29.0*	26.6	6.84
V23-234F	CERAMIC CUPS AND BOWLS	912	SETS	228	CTNS	4	11.8	9.6	38.9*	29.0*	26.6	6.84
V23-235	CERAMIC CUPS AND BOWLS	1,520	SETS	190	CTNS	8	15.0	12.8	48.6*	31.6*	43.6	12.72
V23-236	CERAMIC CUPS AND BOWLS	1,512	SETS	189	CTNS	8	10.6	8.4	50.4*	27.0*	.34.8	8.95
V23-237	CERAMIC CUPS AND BOWLS	1,488	SETS	186	CTNS	8	8.4	6.4	31.0*	28.2*	39.2	6.37
V23-2348	CERAMIC CUPS AND BOWLS	1,520	SETS	190	CTNS	8	10.5	8.0	48.6	28.2*	39.2	10.21
36-062	CERAMIC CUPS AND BOWLS	1,528	SETS	191	CTNS	8	12.0	9.6	49.0*	28.9*	38.2	10.33
36-063	CERAMIC CUPS AND BOWLS	1,496	SETS	187	CTNS	8	8.4	6.4	34.4*	33.0*	27.6	5.86
	Total:	10,888	SETS	1,589	CTNS				17,654.4	14,138.0		68.13

ALL PACKED IN CARTONS

SAY TOTAL: ONE THOUSAND FIVE HUNDRED AND EIGHTY NINE (1,589CTNS) CARTONS ONLY

5. 保险单：

<table>
<tr><td colspan="2">**PICC**</td><td colspan="3">中国人民保险公司
The People's Insurance Company of China
总公司设于北京　一九四九年创立
Head Office Beijing　Established in 1949</td></tr>
<tr><td colspan="5">货物运输保险单
CARGO TRANSPORTATION INSURANCE POLICY</td></tr>
<tr><td>发票号(INVOICE NO.)</td><td>PX21IN1039</td><td rowspan="2">保单号次
POLICY NO.</td><td colspan="2" rowspan="2">SH01/173071</td></tr>
<tr><td>合同号(CONTRACT NO.)</td><td>CB121039</td></tr>
<tr><td>信用证号
(L/C NO.)</td><td colspan="4">DC HMN214479</td></tr>
<tr><td>被保险人：
INSURED:</td><td colspan="4">LILING PENGXING CERAMIC FACTORY WUSHI JIASHU LILING HUNAN, CHINA</td></tr>
<tr><td colspan="5">中国人民保险公司(以下简称本公司)根据被保险人的要求，由被保险人向本公司缴付约定的保险费，按照本保险单承保险别和背面所载条款与下列特款承保下述货物运输保险，特立本保险单。
THIS POLICY OF INSURANCE WITNESSES THAT THE PEOPLE'S INSURANCE COMPANY OF CHINA (HEREINAFTER CALLED "THE COMPANY") AT THE REQUEST OF THE INSURED AND IN CONSIDERATION OF THE AGREED PREMIUM PAID TO THE COMPANY BY THE INSURED, UNDERTAKES TO INSURE THE UNDERMENTIONED GOODS IN TRANSPORTATION SUBJECT TO THE CONDITIONS OF THIS POLICY AS PER THE CLAUSES PRINTED OVERLEAF AND OTHER SPECIAL CLAUSES ATTACHED HEREON.</td></tr>
<tr><td colspan="2">标　记
MARKS&NOS</td><td>包装及数量
QUANTITY</td><td>保险货物项目
DESCRIPTION OF GOODS</td><td>保险金额
AMOUNT INSURED</td></tr>
<tr><td colspan="2">AS PRE INVOICE NO. PX12IVN1039</td><td>1,589 CTNS</td><td>CERAMIC CUPS AND BOWLS</td><td>US$29,588.59</td></tr>
<tr><td>总保险金额
TOTAL AMOUNT INSURED:</td><td colspan="4">SAY U.S.DOLLARS TWENTY NINE THOUSAND FIVE HUNDRED AND EIGHTY EIGHT AND CENTS FIFTY NINE ONLY</td></tr>
</table>

保费: PERMIUM:	AS ARRANGE D	启运日期 DATE OF COMMENCEMENT:	AS PER B/L	装载运输工具: PER CONVEYANCE:	COSCO SEATTLE VOY. NO.0078E
自 FROM:	SHENZHEN	经 VIA		至 TO	PRINCE RUPERT

承保险别:
CONDITIONS:

COVERING ALL RISKS OF CIC OF PICC(1/1/1981) INCL.WAREHOUSE TO WAREHOUSE

所保货物，如发生保险单项下可能引起索赔的损失或损坏，应立即通知本公司下述代理人查勘。如有索赔，应向本公司提交保单正本(本保险单共有 1 份正本)及有关文件。如一份正本已用于索赔，其余正本自动失效。

IN THE EVENT OF LOSS OR DAMAGE WHICH MAY RESULT IN A CLAIM UNDER THIS POLICY, IMMEDIATE NOTICE MUST BE GIVEN TO THE COMPANY'S AGENT AS MENTIONED HEREUNDER. CLAIMS, IF ANY, ONE OF THE ORIGINAL POLICY WHICH HAS BEEN ISSUED IN ONE ORIGINAL(S) TOGETHER WITH THE RELEVANT DOCUMENTS SHALL BE SURRENDERED TO THE COMPANY. IF ONE OF THE ORIGINAL POLICY HAS BEEN ACCOMPLISHED. THE OTHERS TO BE VOID.

		中国人民保险公司 The People's Insurance Company of China
赔款偿付地点 CLAIM PAYABLE AT	PRINCE RUPERT IN USD	SHENZHEN
出单日期	Aug.25,2012	* * * * * *

6. 海运提单：

1. Shipper Insert Name, Address and Phone LILING PENGXING CERAMIC FACTORY WUSHI JIASHU LILING HUNAN, CHINA		许可证号 B/L No. COSFMT3821018 中远集装箱运输有限公司 **COSCO CONTAINER LINES** TLX: 33057 COSCO CN FAX: +86(021) 6545 8984 **ORIGINAL** **Port-to-Port or Combined Transport** **BILL OF LADING**
2. Consignee Insert Name, Address and Phone TO THE ORDER		
3. Notify Party Insert Name, Address and Phone (It is agreed that no responsibility shall attach to the Carrier or his agents for failure to notify) ELBY GIFTS INC. 879 INDUSTRIEL BOIS DES FILION		RECEIVED in external apparent good order and condition except as otherwise noted. The total number of packages or units stuffed in the container, the description of the goods and the weights shown in this Bill of Lading are furnished by the Merchants, and which the carrier has no reasonable means of checking and is not a part of this Bill of Lading contract. The carrier has issued the number of Bills of Lading stated below, all of this tenor and date, one of the original Bills of Lading must be surrendered and endorsed or signed against the delivery of the shipment and whereupon any other original Bills of Lading shall be void. The Merchants agree to be bound by the terms and conditions of this Bill of Lading as if each had personally signed this Bill of Lading. SEE clause 4 on the back of this Bill of Lading (Terms continued on the back hereof, please read carefully). *Applicable Only When Document Used as a Combined Transport Bill of Lading.
4. Combined Transport * Pre-carriage by TRAIN NO.:67589	5. Combined Transport* Place of Receipt CHANGSHA	
6. Ocean Vessel Voy. No. COSCO SEATTLE V.0078E	7. Port of Loading YANTIAN,SHENZHEN, CHINA	
8. Port of Discharge PRINCE RUPERT, BC, CANADA	9. Combined Transport * Place of Delivery BOIS DES FILION, CANADA	

Marks & Nos. Container/Seal No.	No. of Containers or Packages	Description of Goods (If Dangerous Goods, See Clause 20)	Gross Weight Kgs	Measurement
N/M	1589CTNS CONTAINER NO.: CBHU8150082/ B45171/40'HQ	SHIPPER'S LOAD & COUNT & SEAL 1X40'HQ (F.C.L) S.T.C CY/CY ONE THOUSAND FIVE HUNDRED AND EIGHTY NINE(1589CTNS)CARTONS OF CERAMIC CUPS AND BOWLS FOB SHENZHEN, CHINA THIS SHIPMENT CONTAINS NO SOLID WOOD PACKING MATERIALS.	17,654.40 KGS	68.130 CBM
		Description of Contents for Shipper's Use Only (Not part of This B/L Contract)		

10. Total Number of containers and/or packages (in words) SAY ONE THOUSAND FIVE HUNDRED AND EIGHTY NINE CARTONS ONLY.

11. Freight & Charges	Revenue Tons	Rate	Per	Prepaid	Collect
FREIGHT COLLECT	AS ARRANGED				

Ex. Rate	Prepaid at	Payable at	Place and date of issue
			SHENZHEN, CHINA AUG. 24, 2012
	Total Prepaid	No. of Original B(s)/L 3	Signed for the Carrier, COSCO CONTAINER LINES COSCO AS CARRIER XXXX

7. 原产地证：

1. Goods consigned from (Exporter's business name, address, country) PENGXIANG IMP&EXP CORP. WUSHI JIASHU LILING HUNAN, CHINA	Reference No. Z12470ZC40401388 GENERALIZED SYSTEM OF PREFERENCES FORM A CERTIFICATE OF ORIGIN (Combined declaration and certificate)
2. Goods consigned to (Consignee's name, address, country) ELBY GIFTS INC.879 INDUSTRIEL BOIS DES FILION, QUEBEC, J6Z 4T3	FORM A Issued in THE PEOPLE'S REPUBLIC OF CHINA (country) See Notes overleaf
3. Means of transport and route (as far as known) FROM SHENZHEN CHINA TO BOIS DES FILION, CANADA BY VESSEL	4. For official use

5. Item number	6. Marks and numbers of packages	7. Number and kind of packages; description of goods	8. Origin criterion (see Notes overleaf)	9. Gross weight or other quantity	10. Number and date of invoices
1	N/M	CERAMIC CUPS AND BOWLS TOTAL: ONE THOUSAND FIVE HUNDRED EIGHTY NINE (1589) CARTONS COUNTRY OF ORIGIN: CHINA **	"P"	10888SETS	PX12IVN1039 AUG. 16, 2012

11. Certification It is hereby certified, on the basis of control carried out, that the declaration by the exporter is correct. **C.I.Q** SHENZHEN, AUG 19, 2012 -- Place and date, signature and stamp of certifying authority	12. Declaration by the exporter The undersigned hereby declares that the above details and statements are correct, that all the goods were **CHINA** produced in .... (country) and that they comply with the origin requirements specified for those goods in the Generalized System of Preferences for goods exported to **CANADA** .... SHENZHEN, AUG. 19, 2012 -- Place and date, signature and stamp of authorized signatory

8. 汇票：

凭 信用证 第 号

Drawn under HSBC BANK CANADA L/C No. DC HMN214479

日期 按 息 付款

Dated JULY 20, 2012 Payable with interest @.................% per annum

号码 汇 票 金 额 中 国，长 沙 年 月 日

No.: PX12IVN1039 Exchange for USD26,898.00 Changsha, China AUG.26,2012

见票 日后（本 汇 票 之 副 本 未 付）

At *** Sight of this FIRST of Exchange(Second of exchange being unpaid)

Pay to the order of BANK OF CHINA, HUNAN BRANCH 或其指定人付金额

The sum of U.S. DOLLARS TWENTY SIX THOUSAND EIGHT HUNDRED AND NINETY EIGHT ONLY.

To: HSBC BANK CANADA

LILING PENGXING CERAMIC FACTORY
李 望

经过认真审核后，李望发现上述单据中主要存在以下不符点，并予以修改：

1. 商业发票中的抬头错误，应改为 ELBY GIFTS INC.
2. 商业发票中的贸易术语错误，应改为 CIF PRINCE RUPERT, BC
3. 装箱单中的总箱数错误，应改为 1,589 CTNS

4. 保险单中的发票号码错误，应改为 PX12IVN1039

5. 保险单的险种错误，应改为 COVERING ALL RISKS AND S.R.CC. OF CIC OF PICC (1/1/1981) INCL.

6.保险单的签发日期不得晚于提单，应改为 Aug. 23, 2012

7. 海运提单的抬头与信用证规定不符，应改为 TO THE ORDER OF HSBC BANK CANADA

8. 海运提单的费用记载应与贸易术语一致，改为 FREIGHT PREPAID

9. 海运提单的正本份数描述错误，应改为 THREE

10. 原产地证中给惠国漏打了国名，应改为 ELBY GIFTS INC.879 INDUSTRIEL，BOIS DES FILION, QUEBEC, J6Z 4T3, CANADA

11.汇票的期限错误，应改为***

12. 汇票的小写金额错误，应改为 USD26,898.72

13. 汇票中的付款人漏打了地址，应改为：HSBC BANK CANADA, TRADE AND SUPPLY CHAIN, 5100 SHERBROOKE STREET EAST, SUITE 190, MONTREAL, QUEBEC, H1V 3R9 CANADA.

子项目三　开证及改证拓展业务操作

能力实训项目 1：全套单据审核与修改

2013 年 9 月 10 日，单证员黄柯在制作完第 DC 130720 号信用证项下全套单据后根据合同、信用证对单据进行了认真审核，该业务的信用证、合同及所制作的单据如下：

1. 信用证：

SEQUENCE OF TOTAL	27:	1/1
FORM OF DC	40A:	IRREVOCABLE
DC NO.	20:	DC 130720
DATE OF ISSUE	31C:	130720
APPLICABLE RULES	40E:	UCP 600
EXPIRY DATE AND PLACE	31D:	130920 IN CHINA
APPLICANT	50:	CONSTRUCTION MOUDULAR SPECIALIST POSTAL: 13 HARVEY RD., SHENTON PK, WA 6008 AUSTRALIA
BENEFICIARY	59:	PRIMA CONSTRUCTION MATERIOLS CO., LTD 1401 ROOM, 38 BUILDING, CHUANGYE GARDEN BAOAN DISTRICT, SHENZHEN, CHINA
AMOUNT	32B:	USD6,840.00
AVAILABLE WITH/BY	41D:	ANY BANK BY NEGOTIATION
DRAFTS AT	42C:	AT 30DAYS AFTER SIGHT

DRAWEE	42A:	DRAWN ON US
PARTIAL SHIPMENTS	43P:	ALLOWED
TRANSHIPMENT	43T:	ALLOWED
LOADING PORT	44E:	CHINA MAIN PORT
DISCHARGE PORT	44F:	FREMENTLE, AUSTRALIA
LATEST DATE OF SHIPMENT	44C:	130905
DESCRIPTION OF GOODS	45A:	BAMBOO FLOORING ITEM 1 100 SQM U.S.D20.00/SQM ITEM 2 100 SQM U.S.D39.50/SQM ALL PACKING IN SEA WORTHY CARTONS CIF FREMENTLE AS PER PI NO.: BFF0610
DOCUMENTS REQUIRED	46A:	+ MANUALLY SIGNED COMMECIAL INVOICE 3 ORIGINALS PLUS THREE COPIES. + FULL SET(3/3) OF MARINE BILLS OF LADING, MADE OUT TO ORDER, MARKED FREIGHT PREPAID, AND NOTIFY APPLICANT (STATING FULL NAME AND ADDRESS). + INSURANCE POLICY OR CERTIFICATE IN TRIPLICATE, BLANK INDORSED, FOR THE INVOICE VALUE PLUS 10% COVERING ICC(A) RISK AND ICC(STRIKE). FROM WAREHOUSE TO WAREHOUSE AND I.O.P, PAYABLE AT FREMENTLE IN U.S.D. + PACKING LIST 3 ORIGINALS AND 2 COPIES. +CERTIFICATE OF ORIGIN IN CHINA ISSUED BY OFFICIAL AUTRORITY. + BENNIFICIALRY'S CERTIFICATE SHOWING THAT A SET OF ORIGINAL SHIPPING DOCUMENTS HAS BEEN MAIL TO THE APPLICANT BY EXPRESS AFTER 2 DAYS OF SHIOMENT.
CHARGES	71B:	ALL BANKING CHARGES OUTSIDE COUNTRY OF ISSUE ARE FOR BENEFICIARY/'S ACCOUNT.
PERIOD OF PRESENTATION	48:	WITHIN 15 DAYS AFTER THE DATE OF SHIPMENT BUT WITHIN THE VALIDITY OF THE L/C
CONFIRMATION INSTRUCTIONS	49:	WITHOUT

2. 合同：

CONTRACT

Contract No.: BFF0606

Date: JUL. 1, 2013

THE SELLER: PRIMA CONSTRUCTION MATERIOLS CO., LTD
1401 ROOM, 38 BUILDING, CHUANGYE GARDEN
BAOAN DISTRICT, SHENZHEN, CHINA

THE BUYER: CONSTRUCTION MOUDULAR SPECIALIST
POSTAL: 13 HARVEY RD.,
SHENTON PK, WA 6008 AUSTRALIA

This Contract is made by and between the Buyer and Seller, whereby the Buyer agrees to buy and the Seller agrees to sell the under mentioned goods on the terms and conditions stated below:

Description of Goods, Specifications,	Quantity (SQM)	Unit Price (U.S.D/SQM)	Amount (U.S.D)
BAMBOO FLOORING ITEM 1 ITEM 2 AS PER PI NO.: BFF0610	 100 100	CIF FREMENTLE 20.00 39.50	 2,000.00 3,950.00
Total	200		5,950.00

Say total: U.S DOLLARS FIFTY NINE HUNDRED AND FIFTY (USD5,950) ONLY.

PACKING: ALL PACKING IN SEA WORTHY CARTONS.

TRANSPORT DETAILS: the goods should be shipped on or before: 20th Sep, 2013, from Shenzhen, China to Frementle Australia, transshipment and partial shipment are all allowed.

INSURANCE: To be effected by the Seller for 110% of invoice value covering ICC(A) risk and ICC(War Risk).

PAYMENT: By irrevocable documentary letter of credit at 30 days after sight, reaching the seller not later than Jul 30,2013 and remain valid for negotiation in China for 15 days after shipment.

DOCUMENTS:

+ Signed commercial invoice three originals and three copies.
+ Full set of clean on board ocean Bill of Lading made to order.
+ Packing List three originals and two copies.
+ Insurance policy endorsed in blank and in triplicate.
+ Certificate of Origin in China issued by official authority.

3. 商业发票：

Prima Construction Materials Co., Ltd.

Add: 1401Room, 38building, Chuangye Gardern, Baoan District, Shenzhen China

Tel: 0086-755-32076630 Fax: 0086-755-32076630

COMMERCIAL INVOICE

To: CONSTRUCTION MOUDULAR SPECIALIST
POSTAL: 13 HARVEY RD., SHENTON PK, WA 6008 AUSTRALIA

Contract No.: CBF130724		**No.:PR-20130820**		
L/C No.: DC 13724		**Date: AUG. 22, 2013**		
From: SHENZHEN		**To: FREMENTLE**		
Marks&Nos. No	**Description of Goods**	**Quantity**	**Unit Price**	**Amount**
	BAMBOO FLOORING		CIF shenzhen	
CMS FREMENTLE CBF130724 NO.:1-109	CARBONISED BAMBOO FLOORING	100SQM	$ 20.00	$2,000.00
	STRAND WOVEN BAMBOO FLOORING DECKING	100SQM	$39.50	$3,950.00
TOTAL			EXW PRICE	$5,950.00
			LCL CHARGE	$ 450.00
			INSURANCE COST	$ 60.00
			FREIGHT	$ 380.00
			CIF VALUE	$6,480.00

Prima Construction Materials Co., Ltd.

黄 柯

4. 海运提单：

1. Shipper Insert Name, Address and Phone

PRIMA CONSTRUCTION MATERIOLS CO.,
LTD 1401 ROOM, 38 BUILDING,
CHUANGYE GARDEN BAOAN DISTRICT,
SHENZHEN, CHINA

2. Consignee Insert Name, Address and Phone

TO ORDER OF CONSTRUCTION
MOUDULAR SPECIALIST

3. Notify Party Insert Name, Address and Phone
(It is agreed that no responsibility shall attach to the Carrier or his agents for failure to notify)

CONSTRUCTION MOUDULAR SPECIALIST
POSTAL: 13 HARVEY RD.,
SHENTON PK, WA 6008

4. Combined Transport * Pre-carriage by	5. Combined Transport* Place of Receipt
6. Ocean Vessel Voy. No. MOL INTEGRITY/ 102W	7. Port of Loading SHANGHAI, CHINA
8. Port of Discharge FREMENTLE, AUSTRALIA	9. Combined Transport * Place of Delivery

许可证号

B/L No.
COSFMT3821018

中远集装箱运输有限公司
COSCO CONTAINER LINES

TLX: 33057 COSCO CN
FAX: +86(021) 6545 8984

ORIGINAL

Port-to-Port or Combined Transport

BILL OF LADING

RECEIVED in external apparent good order and condition except as otherwise noted. The total number of packages or units stuffed in the container, the description of the goods and the weights shown in this Bill of Lading are furnished by the Merchants, and which the carrier has no reasonable means of checking and is not a part of this Bill of Lading contract. The carrier has issued the number of Bills of Lading stated below, all of this tenor and date, one of the original Bills of Lading must be surrendered and endorsed or signed against the delivery of the shipment and whereupon any other original Bills of Lading shall be void. The Merchants agree to be bound by the terms and conditions of this Bill of Lading as if each had personally signed this Bill of Lading.

SEE clause 4 on the back of this Bill of Lading (Terms continued on the back hereof, please read carefully).

*Applicable Only When Document Used as a Combined Transport Bill of Lading.

Marks & Nos. Container/Seal No.	No. of Containers or Packages	Description of Goods (If Dangerous Goods, See Clause 20)	Gross Weight Kgs	Measurement
CMS FREMENT CBF1324 NO.:1-109	109CTNS	BAMBOO FLOORING 109 CTNS PACKED IN 2 PLTS	3,128.000 KGS	5.280 M^3
		Description of Contents for Shipper's Use Only (Not part of This B/L Contract)		

10. Total Number of containers and/or packages (in words) SAY ONE HUNDRED AND NINE CARTONS ONLY

Subject to Clause 7 Limitation

11. Freight & Charges	Revenue Tons	Rate	Per	Prepaid	Collect
FREIGHT COLLECT	AS ARRANGED				
Declared Value Charge					

Ex. Rate	Prepaid at	Payable at	Place and date of issue
			SHANGHAI SEP. 5, 2013
	Total Prepaid	No. of Original B(s)/L	Signed for the Carrier, COSCO CONTAINER LINES
		THREE	COSCO AS CARRIER XXXX

LADEN ON BOARD THE VESSEL

AS AGENT FOR THE CARRIER NAMED ABOVE

DATE SEP 5, 2013 BY

5. 装箱单：

Prima Construction Materials Co., Ltd.

Add: 1401Room, 38building, Chuangye Gardern,
Baoan District, Shenzhen China

WEIGHT LIST

To: CONSTRUCTION MOUDULAR SPECIALIST
POSTAL: 13 HARVEY RD.,SHENTON PK, WA
6008 AUSTRALIA

Date AUG. 18, 2013
Invoice No.: PR-20130820

From: SHANGHAI, CHINA **To:** FREMENTLE, CANADA

Item No.	Description of goods	Quantity (CTN)	G.W (KGS)	N.W (KGS)	Meas. (CBM)
	BAMBOO FLOORING				
CMS FREMENTLE CBF130724 NO.:1-109	CARBONISED BAM-BOO FLOORING	55CTNS	1,600KGS	1,519KGS	2CBM
	STRAND WOVEN BAMBOO FLOORIN-G DECKING	54CTNS	1,528KGS	1,500KGS	2CBM
Total:		109 CTNS	3,128KGS	3,019KGS	4CBM

TOTASAY ONE HUNDRED AND NINE(109CTNS)CARTONS ONLY

请对照合同与信用证审核并修改单据中的错误：

项目十三　交单结汇及单证归档业务

项目预期目标

通过对该业务中全套单据的管理，在收到银行结汇收账通知后填写客户交单联系单，并对单据进行归档管理，作为国际商务单证员，至此完成一笔完整的单证业务，在今后的工作中能基本独立完成单证相关工作。

表 13-1　　项目预期目标

目标类型	交单结汇及单证归档业务
知识目标	了解单证归档的重要性
	掌握客户交单联系单的填制
能力目标	能根据银行水单填写客户交单联系单
	能有效进行单证归档
职业素质目标	独立业务操作能力
	认真、细致、严谨的工作态度
	与银行的沟通衔接能力

项目实施条件

1. 组织学生熟悉几种常见的银行水单类型及客户交单联系单
2. 银行国际结算部能提供水单及联系单副本作为教学参考
3. 专业教师具备扎实的国际结算业务知识

开篇业务引入

2012 年 8 月 31 日，长沙鹏兴进出口有限公司单证员李望在完成了第 L-12017 号信用证业务下全套结汇单据的制作及审核工作之后准备向中国银行湖南省分行交单结汇。

子项目一　交单业务办理及单证归档

一、交单结汇业务办理

单证员在备齐全套单据之后应在规定的时间和规定的地点交单。实际交单时间应控制在运输单据出单日期之后的 21 天内，且不得超过信用证的有效期，否则视为单据过期，银行将不予接受。而交单地点一般选在受益人所在国，如果对方提出在申请人所在国交单，则很有可能因为单证不符或单据运送途中需要占用时间而导致单据过期或失误无法挽救，对受益人极为不利。

单据提交后如果被查出不符点则有可能影响受益人顺利结汇，此时的做法应该采取以下几个步骤：

1. 在开证行电提不符点后首先判断不符点的提出是否有效并符合 UCP600 及 ISBP 的规定。

2. 如果确有不符点，则应当尽快联系开证申请人请对方放弃不符点，即接受不符点单据，这样仍可正常结汇。

3. 如果对方不愿意直接接受不符点单据，而据此提出延期付款等条件则应当及时与公司主管沟通决定是否答应此类条件。

4. 如果不符点较多且属于实质性单证不符遭到开证行拒付，此时就应当与开证申请人协商寻找其他结汇方式，如托收、汇付等，但结汇麻烦且必须承担一定的费用。

5. 如果申请人恰好想据此拒付并拒收货物，则只能设法在进口国另寻买主或进口安排承运人将货物运回，这时的损失就比较严重了。

二、单证归档业务管理

在进出口业务中，全套单证的准确制作及有效管理是至关重要的，稍有不慎就有可能导致整笔业务的结汇失败，因此，作为一名合格的国际商务单证员，不仅需要时刻以业务为中心制作单据，更应该严格遵守公司的单证管理制度，将单据进行及时归档并有效管理，同时及时与银行保持联系，保证业务的顺利进行。

一般来说，出口业务的单证归档应遵循以下原则：

1. 按出运批次归档，按客户分类归档。

2. 每套单据都需保留一套副本及一份电子单据存档备查。

3. 需要存档的单据包括销售合同、生产合同、运输单据及报关单据等。

子项目二　客户交单联系单典型业务演示

上接项目十二，鹏兴公司单证员李望在将全套单据交银行之后，经开证行审单合格后，于 2012 年 9 月 25 日收到中国银行湖南省分行一式三联的结汇收账通知（即银行水单)，此时，单证员李望的工作任务是：

任务 1：根据水单填写中国银行的客户交单联系单

任务 2：业务结束后将单证归档

1. 结汇收账通知：

T 中 1008F　出口结汇收账通知（3-1）

2012 年 9 月 25 日

结汇单位	全称	长沙鹏兴进出口有限公司	
	账号	430781008888	
外　汇　金　额		牌　价	折合人名币金额
U.S.D 26,898.72		USD1=CNY6.4602	￥173,771.11
摘要			

注：第 2 联、第 3 联略。

据此，单证员李望填写了客户交单联系单：

客户交单联系单

致：中国银行

兹随附下列出口单据一套，信用证业务请按国际商会现行《跟单信用证统一惯例》办理，跟单托收业务请按国际商会现行《托收统一规则》办理。				
信用证	开证行：HSBC BANK CANADA		信用证号：DCHMN214479	
	通知行号：CH200289210666	提单日期: 120824	效期: 120919	交单期限: 15 天
无证托收	付款人全名及详址：			
	代收行外文名称及详址（供参考）：			
	交单方式：（　）D/P（　）D/A		付款期限：	
发票编号：PX12IVN1039			核销单编号：772335670	金额：U.S.D 26,898.72

单据	名称	汇票	发票	海关发票	装箱/重量单	产地证	GSP FORM A	数量/质量/重量证	检验/分析证	出口许可证	保险单	运输单据	电抄	受益人证明	船公司证明	提单	装运通知			
	份数	2	3		3		1				2					3	1			

委办事项：（打“×”者）

（　）上述单据请按我司与贵行签订之总质押书办理押汇。

（　）上述单据系代理出口项下业务，收妥后请原币划______________________________

（　）开户行：中国银行　　　　　　账号：6227004951132250

（　）若付款人拒绝/承兑，不必作成拒绝证书，但须以电传通知我司。

（　）附信用证及修改书共　　　　　纸。

（　）单据中有下列不符点：（　）请向开证行寄单，我司承担一切责任。

（　）请电询开证行同意后再寄单。

（　）______________________________

（　）______________________________

公司联系人：　　　　　　　　联系电话：　　　　　　公司公章：

<table>
<tr><td rowspan="10"></td><td colspan="3">银行接单日期：</td></tr>
<tr><td colspan="2">索汇金额：</td><td>BP NO.</td></tr>
<tr><td colspan="2">寄单日期：</td><td>OC NO.</td></tr>
<tr><td rowspan="6">银行费用</td><td>通知/保兑：</td><td rowspan="3">索汇方式：</td></tr>
<tr><td>议/承/付：</td></tr>
<tr><td>邮费：</td></tr>
<tr><td>电传：</td><td rowspan="4">寄单方式：</td></tr>
<tr><td></td></tr>
<tr><td>小计：</td></tr>
<tr><td colspan="2">费用由　　　　　　承担</td></tr>
<tr><td>退单记录：</td><td colspan="2">银行经办：</td><td>银行复核：</td></tr>
</table>

参考文献

［1］章安平. 外贸单证操作［M］. 北京：高等教育出版社，2008.

［2］刘启萍，周树玲. 外贸单证 ［M］. 北京：对外经贸大学出版社，2008.

［3］林文斌，涂奇. 外贸单证［M］. 南京：南京大学出版社，2011.

［4］全国国际商务单证培训认证考试办公室. 国际商务单证理论与实务［M］. 北京：中国商务出版社，2014.

［5］国际商会中国国家委员会. ICC 跟单信用证统一惯例（UCP600）［M］. 北京：中国民主法制出版社，2006.

［6］江舟子. 国际贸易结算单据［M］. 广州：广东经济出版社，2006.

工学结合新思维高职高专财经类“十二五”规划教材

（一）基础课程

1. 经济应用数学
2. 大学语文
3. 统计学原理
4. 经济学基础——宏微观经济的理性选择

（二）国际经贸

1. 国际贸易环境分析
2. 进出口单证实务
3. 进出口贸易操作实务
4. 进出口业务流程综合实训
5. 国际贸易理论与实务
6. 保险实务
7. 国际结算实务
8. 国际金融实务
9. 报关实务
10. 新编商务英语函电
11. 商务英语写作
12. 商务英语谈判
13. 外贸英语函电
14. 国际商务单证操作

（三）财会金融

1. 会计学原理
2. 会计报表分析
3. 会计信息化教程
4. 外贸会计实务
5. 经济法实务
6. 商业银行综合柜台业务

（四）工商管理

1. 管理咨询实务
2. 人际沟通与礼仪
3. 市场营销实务
4. 商务信息检索
5. 国际市场开发
6. 商务沟通技巧
7. 房地产销售实务

（五）物流管理

1. 企业物流管理
2. 物流市场调研与开发
3. 物流服务营销

（六）电子商务

1. 电子商务
2. 网络营销

（七）旅游与酒店管理

1. 旅行社经营与管理
2. 酒店经营与管理
3. 饭店前厅与客房管理实务
4. 酒店实用英语
5. 旅游英语